LEGAL RESEARCH

...WITHOUT LOSING YOUR MIND

By C. Edward Good

Writer-in-Residence
Finnegan, Henderson, Farabow, Garrett & Dunner
Washington • Brussels • Tokyo

LEGAL RESEARCH . . . WITHOUT LOSING YOUR MIND

by C. Edward Good

Published by
Word Store
P.O. Box 5345
Charlottesville VA 22905
(804) 979-3595
(800) 662-9673 (orders only)

ISBN 0-9648247-2-8

PREFACE

Fear

It struck at my heart as I began my study of the law. Hostile-looking law professors glared at me from my very first class. I avoided all eye contact, fearful it might acknowledge some willingness on my part to answer the unanswerable questions flung at me each day. As paranoia grew, I looked around nervously, convinced that all classmates had 4.0 GPAs and 99.99 percentiles on their LSATs, that somehow I managed to slip in, perhaps as some sort of colossal blunder by the Admissions Committee. Surely everyone else understood all this stuff. Surely no one else was as confused as I. Surely this would all sink in one day. "Why am I here?" I moaned.

And then fear struck again, this time more cruelly, when I attended my first class in Legal Research and Writing. I was told to research a real case. I even went on a library tour where all the sources were pointed out to me. "Simple," everyone else seemed to say, "this course'll be a cakewalk."

Everyone else, I deduced, suspiciously glancing at my classmates, undoubtedly worked as paralegals for fat-cat law firms before entering law school. They knew all about this stuff. I didn't. I thought I was losing my mind.

So much for fond memories of law school.

A Method to the Madness

It doesn't have to be that way, at least not in your course in Legal Research and Writing. Despite its brooding appearance, the law library is really a rather friendly place, once you understand a few basic principles. There is a method, after all. To all this madness.

That's what this book is all about: a foolproof method of legal research. To share it with you, I've divided all law into two groups: (1) case law and (2) legislative and administrative law. For each I've devised two sets of facts, one fictitious for case law, the other quite real and famous for legislative and administrative law. As the chapters unfold, you'll learn a method for researching case law and then one for legislative and administrative law.

Chapter Outline

Case Law. In Chapter 1, I'll kid around with you and explain the name of this book. In Chapter 2, you'll find your first set of facts. It involves the fictitious Wally and Mipsie and their lawsuit against your client, Dr. Cynthia Schwartz, for a negligent sterilization operation resulting in the birth of their unwanted children. In Chapters 3 and 4, you'll learn all about the American judicial system and the publication of American case law. In Chapter 5, you'll learn some vital preliminary steps for your first foray in the law library. Chapters 6-9 present a four-step approach to case law legal research, a method you may follow to solve any legal research problem governed by state or federal cases. Chapter 10 then looks back and reviews the strategy of the four-step method of case law legal research.

Legislative and Administrative Law. Chapter 11 reviews the federal legislative system and techniques of publishing legislative law. Chapter 12 introduces you to your second set of facts, this time the very real facts involved in the confirmation hearing of Judge Clarence Thomas. Then, in the same chapter, you'll learn a step-by-step method for researching federal legislative problems. Chapter 13 concludes with a look at the federal administrative process, the publication of administrative law, and a step-by-step method of researching federal regulations.

What About State Law?

The research method in Chapters 6-9 teaches you to retrieve state and federal case law. Chapters 12 and 13, however, limit the discussion to retrieving federal statutes and federal regulations. You will find, however, that when you learn how to research federal legislative law, you'll be able to transfer those skills easily to any of the state legislative systems. The publication techniques, after all, are virtually the same.

The Visual Aids Booklet

Teaching legal research successfully is an exercise in "show and tell." I can describe lawbooks far into the night without your comprehending a thing. To learn it, you must see it.

To enable you to *see* the research process unfold, I have prepared a collateral booklet of Visual Aids. There you will find actual pages from real lawbooks, along with my commentary superimposed on the pages themselves. The pages are sample pages you would encounter when researching the case law problem in Chapters 2-10 (Wally & Mipsie's Case) and the legislative-administrative problem in Chapters 12-13 (the Thomas-Hill Case).

Printing considerations limited the Visual Aids to 85 sample pages. Thus, the Visual Aids booklet does not include all pages you would encounter in the research process. Quite the contrary. The Visual Aids represent just a small portion of the pages you would use in solving either of the research projects. In the real world, you'd surely bump up against more pages, many from dead ends that inevitably arise in the real, and oftentimes crazy, world of legal research.

Welcome to the World of Legal Research

So welcome. The world of legal research is a strange world indeed, full of bizarre time zones, weird characters, and puzzling words and numbers. But it's full of something else as well. It's full of what you seek: cases on point, authority that you must find and read and analyze when representing the interests of your client. That's your objective: to find *all* cases and statutes and regulations on point.

Or put another way: your objective is not to *miss* a case or statute or regulation on point. For if you do, you can count on one absolute rule of nature, one 100% guarantee: your *opponent* will find that law and smugly serve it up to the judge in a trial or appellate brief. Much to your horror and dismay.

Fear.

It strikes at the heart in the study of the law.

But fear not. Help is on the way.

C. Edward Good
Charlottesville, Virginia
January 17, 1993

CONTENTS

THE ROADMAPS FOR RESEARCH

FIGURES

TABLES

TABLES (continued)

GOOD'S RULES OF RESEARCH

Appreciation

My heart-felt thanks go to William Van Doren, whose book design and unforgettable artwork help bring this subject alive.

CHAPTER 1

TAKE A DEEP BREATH

So you've made it to law school, paralegal school, college, or some other kind of school that forces you—much against your will—to spend time, lots of time, in that most frightening, intimidating, and bewildering of places on the face of the earth:

The Law Library.

Just look at the place. Stacked from floor to ceiling on shelves without end, those crusty, mean-looking lawbooks sit there smirking at you, almost daring you to come over, pick one up, in front of everybody. "Hey, Rookie!" the books seem to say. "Don't worry, you won't make a fool of yourself, pick one up, just try opening one," the books urge. "Try me, try me! You won't look stupid. Trust me. You'll do fine. You'll be efficient. We'll have you researching just like a lawyer in no time."

Not.

The Law Library, you'll soon learn, is not far away from *Wayne's World.*

Without knowing it, however, you are indeed fortunate. At least you've got a sympathetic, understanding, sensitive legal research professor.[1] Not like mine, some years ago at the University of Virginia School of Law. In those days—the period just after the last ice age—there were no such things as "Legal Research and Writing Professors." In those days, legal research was "taught" by reluctant Law Professors who had to teach legal research and writing to a section of their students taking Torts, Contracts, Property, or Whatever. These good Law Professors, no doubt, had the best of intentions, but their pedagogy consisted of devising an incredibly ridiculous fact situation full of red herrings, dead ends, and stale humor, pointing you in the direction of the law library, and instructing you to:

"Turn in your completed Memorandum of Law no later than next Friday." Naturally, it was Monday at the time.

So consider yourself fortunate. Your legal research professor really does know what he or she is doing; your legal research topic is timely, funny, and intriguing;

[1]The reader might think that such a statement is a ploy to get legal research professors to adopt this terrific legal research book. The reader just might be right.

you've brainstormed the issue with your classmates; and the due date is, no doubt, reasonable. Yeah, sure.

But your one, slightly nagging question remains:

"So what do I do now?"

"What do I do first?" you legitimately ask anyone willing to listen. Which book do I go to and what will it do for me? Then what do I do? Is there any method to this madness? Any system? Surely somewhere there's a set of instructions I can find and follow that'll tell me where to go first, second, third, and so on. There has got to be someone who can take me step by step through the, uh, "process." *Is* there a "process"? A beginning, a middle . . . an end? Surely there's an end. What if there's no end? What if I get caught in some sort of legal research loop, some repeating procedure spinning me forever toward infinity, some time warp, some new dimension in time, maybe there are *lost* legal researchers floating in this new dimension in the stacks of the law library, maybe students from generations ago are still there researching their topics due next Friday . . . next Friday . . . next Friday. . . .

"Help!" you scream, daring "them" to send the guys in the white coats with the Velcro Restraint Jackets. Don't worry. Be happy. We know you're mad. You've got perfectly sane reasons for insanity.

But help is on the way. In fact, help is sitting right in your hot little hands. Help is right here, in this sizzling, runaway bestseller, in this soon-to-be-a-major-motion-picture, don't-read-it-if-you-have-to-get-a-good-night's-sleep thriller, in this towering academic tour de force, in this mesmerizing new book entitled . . . .

Well, just what do I name it? No way can I write a book without a name, a name that'll grab the reader's attention right from the beginning. Some might ask, "What's in a name?" but what do they know? I thought, at first, I'd name it:

Comma Supra, A Bizarre Guide to Smarmy Sex Among the Stacks. But then I figured the librarians of this world would have a hard time figuring out the right subject matter headings when they catalogued the work in hundreds of thousands libraries across the globe.

And then I thought I'd follow the precedent set by other distinguished treatise authors, stroke my own swollen ego,[2] and name it after . . . well, after . . . Me! *Good on Legal Research.*

And then I thought that I'd play around with that preposition "on" and give it a little twist:

Good for Legal Research. And then I really got going with *Damn Good Legal Research* or *The Goods on Legal Research* (but my wife objected to that, saying she wanted nothing to do with some weird legal research book). Smart wife.

So I decided to give it a descriptive title:

Legal Research . . .

[2]All treatise writers have swollen egos. It's a documented fact.

Catchy, huh? The ellipses add an appealing academic dimension, don't you think?

But the subtitle says it all:

Without Losing Your Mind

The subtitle captures the entire approach and philosophy of this book: as a newcomer, you don't need a book explaining everything there is to know about the law library. Such a book would drive you bats. You don't need, not now anyway, a complete description of legislative histories, a detailed treatment of looseleaf services, chapters on international materials, and complex discussions of other sources that will never pass through your hands in your first year of law school or paralegal school. That text would just gather dust on your shelf while you open your window and prepare to jump.

And you don't need, not now anyway, much instruction on computer legal research. In the law schools, most legal research programs prohibit first-year students from using LEXIS or WESTLAW during their first year. Most paralegal students don't even have access to computer-assisted legal research systems. So computers can wait.

What you do need, and will indubitably get in this chartbuster, is down-to-earth advice on (1) where to go first, (2) what to do next, and (3) how to figure out when you've finished. Step 3, of course, is crucial so that you can leave the law library—at some point in the distant future—go home, and get some needed and well-deserved sack time.

So that's my approach. I intend to share with you a tried and true method of legal research that will enable you to research two basic types of legal research assignments: (1) a pure case law problem and (2) a problem governed by legislation and administrative regulations.

In presenting this down-to-earth advice, I will treat each form of law in a way similar to the approach in my other sizzling page-turner, *Citing & Typing the Law—A Guide to Legal Citation and Style* (LEL Enterprises 1992).[3] I will first describe the nature of the legal process that produces law in the first place. Second, I will introduce you to the books that publish that law. Third, I will review, book by book, the lawbooks you should use in the order you should use them to solve a legal research problem based on that form of law.

To make it interesting, I will introduce you to "Good's Rules of Research," to a new dimension of time known as the "NO ZONE," to "The Single Most Important Page in All of Legal Research," to "Wilbur" (the wimpy author of all lawbooks), to the "Nope-Nope-Nope Approach" (a legal index method guaranteed to crack your fingernails), and myriad other devices that will help you survive—no, win!—your first bout with the law library.

[3]Another ploy to encourage you to encourage your law professor to adopt this terrific book, which explains the mysteries of legal citation found in the Harvard *Bluebook*.

So welcome to bafflement and befuddlement. Welcome to the most complex body of information on earth: American law. Welcome to the law library.

Welcome to *Legal Research . . . Without Losing Your Mind.*

CHAPTER 2

THE STATEMENT OF FACTS: WALLY AND MIPSIE'S CASE

All legal research problems begin with a "Statement of Facts." Typically, this "Statement of Facts" is full of all sorts of details, most of which don't make the slightest bit of difference in your legal analysis and your ultimate Memorandum of Law. The "Statement of Facts" will also have all sorts of dead ends, red herrings, curve balls, and a mixture of various other metaphors so that you have to rewrite the "Statement of Facts" into a proper Statement of Facts in the Memorandum of Law. Actually, truth be known, the "Statement of Facts" gives your legal research professors the only chance in their lives to pretend they're the writers of great works of fiction, so they warm to the task and go stark raving mad as they weave an impossible plot and create unforgettable characters (with whom you will intimately live for the rest of your days—trust me, you will *never* forget, no matter how hard you try, your first "Statement of Facts"). They are sure to take a stab at some dialogue, throw in some mood-producing imagery of color, and (you can count on this) riddle the entire scenario with knee-slapping humor, which they, and they alone, find incredibly funny. (How do I know? Simple. Read my facts below.)

They type it all up (usually in the form of a confidential law firm memo—you know, "Our client has asked our advice . . . "), deliver it to the school's Reproduction Department (we used to call it the "Copy Center"), get a supply of copies for all their students, and deliver to you your very own copy of:

To: Summer Associate
From: The Senior Partner[1]
Re: Dr. Cynthia Schwartz

Our client has asked our advice[2] with respect to[3] the following [uh oh, here it comes] Statement of Facts:

[1]A truly terrifying bit of information.

[2]Told you so.

[3]Lawyers love to say "with respect to." Get used to it.

Wally and Mipsie Stevens are two young urban professionals on their way up in the world. Mipsie is an attorney with one of the smaller law firms in this city. Wally, I fear, is a professional stamp collector. After much thought and late-night discussion, Mipsie and Wally decided not to have children. In Mipsie's words, "The little brats just get in the way of our sophisticated lifestyle."[4] Wally, as usual, agreed with his wife. Mipsie, after some research in her law firm's rather limited medical library, found that her risk in undergoing a tubal ligation was greater than Wally's risk in undergoing a vasectomy. Wally, as usual, agreed with his wife. Mipsie researched the issue and found that Dr. Cynthia Schwartz was the most well-known urologist in the area and promptly made an appointment for Wally.

On the appointed day, Wally presented himself at Dr. Schwartz's office. The doctor explained the operation and pointed out that it was not 100% foolproof. Postoperative tests would show whether the operation was a success. Wally said that Mipsie said that this was the best procedure for them and that he was willing to go forward. Dr. Schwartz performed the operation that day, and Wally was released to return home for one day of bed rest.

Three months later, Mipsie discovered to her horror that she was pregnant. Outraged, she screamed at Wally, "We'll sue that incompetent worm for everything she's worth."

"On what grounds?" Wally asked.

Surprised that Wally knew a legal word like "grounds," Mipsie replied, "How do I know? I specialize in antitrust law. I'll have to ask our medical malpractice department."

That night, Mipsie returned home with the news that the doctor might very well be liable for the costs of rearing their child, which, she pointed out, would include at least the best private schools, the best summer camps, exchange programs abroad, cotillion, four years of tuition at Bennington, and braces.[5] After the child was born, Mipsie reported, they would file suit against Dr. Schwartz and seek to recover all costs of rearing their child and whatever else they could pry out of the insurance company. "This could be the financial break we've been waiting for," Mipsie mused as she searched through the Yellow Pages[6] for the number of the local Merrill Lynch office.

Subsequently, Mipsie gave birth to beautiful, healthy quintuplets.

Dr. Schwartz has asked our advice on the extent of her liability. I would like you to go to the law library and find every on-point case in the country no later than this afternoon. Then I would like you to prepare a short Memoran-

---

[4]How the Senior Partner knows what Mipsie said is left unexplained. The "Statement of Facts" is typically written from an omniscient point of view.

[5]See how funny this is?

[6]This is the color imagery part.

dum of Law (25 pages or so) analyzing the damages that Mipsie and Wally might recover from Dr. Schwartz.

By the way, your Memorandum of Law is due this Friday.

Panic begins to set in. "Every on-point case?" you ask no one in particular. Then an idea strikes, from out of the blue. "Ah," you say, "I'll just have to find the cases in our state. Can't be that many. Let's see, where did this Wally and Mipsie business take place, anyway?"

Your legal research professor then informs you that the entire "Statement of Facts" occurred in a . . . Mythical Jurisdiction.

"A what?"

Mythical Jurisdiction. In my case, back in the ice age, my "Statement of Facts," an incredibly stupid story about Baldwin Gwinn who fell in a hole on a college campus—I told you it will haunt you for the rest of your life—well, my "Statement of Facts" occurred in the "State of Monroe."

So your legal research professor is likely to tell you that your facts happened in the State of Ecstasy. Or some such place.

Thus, if your "Statement of Facts" occurred in a Mythical Jurisdiction, then you've got to research case law in the entire country, find all on-point cases, read scads of cases, take reams of notes, and write a Memorandum of Law. By Friday.

But first, it's time to learn a few basics about the American legal system, specifically about the American judicial system. Before you can possibly be turned loose in the dreaded law library to find on-point cases, you must first gain a thorough understanding of the judicial system, the federal and state court systems, and the techniques of publishing case law in the United States.

So before we join Wally and Mipsie and attempt to destroy their chances for recovering a solitary dime from the good Doctor Schwartz, let's take a trip through the case law system and learn some of the basics of the American judiciary.

CHAPTER 3

THE AMERICAN JUDICIAL SYSTEM

§ 3.1 Introduction

Before you prepare to attack the law library and find every on-point case governing Wally and Mipsie's rather bizarre set of facts, you need to take a step back and reflect on the nature of case law and its origins in the American legal system. To understand the strategies you will use to ferret out the cases governing Wally and Mipsie's case, you must first learn about the American judicial process, the court structures in the United States, and the techniques used to publish or "report" court opinions.

Having already described the American judicial system and the techniques of publishing American case law in *Citing & Typing the Law* (LEL Enterprises 1992), I am borrowing from chapters 4 and 5 of that book and shifting their focus away from legal citation and style to our subject, methods of legal research.

§ 3.2 The American Judicial System

§ 3.2(a) Anatomy of a Lawsuit

Basically, there are two types of court cases: civil and criminal. Criminal cases, of course, are not called "lawsuits"; they always involve the state or city or county government or the federal government proceeding against individuals. For the purpose of this discussion, we'll focus on civil suits, primarily those between two private citizens. Keep in mind, however, that state or federal governments are often involved in civil cases as well, either as a defendant when a government is being sued or as a plaintiff when a government is bringing a civil enforcement or collection action against a private party.

Also when discussing the anatomy of a lawsuit, I'll focus on the federal court system, federal civil procedure, and federal cases. You will soon learn that, with only a few exceptions, techniques of legal research apply equally to federal and state case law.

§ 3.2(b) Jurisdiction of the Federal Courts

All federal criminal cases must be brought in federal court. For civil cases, the federal courts have the power or "jurisdiction" to hear two types of cases: those involving a "federal question" and those involving disputes between citizens of different states.

The first type, "federal question" jurisdiction, is given to the federal courts by statute. A federal statute empowers the federal courts to hear cases involving cases or controversies arising under the laws of the United States. Thus, if a government official acting "under color of law" denies you your civil rights, you may bring a federal court civil action for damages against that officer. Such a case involves the law of the United States as found in 42 U.S.C. § 1983 (1988).

Another type of "federal question" jurisdiction is found in individual statutes that expressly confer jurisdiction on the federal courts to hear claims arising under the statute. The Federal Torts Claim Act, for example, provides that private citizens can sue the federal government for torts caused by employees of the federal government. The statute goes on to provide that the federal courts are empowered to hear cases arising under the Federal Torts Claim Act.

So a case might go to federal court under the blanket "federal question" statute or under a specific statute giving the federal courts power to hear the case. These "federal question" cases constitute a large part of the federal courts' caseload.

The second type of civil case heard in federal court is called a "diversity of citizenship" case. These cases really have nothing to do with federal law. Suppose in Wally and Mipsie's case the doctor resides in a different state. For example, maybe Wally and Mipsie live in the northern Virginia suburbs and went to Dr. Schwartz, practicing in southern Maryland. Wally and Mipsie could then bring their case in federal court even though state case law would govern the outcome.

In the early 1800s when Congress was creating the federal court system, it was concerned about the out-of-state litigant getting a fair shake in the courts of another state. To protect this nonresident litigant, Congress enacted a statute giving the federal courts the power—the "jurisdiction"—to hear cases brought between citizens of different states. Today, the statute remains in force, although the amount involved in the controversy must be more than $50,000 for the federal courts to have the power to hear the case.

§ 3.2(c) United States District Courts

Before following a civil case through the trial process, we should review the structure of the federal trial court system. You will soon see that efficient legal research strategy depends upon your thorough understanding of federal and state court systems. Knowing the status of a court deciding a case you've uncovered in the research process might very well determine your next research move.

The United States and its territories have 94 trial courts called the United States District Courts. Each of these courts resides within the geographic boundaries of a single state or territory. In some states, there is only one federal district court. These federal courts are named: the United States District Court for the District of (name of state). Examples include the United States District Court for the District of Massachusetts or the United States District Court for the District of Columbia.

Other states, the larger and more populous ones, or the ones with Senators who have enough clout to get more federal district courts established in their states, have as many as four United States District Courts. In a multicourt state, the state is divided into "geographic districts." There are only six possible geographic districts, although no state has more than four. The table below shows the names of the six federal district courts and the correct abbreviation that should show up in a citation to a case from each court:

Geographic District	Abbreviation
Northern District	N.D.
Southern District	S.D.
Eastern District	E.D.
Western District	W.D.
Central District	C.D.
Middle District	M.D.

The courts in these multicourt states are named: the United States District Court for the Northern (Southern, Eastern, Western, Central, or Middle) District of (name of state). Examples include: the United States District Court for the Southern District of New York (S.D.N.Y.) or the United States District Court for the Eastern District of Virginia (E.D. Va.).

Although I'll talk about the "circuits" shortly, it is important to point out here that each federal district court is in a particular circuit. Thus, the Southern District of New York is in the Second Circuit, and the Eastern District of Virginia is in the Fourth Circuit.

§ 3.2(c)(i) The Case Begins: Pleadings and Motions

Now let's follow a hypothetical lawsuit through the federal court system. The case begins by the plaintiff filing a "complaint" with the clerk of a United States District Court. The complaint describes the facts of the controversy and the legal grounds upon which the lawsuit is based. It does so in numbered paragraphs, each alleging a particular fact or a particular legal ground for relief. Finally, the complaint asks the court for particular relief such as money damages. The plaintiff might seek "compensatory" damages for the harm done and perhaps "punitive" damages to "punish" the defendant for particularly reprehensible conduct. The complaint might also ask for "equitable relief" like an "injunction" ordering the defendant to stop doing something, or some other form of equitable relief.

Once the complaint is filed with the clerk of the federal district court, "process" is "served" on the defendant, a fancy way of saying that the summons and the complaint are delivered to the defendant. This "service of process" might be in person, or it might take place as "substituted service of process" through the mail. The important point is that once the defendant has been served, the court has power over the defendant's person. The court has what is called "in personam" jurisdiction. This means if the defendant fails to show up at trial or fails to "answer" the complaint, the court might order a "default judgment" in favor of the plaintiff. Most defendants, naturally, hire a lawyer and defend the suit.

When the defendant receives the complaint, the defendant's lawyer files either an "answer" or a "motion to dismiss." The answer responds to the complaint, perhaps by admitting certain facts and denying other facts. The answer might also plead certain "affirmative defenses," which are defenses that must be pleaded or the defendant "waives" them (gives them up).

A "motion to dismiss" might be based on a variety of grounds. Perhaps the "statute of limitations," the time allowed by statute to bring a particular kind of claim, has elapsed. Or perhaps the defendant believes the plaintiff has no legal right to relief. The defendant then files a motion to dismiss for "failure to state a claim upon which relief can be granted." In such a motion, the defendant is saying that even if every fact the plaintiff alleges is true, the plaintiff has no remedy in law.

In Wally and Mipsie's case, for example, perhaps your legal research will reveal that most courts refuse to allow damages for the costs of rearing an unplanned child. Your law firm, using *your* legal research and perhaps *your* Memorandum of Law, would file a motion to dismiss the claims for the cost of rearing the children.

When filing a motion to dismiss, the defendant's attorney will likely write and submit a Memorandum of Law in Support of Defendant's Motion to Dismiss. In that memo, of course, the attorney will be arguing about what the law means. In so doing, the attorney will cite cases, statutes, constitutional provisions, and any other applicable primary or secondary authority—all found in the legal research process and all cited, of course, in compliance with the exacting standards of the Harvard *Bluebook*.[1]

§ 3.2(c)(ii) Discovery: Who Knows What?

If the court refuses to grant any motion to dismiss, the case is docketed for trial. Before trial, however, the plaintiff wants to learn what the defendant knows about the case and vice versa. So the parties engage in what is called "pretrial discovery," which can take a variety of forms.

One party might take "oral depositions" of the other party or the other party's witnesses. These oral depositions are question-and-answer sessions where the

[1] *A Uniform System of Citation* (15th ed. 1991) is commonly referred to as the Harvard *Bluebook*. If you haven't yet encountered it, then you're in for a real treat. The *Bluebook* governs the rules of legal citation and style for most of legal writing throughout the legal profession. If you find the *Bluebook* confusing, then please read *Citing & Typing the Law* (LEL Enterprises 1992), written by yours truly.

"deponent" is under oath and a "reporter" transcribes everything that is said.

One party might submit "written interrogatories" to the other party or the other party's witnesses. Interrogatories are questions that must be answered in writing unless the information they seek is "privileged."

Other forms of discovery include "requests for the production of documents," which ask one party to give documentary evidence to the other party, and "motions for physical examinations," which if granted require a party to submit to a court-ordered medical examination.

The overall purposes of modern forms of discovery are to reduce the element of surprise at trial, to expedite the proceedings, and to narrow the legal issues involved. Sometimes, however, the litigants use the discovery mechanism to delay the trial—a source of much criticism of discovery in recent times.

§ 3.2(c)(iii) More Motions: Summary Judgment

After discovery, a party might make a motion for "summary judgment." This motion essentially asks the court to look at these pleadings—the complaint and the answer—and at the affidavits filed and then to decide the case without a trial. The moving party tries to convince the court that there is "no material dispute of fact" (and hence nothing for the jury to do) and that the legal issues can be decided "as a matter of law." When making such a motion, a party will likely submit a Memorandum in Support of Plaintiff's (or Defendant's) Motion for Summary Judgment. In the memo, the attorney argues about the meaning and applicability of the law. Again, in so doing, the attorney cites cases, statutes, procedural rules, and a host of other legal materials—all, naturally, found by you efficiently and effortlessly in the law library and then cited in strict compliance with the Harvard *Bluebook*.

§ 3.2(c)(iv) The Trial: Winners and Losers

Once discovery has taken place and pretrial motions have been disposed of, it is time for the trial. At trial, the dispute contains two basic types of issues: factual and legal. The jury decides which facts are true and which are not true. The judge gives "instructions to the jury" to guide the jury in its resolution of factual issues and also to inform the jury what the legal result has to be if the facts are decided in a particular way. The judge also applies the procedural rules at trial governing the evidence to be admitted, the kinds of questions to be asked of witnesses, and many other procedural details.

Before the case goes to the jury, however, each party might decide to make a "motion for a directed verdict." Comparable in many ways to the motion for summary judgment, the motion for a directed verdict asks the court to look at the evidence and to conclude that no rational jury could decide the case against the moving party. The facts, therefore, must be strongly in favor of the moving party before a judge will enter a directed verdict. If the judge denies the motion, which is usually the case, the case goes forward to the jury itself.

After the plaintiff's and defendant's witnesses have testified, the jury must reach its decision. Using the "jury instructions," the jury meets in secret and votes on the essential factual issues. Once it reaches a unanimous decision on each factual issue, it "applies the law" as found in the instructions to reach its "verdict." The jury might decide that the plaintiff wins and that the "recovery" is, oh, say about $10,000,000.

Losers, of course, do not routinely take defeat lying down. The loser's attorney typically will make yet another motion, sort of a last-ditch effort to prevail. The losing party may make a "motion for judgment notwithstanding the verdict," or, in the Latin, a motion for a judgment *non obstante verdicto,* or, in the inevitable abbreviated form, a motion for a judgment n.o.v. This motion gives the power to the judge to negate an irrational jury's verdict, but because of their faith in the jury system, judges rarely use the power provided by the motion and instead let the jury's verdict stand. The loser is miffed even more.

So it's bad news for the loser: the inevitable result of our adversarial system of resolving disputes—one side wins—one side loses. You can rest assured that losers are not happy people. Our defendant does not happily whip out the old checkbook and write plaintiff a check for a cool ten million. No, the loser is quite likely to "appeal."

§ 3.2(c)(v) Court Opinions

Before turning to the appellate process, let's learn about some highly important legal information that comes from the trial itself. Often the trial judge is asked in a motion to reach a legal decision. Perhaps the trial judge must rule on a motion to dismiss for "failure to state a claim upon which relief can be granted." In ruling on such a motion, the court decides that one side wins and one side loses. Sometimes the trial judge might rule on such a motion from the bench or in chambers. But the trial judge might also decide that a full explanation of the ruling is needed. The trial judge, then, might write an "opinion of law," which is also called an "opinion," a "decision," or a "case." It is this opinion that is published and subsequently located by a legal researcher and subsequently "cited" by a legal writer. As we shall see, the opinion becomes "law." It becomes part of the vast body of law known as "case law." I shall return to a more detailed discussion of what court opinions are and how they are published after we continue our tour of a typical court proceeding.

§ 3.2(d) The Case Continues: United States Courts of Appeals

The loser at trial might want another chance to prevail. If the loser's attorney can identify "legal error" in the proceedings of the trial court, there just might be a chance for a successful appeal.

All appeals in the federal system are "heard" by the United States Courts of Appeals. These thirteen courts are known as the "circuits." Eleven of the circuits are numbered, First through Eleventh. The twelfth and thirteenth are the United States Court of Appeals for the District of Columbia Circuit and the United States Court of Appeals for the Federal Circuit. Each of the eleven numbered circuits contains more than one state, and no state is split between two circuits.

The circuits begin in the northeast with the First Circuit, and continue to the New York area (Second Circuit), to the Pennsylvania area (Third Circuit), to the Virginia area (Fourth Circuit), to the Georgia, Alabama and Florida area, which used to be part of the Fifth Circuit but is now the new Eleventh Circuit. The Louisiana area is the Fifth Circuit, the Ohio area is the Sixth Circuit, and the Illinois area is the Seventh Circuit. The Eighth Circuit is the Nebraska area, the Ninth is the California area, and the Tenth is the Colorado area.

§ 3.2(d)(i) A Geography Lesson: Map of the Circuits

To qualify as an Ace Legal Researcher, you must become intimately familiar with the geographic arrangement of the circuits. You will find out later, to your dismay, that the West Publishing Company arranges references to circuit court opinions *alphabetically by state*, not numerically by circuit. Thus, in many books published by West, you'll find references such as "C.A. Cal.," which means the United States Court of Appeals that Sits in California. The Ace Legal Researcher will immediately recognize that court as the Ninth Circuit.

If you wish to qualify as an Ace Legal Researcher, study the map appearing on the next page:

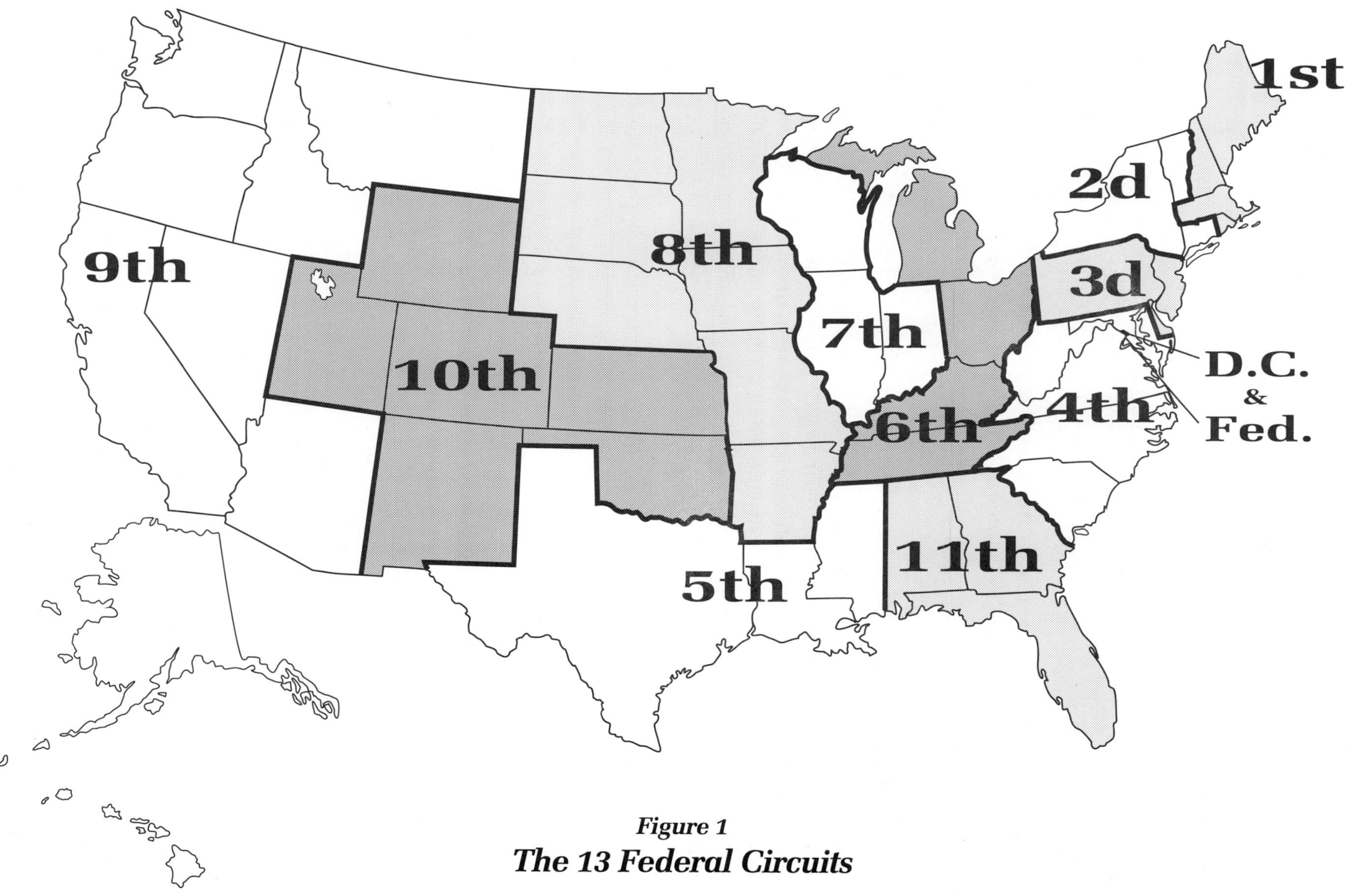

Figure 1
The 13 Federal Circuits

§ 3.2(d)(ii) Appellate Panels

Each court of appeals has at least three judges "sitting" on the court. A larger circuit, like the Ninth Circuit, might have more than twenty judges on the court. Not all circuit judges, however, hear each case. The court divides into panels of three judges for each case heard. For extremely important cases, those involving crucial legal issues, the court might elect to sit "en banc," meaning that all judges sit to hear and decide the case. At the appellate level, usually only legal issues are involved. Rarely does an appellate court disturb the jury's findings of fact.

To appeal a case, the loser, who is called the "appellant," files a "notice of appeal" with the district court clerk. The notice reveals the fact that an appeal will be filed and the grounds upon which the appeal is based. The district court clerk compiles the "record" of the proceedings at trial and sends the record to the appropriate court of appeals. Any appeal from a district court in the Second Circuit, for example, must be filed with the Second Circuit.

§ 3.2(d)(iii) Appellate Briefs

When the circuit receives the record, the time clock starts to tick, and the appellant has forty days to file the "appellant's brief." After the appellant's brief is filed, the winner at trial, who is called the "appellee," has twenty-one days to file the "appellee's brief."

A brief, which must be typed according to exacting rules of format and style, contains a title page, a statement of jurisdiction, an index of authorities, a statement of facts, a statement of the case, and an argument. The argument rigorously challenges the legal decisions of the trial court and tries to convince the appellate court that the trial court committed "reversible error." Again, the parties are not arguing the factual decisions of the jury but the legal decisions of the trial judge. In so doing, of course, the attorney cites a host of cases, statutes, law review articles, constitutional provisions, and other forms of legal material—all uncovered in the legal research process and then cited in strict compliance with the rules of citation and style found in the Harvard *Bluebook*.

Law students, early in their legal careers, will be asked to write appellate briefs. Most first-year legal writing programs require the preparation of an appellate brief and an oral argument before a panel of "judges." Those law students who aspire to be litigators will then participate in "Moot Court," an elaborate competition of appellate advocacy, oral and written.

§ 3.2(d)(iv) Oral Argument

After the appellate court receives both briefs, an "oral argument" might be scheduled. In many of the circuits, however, a team of staff attorneys reviews the briefs first and recommends to the judges that certain appeals are "frivolous" and should be dismissed without oral argument. The judges review the briefs, and the staff attorneys' recommendations, and usually follow the recommendations of the staff attorneys. This practice of screening appeals, which began in the Fifth Circuit, has effectively dealt with the burgeoning caseload facing the federal appellate courts, which exceeds 36,000 appeals each year.[2]

If a case is granted an oral argument, the appellant's attorney and the appellee's attorney go to the court at an appointed time and actually argue the case orally before the panel of three judges. Each side is given thirty minutes to argue the case.

During the argument, the judges frequently ask probing questions of the attorneys. Through these questions, the judges seek to resolve the dispute between the parties and, perhaps even more importantly, to render an opinion that represents good law. The judges know that the opinion will have major implications not only on the parties' lives but on society as well. They seek to be informed, often through oral argument, about the consequences of holding one way or the other.

At the end of oral argument, the judges retire to their chambers, later to reach their decision. The judges have read both briefs, they have researched the law, and they have read "bench memos" prepared by their law clerks. They discuss the case with each other. Ultimately, the three judges vote on the result. The side that gets at least two votes wins.

§ 3.2(d)(v) More Court Opinions

Once again we have one winner and one loser. The court does not send a Hallmark sympathy card to the loser and an Express Mail letter of congratulations to the winner. Rather, the court writes a full "opinion of law." The opinion is sent to the appellant and the appellee, but the opinion is also published, later to be found by legal researchers and cited by legal writers. I shall return to a more detailed discussion of court opinions or "case law" below.

But now in our hypothetical lawsuit we have another loser. The loser now might pound his fists on the table and say, "I'll take this case all the way to the Supreme Court of the United States." Well, maybe, but we'll see that the odds are against it.

§ 3.2(e) The Final Step: Supreme Court of the United States

Sitting atop the federal court pyramid, and atop the state court systems on matters of federal or constitutional law, is the Supreme Court of the United States. Consisting of nine "Justices," one of whom is the "Chief Justice," the Supreme Court has the ultimate authority to interpret federal law. It has the power to reverse any lower court, if the losing party in that case brought the appeal to the Supreme Court. It has the

[2]In the fiscal year ending June 30, 1971, the number of appeals filed in the federal circuits totalled 10,798. *Annual Report of the Administrative Office of United States Courts* 252 (1971). By the end of the fiscal year ending June 30, 1990, this figure had jumped to 36,609. *Annual Report of the Administrative Office of United States Courts* 130 (1990).

power to negate an entire federal or state statute as being in violation of the Constitution of the United States. It has the final say in interpreting the laws of Congress. It also has a very small amount of time and resources to carry out these enormous tasks, so little time and so few resources that very few cases actually make it to the Supreme Court.

§ 3.2(e)(i) "Cert" Is Not a Breath Mint

The loser in our hypothetical lawsuit has two ways to get to the Supreme Court of the United States: by appeal or by writ of certiorari. The losers in certain kinds of cases enjoy a "right" to appeal to the Supreme Court, e.g., a case in which the lower federal court has declared a state statute to be unconstitutional. In many of these "right of appeal" cases, however, the Supreme Court dismisses the appeal if the issues involved do not appear significant or substantial. For all practical purposes, the Supreme Court exercises its discretion in deciding whether it wants to hear these "right of appeal" cases.

The other route, by certiorari, is both theoretically and actually a "discretionary" review on the part of the Court. The loser, who is now called a "petitioner," files a "petition for certiorari" with the Supreme Court. The petition for "cert" seeks to demonstrate to the Court why this particular issue merits the attention of the Supreme Court. The petition tries to point to matters of national interest the case represents, to "conflicts in the circuits," and to the need for "uniformity" in federal law.

The petition for cert, however, faces a great deal of competition. Each year, nearly 5,000 petitions and appeals are filed in the Supreme Court. There is no way that nine Justices can hear, decide, and write opinions on 5,000 cases. So most of the petitions for cert and the right to appeal cases are "denied" or "dismissed." Anyone who has ever read any legal writing has seen the phrase "cert. denied" typed after a case citation. It means the ball game is over, Jack. You lose. There's nowhere else to go.

In reaching the "cert. denied" decision, the Justices read memoranda of law prepared by their law clerks. In the Supreme Court itself these memos are known as "flimsies," not so named by the quality of their content but by the onion skin paper upon which they used to be typed by the law clerks themselves. (Typing ability used to be a significant qualification for a judicial clerkship with the Supreme Court.)[3]

§ 3.2(e)(ii) More Briefs and More Oral Arguments

If the Court grants certiorari, then the appeal proceeds. The petitioner writes a petitioner's brief. The respondent writes a respondent's brief. At an appointed time, each side goes to the Supreme Court for oral argument.

All nine Justices sit to hear each oral argument. Each side has thirty minutes, unless lengthened by the Court. Many of the male attorneys follow ancient tradition

[3]Just kidding.

and wear "morning suits" for the oral argument. The Solicitor General of the United States, who argues all Supreme Court cases involving the United States as a party, has followed this fashionable tradition.

After oral argument, sometimes many months after oral argument, the Justices reach a decision. Each Friday afternoon while the Court is in session, all nine Justices meet in the Conference Room of the Supreme Court. No one else is allowed in. The junior-most Justice must go to the door for messages. At these conferences, the Justices discuss the case and ultimately vote on a result. The side that gets five votes wins.

§ 3.2(e)(iii) More Court Opinions

The Chief Justice then appoints one member of the "majority," the side that prevailed, to write the "majority opinion." Any other member of the majority may write a "concurring opinion," which usually means the Justice agrees with the result but disagrees with the reasoning used to reach that result. Any member of the losing side may write a "dissenting opinion."

For legal research purposes, of course, these opinions are not just sent to the parties involved in the lawsuit. They are published. They become the supreme law of the land. They are found by legal researchers, analyzed by armies of law professors, pored over by the press, and cited by legal writers.

When the Supreme Court has acted, the appellate process is at an end on those issues disposed of by the Supreme Court. The lawsuit, however, might not be over. The Supreme Court might have "reversed and remanded" the case back to the trial court for a new trial "not inconsistent with this decision." Indeed, the lawsuit could go all the way back to the trial court and then, once again, come up through the appellate court system on a completely different legal issue.

§ 3.2(f) State Court Systems

The above "anatomy of a lawsuit" has dissected a typical court case as it winds its way through the federal court system. I must point out that a similar process takes place in the state court systems of the fifty states.

§ 3.2(f)(i) State Trial Courts

Most states have three-level court systems. At the bottom, a network of trial courts covers the entire state. These courts might be divided by cities, counties, or districts. The trial courts might be of various types. Small claims courts resolve minor claims. Some might only have criminal jurisdiction. Some might be a family court or an orphans court or a probate court. Regardless of their type, the process described above is at work.

§ 3.2(f)(ii) State Intermediate Appellate Courts

Most of the states have an intermediate appellate court system comparable to the United States Courts of Appeals. These courts might be called Appellate Courts, District Courts of Appeal, Special Courts of Appeal, Courts of Civil Appeals, Courts of Criminal Appeals, and the list goes on and on. Panels of three judges hear appeals from the trial courts. Oral argument might take place. Opinions are written, published, later found by legal researchers, and cited and analyzed by legal writers.

Some states, however, do not have an intermediate level of appellate courts. Appeals from trial courts go directly to the supreme court of the state, which usually exercises its discretion in deciding whether to hear an appeal or not. Until 1985, for example, Virginia did not have an intermediate court of appeal. Before that time, when the Virginia Court of Appeals was created, appeals went straight from trial courts to the Virginia Supreme Court. Now they first go to the intermediate court of appeals, much like a federal case goes to a circuit court before an appeal may be taken to the Supreme Court.

§ 3.2(f)(iii) State Supreme Courts

Losers at the intermediate appellate level then appeal to the highest state court, generally called a "Supreme Court," although some states call their highest courts the "Court of Appeals" (Maryland and New York), the "Supreme Judicial Court" (Maine), or the "Supreme Court of Appeals" (West Virginia). Regardless of its name, the same appellate process is at work. Briefs are filed, oral arguments made, decisions reached, opinions written, opinions published, case law ultimately found and cited and analyzed by legal writers.

As you gain familiarity with the research process, you should pay special attention to the courts deciding the cases you uncover in the research process. For example, if you find a case decided by the supreme court of a state and the issue involved is a pure state law issue (not a federal or constitutional law issue), then such an opinion is a "safe" opinion—that is, there is no higher court that could reverse such an opinion.

If, on the other hand, you find a case decided by the intermediate court of appeal, such an opinion is distinctly not "safe." The loser in that case might have appealed the decision to the state's supreme court. The supreme court might very well reverse that opinion. The appeal culminating in such a reversal takes place *after* the opinion at the intermediate level was published. So nothing on the title page of the case you found gives you the slightest hint that you are about to cite and use a case that is no longer good law.

As you develop your skills and slowly but surely attain the status of Ace Legal Researcher, you will of course commit to memory all of Good's Rules of Research. There will be many. Here's the first:

GOOD'S RULE OF RESEARCH #1:

Woe be unto the legal researcher who fails to notice the status of the court deciding the case.

By noticing the status of the court, e.g., that it is an intermediate court of appeal, the Ace Legal Researcher would immediately Shepardize such a case to ascertain that the case is still good law. By the same token, the Ace Legal Researcher would notice that an opinion was decided by a state's supreme court and would realize that immediate Shepardizing is not necessarily required.[4]

§ 3.3 Case Law and the Doctrine of Stare Decisis

Pouring out of trial courts, especially in the federal court system, out of state and federal intermediate appellate courts, and out of state and federal supreme courts is a flood of case law, a tidal wave of case law. Each year, thousands of new court opinions are written and published, only to be sought, found, and cited by legal researchers and writers.

Why do attorneys seek these cases? Why do they cite these cases in memos and briefs? Why do scholars pore over the implications of a single court opinion? The answer is found in the doctrine of stare decisis, an ancient doctrine inherited from English common law at the dawn of the legal system in the United States.

Stare decisis literally translates to "let the decision stand." The doctrine means that if the court and previous courts have decided this type of lawsuit in a certain way in the past, then let's continue to decide identical or sufficiently similar disputes the same way today and in the future. For example, if previous court opinions in a state have "held" that a mother and father may not recover the costs of rearing their child, born as the result of a physician's negligent sterilization procedure, then a mother and father cannot expect to recover such damages in a future lawsuit.

Why then would a mother and father bring such a case when they know that the case law of that state denies recovery in those types of cases? Because even though stare decisis is a strong doctrine discouraging rapid and radical change in rules of law, a court is not prevented from changing the law as found in its own decided cases. A lower court, on the other hand, is strictly bound by an "on-point" case rendered by a

[4]Don't worry. We'll cover all the ins and outs of Shepardizing in a later chapter.

higher court. After all, if the lower court refuses to follow the higher court case, the losing party appeals, and the higher court reverses the lower court.

§ 3.3(a) Don't Rock the Boat?

Stare decisis sounds like a crusty old doctrine that absolutely prohibits any change of ancient rules of law. Stare decisis might slow down change, but as noted above, change does come. This slowing down of change, however, is the precise purpose of the doctrine of stare decisis. By knowing the rules of the games of life—the rules of buying, selling, marrying, divorcing, investing, inheriting, giving, and contracting—people can know what to expect from their actions.

Justice William O. Douglas wrote an excellent description of the doctrine of stare decisis in a 1949 law review article:

> Most lawyers, by training and practice, are all too apt to turn their interests and their talents toward the finding not the creating of precedents. This lawyerly search is for moorings where clients can safely be anchored. But the search has, as well, a deeper, more personal impetus. For the lawyer himself shares the yearnings for security that is common to all people everywhere. And this yearning grows as the world seems to grow more *insecure* . . . .
>
> Uniformity and continuity in law are necessary to many activities. If they are not present, the integrity of contracts, wills, conveyances and securities is impaired. And there will be no equal justice under law if a negligence rule is applied in the morning but not in the afternoon. *Stare Decisis* provides some moorings so that men may trade and arrange their affairs with confidence. *Stare Decisis* serves to take the capricious element out of law and to give stability to a society. It is a strong tie which the future has to the past.[5]

§ 3.3(b) Cases "On Point"

Thus, the doctrine of stare decisis prompts attorneys to search for "on-point" cases in the law library. They hope to find a case decided by their state court or by their federal circuit court. They hope the case is virtually identical in its facts to their case and favorable in its result. They hope the rule of law found in the court opinion applies directly and favorably to their client's situation. To get the favorable result to apply precisely to their case, the attorneys try to show similarities of their case with the decided case. They "analogize" the favorable opinion.

If the case does not apply favorably, if the result goes the other way, the attorneys try to show that the decided case really differs from their case, that the rule in that unfavorable case really does not apply in their case. They "distinguish" the unfavorable case. If "distinguishing" the case does not work, they must then try to change the law, to meet the doctrine of stare decisis head on and convince the court the time is

[5]William O. Douglas, *Stare Decisis*, 49 Colum. L. Rev. 735, 736 (1949).

ripe for the old rule of law to give way to a new, more modern rule of law, which, naturally, is favorable to their client.

The attorneys' legal research reveals these "on-point" cases. When writing a memo analyzing their client's situation or a brief arguing their client's case to a court, the lawyers "cite" these earlier court opinions, which contain the case law governing their client's lawsuit.

It is almost time for *your* legal research to reveal the on-point cases you'll need for your Memorandum of Law. But before we take a detailed look at techniques for *finding* cases, let's first turn our attention to the techniques used to *publish* cases in the state and federal court systems. It is impossible to understand the intricacies of legal research without first understanding the court structures we've just discussed and the types of lawbooks that publish all cases in American law.

§ 3.4 Conclusion

In this chapter you learned how the judicial process produces "case law," which comprises the overwhelming bulk of law in the United States. Because of the sheer mass of material, you will undoubtedly find the retrieval of cases to be the most difficult part of the legal research process.

In the next chapter I'll carefully review the systems of "court reports" that publish American case law. To ensure your thorough understanding of these lawbooks, I'll ask you to complete a series of library exercises, which will include a self-guided tour of the National Reporter System, a colossal set of court reports totaling nearly 10,000 volumes.

CHAPTER 4

THE PUBLICATION OF AMERICAN CASE LAW

§ 4.1 Court Reports: Chronological Publication of Cases

§ 4.1(a) The Twilight Zone

When a court opinion is filed by the court with its clerk's office, the *case law* of that opinion becomes effective immediately in the territorial jurisdiction of that court. The opinion is binding on all lower courts within that system of courts. The opinion can affect our lives, the marketplace, the rights of criminal defendants, and the relationships between governments and government agencies. Thus, attorneys, and through them the public, want to know about law when it comes into being. This need for speed in legal publishing is satisfied by *chronological publication*. Quite simply, as case law is decided, it is immediately published in chronological systems of lawbooks known as "reports" or "reporters."[1]

Mark "chronological publication of law" down as a crucial concept for the Ace Legal Researcher. As this story unfolds, you will find that Ace Legal Researchers must keep track of time, not billable time but time on a legal research calendar, a moment known as "legal research time," a time dimension not unlike the Twilight Zone.[2]

No doubt the Catalogue of your law school or paralegal school failed to mention these weird time dimensions. But trust me. They do exist, they tend to befuddle, and they definitely threaten your status as Ace Legal Researcher. So early in the game, just accept as fact that time tends to spin in the world of legal research.

Also accept as fact that, just like "the soldier who saw everything twice" in Joseph Heller's *Catch-22*, when you enter the world of legal research, you will see everything twice as well.

---

[1]There is also an official working for the court called the "court reporter." It is his or her job to edit the opinions, make sure they are in publishable form, send them to the contract printer, and maintain the list of people subscribing to the "court reports."

[2]See? There is a plot. You're dying to know all about this time warp. Not telling.

Almost all law—especially cases and statutes—is published twice. That's right, twice. Sometimes thrice. First the government—state or federal—will publish the law in "official sources." Then the private sector comes along, dresses things up a bit, adds some neat features, speeds the process along, turns around, and publishes the same law all over again in "unofficial sources."[3]

So if time and rays of light tend to bend slightly in the dizzying world of legal research, it makes perfectly good sense to do everything twice. Or thrice.

§ 4.1(b) Chronological Publication

Cases are published chronologically in sequentially numbered volumes, each with sequentially numbered pages. These volumes are commonly called "court reports." Following the ordinary rules of legal citation will produce a "cite" to a case that might look like this: 126 N.E.2d 345. In the world of legal citation, we follow a rule I call the "number-book-number" rule, which simply means that whenever you see a number followed by an abbreviated name of a book followed by a number, such a citation means "volume-book-page." Thus, "126 N.E.2d 345" means *volume* 126, *page* 345 of the *North Eastern Reporter, Second Series*, a court report published by the West Publishing Company.

Many courts, most notably the federal circuit courts of appeal, will first publish their opinions individually, as little booklets or as stapled documents. Each opinion is separately published as a "slip opinion." Unfortunately, the slip opinions are not paginated chronologically as they will ultimately appear in the next bound volume of the court report, making the citation of cases to their slip opinion publication more difficult.

§ 4.1(c) Advance Sheets

Many court reports, in particular those published by the West Publishing Company, hasten the publication of cases by first publishing "advance sheets." Instead of waiting around for enough cases to accumulate to warrant the publication of the next bound volume, the publishers print part of the next volume as a paperback advance sheet. An example will illustrate the process.

Suppose the last bound volume of A.2d (the *Atlantic Reporter, Second Series*) is currently volume 601. As shown in Figure 3 on page 28, the next book published will be the advance sheet for volume 602. It will be called Volume 602, No. 1. It will have, say, pages 1 through 428. Then, the next book published will be the advance sheet called Volume 602, No. 2. It will have pages 429 through 986. Its page numbering picks up where the first advance sheet left off. The next separately published advance sheet actually might contain the tail end of volume 602 (pages 987 through 1328) and the beginning of volume 603 (pages 1 through 92). It might be called Volume 602, No. 3, Volume 603, No. 1.

[3]Don't let the name "unofficial" fool you. The unofficial sources usually are better, faster, and more accurate than the official sources.

At the bottom of the spine of these advance sheets you'll find a very important number, the "week number" (see Figure 3, next page). In the West system, advance sheets are published weekly,[4] that is, 52 times each year. The first advance sheet in a calendar year will bear the number "1" at the bottom of its spine. The next, not surprisingly, will have "2" at the bottom of its spine. And so on through the year until the last one has "52" at the bottom of its spine. The next one on the shelf will have "1" and the process repeats.

§ 4.1(d) Bound Volumes

Throughout the year, as bound volumes are received by the law library, the librarian will take the advance sheets encompassed by each bound volume and promptly deposit them in the recycled paper bin. Thus, at the end of each shelf of court reports, you'll find the bound volumes ending and the advance sheets beginning. A typical shelf, using the *Atlantic Reporter* as an example, might look like this:

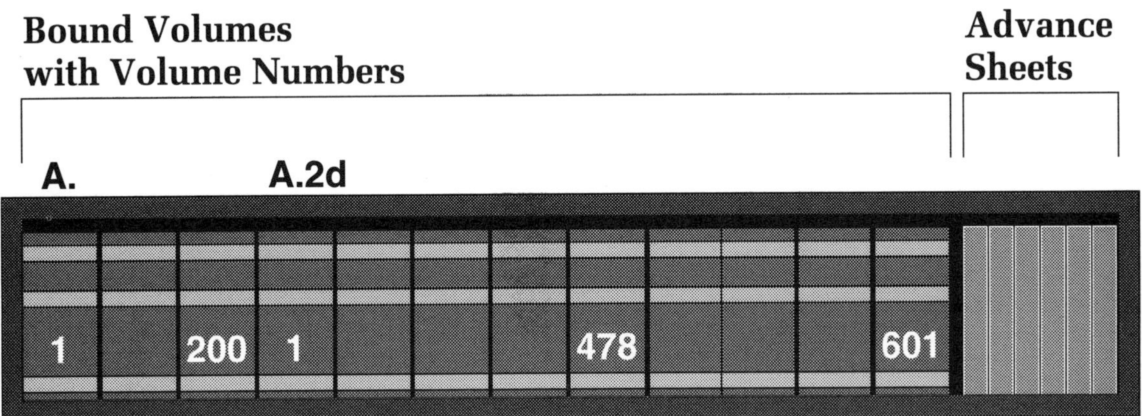

Figure 2

Bound Volumes and Advance Sheets

§ 4.1(e) The NO ZONE

As you make your way slowly toward that coveted status of Ace Legal Researcher, you will find that these "week numbers" on the spines of advance sheets become a crucial bit of information. You will find that one of these advance sheets, and hence one "week number," will mark the beginning of the dreaded "NO ZONE," a strange dimension in time where the laws of physics no longer pertain. The NO ZONE, as you will learn in Chapter 8, comprises the only area of case law legal research where "volume-by-volume" searching becomes mandatory. As you traverse this NO ZONE, you'll find that you never find any on-point cases. And, when the NO ZONE lulls you to sleep and you decide *not* to research through the NO ZONE, you guessed it: on-point cases reside there, waiting for retrieval by you know who—your opponent! The plot thickens.

[4]An exception is the *Supreme Court Reporter*, whose advance sheets appear every other week.

The following figure shows what the tail end of a library shelf might look like, with the end of bound volumes and the beginning of advance sheets. Somewhere near the end of the shelf, the dreaded NO ZONE begins. Exactly where becomes the subject of Chapter 8.

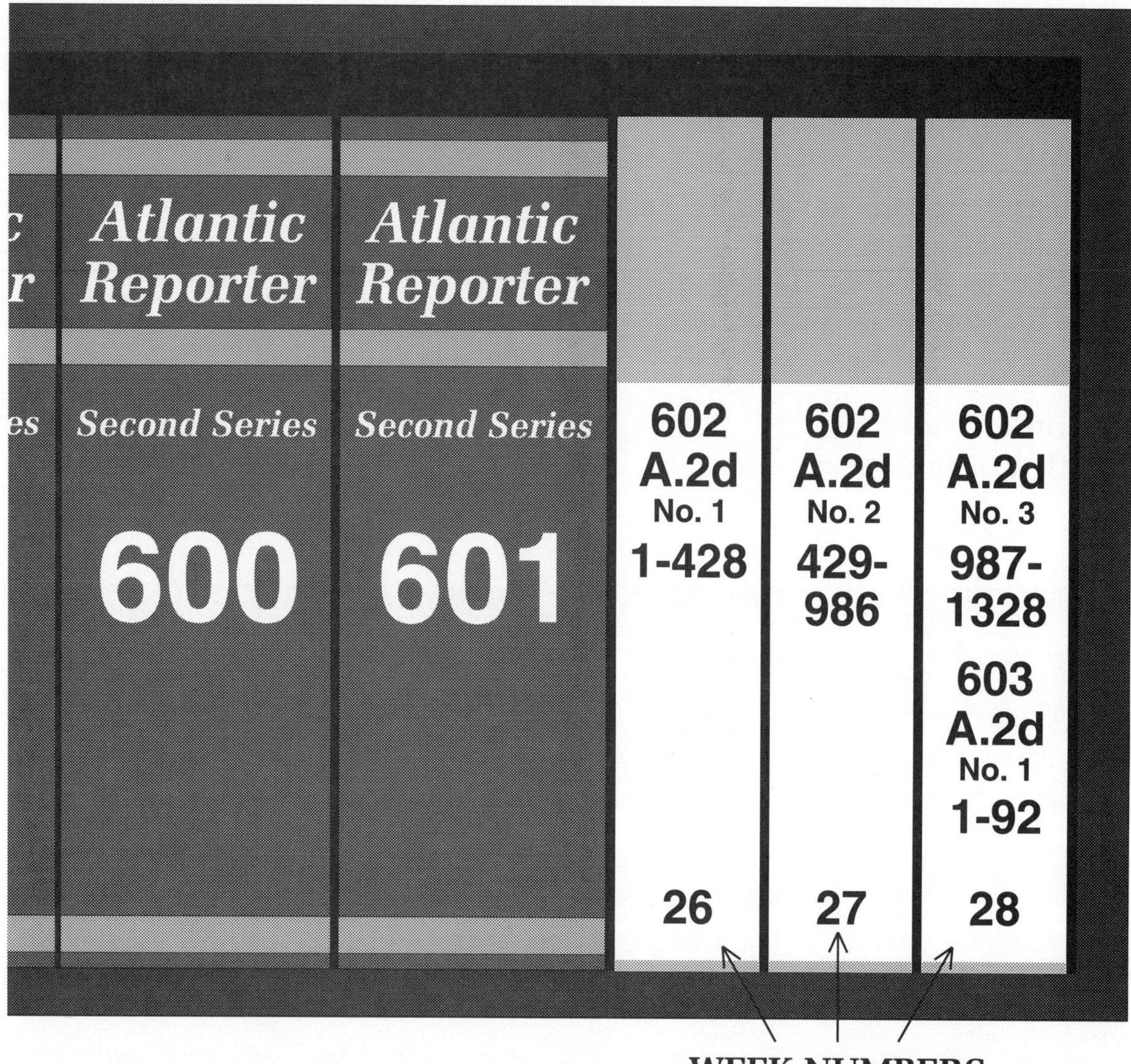

Figure 3
Advance Sheets

§ 4.1(f) Marking Time

You can readily see that a chronological system of court reporting not only satisfies the need for speed but creates a sort of primitive calendar, which prehistoric legal researchers used to tick away moments in time. Thus, as you can see on the above figure, 602 A.2d 1-428 represents "week number 26" whereas 602 A.2d 429-986 hit the shelf one week later. By the same token, you can see that the citation 602 N.E.2d 521 marks a precise "week in time," that is, law librarians of the universe deposited that citation on the shelf at a precise moment in time. The citation 602 N.E.2d 412 occurred earlier, and the citation 602 N.E.2d 992 occurred later.

As you yearn for the status of Ace Legal Researcher, you will find out that membership in this elite club requires your thorough understanding of this "citation calendar." As part of your initiation rites, we will return to the concept of time, time and time again. It is, after all, about time itself.

§ 4.1(g) Tables of Cases and Other Finding Aids

Within each court report volume, you will find an alphabetical listing of the cases reported in that volume with a cross-reference to the page number where each opinion begins. Each case is listed twice (but of course), once under the plaintiff's or appellant's name and once under the defendant's or appellee's name. Thus, the famous case of Jones v. Smith is listed in the case table under the J's as follows:

"Jones v. Smith. . . . . 346"

The same case is listed under the S's as follows:

"Smith; Jones v. . . . . 346"

When you study correct legal citation form, you will see a relationship between the rules of citing case names and the existence of these alphabetical case tables. If we cite cases found in court reports in much the same way as those same cases are listed in the case tables, then we are helping the reader of our brief or memo locate those cases we cite, especially in those instances where the "citation" to the case, 264 N.E.2d *123*, is typed incorrectly as 264 N.E.2d *213*. If the reader is referred to the name of the case the same way the case is listed in the alphabetical table of cases, the reader can find the case in the case tables. You might wonder what happens when the *volume number* is typed incorrectly. How can the reader get to the correct volume to find the correct table of cases? I'll answer this question in Chapter 8, where I discuss the Tables of Cases appearing in the American Digest System.

These case tables are not really helpful in the legal research process. After all, you don't know the name of the case you're looking for. You're just looking for any case on a particular *topic* and could care less about its name. Well, case tables are not the only "finding aids" in court reports. Each volume has a "table of statutes," which sequentially lists federal and state statutes construed by any case reported in that court report volume. While the tables of statutes do serve a more important research function than the case tables, you will find that you use them only rarely in the research process.

Instead, in legal research, you'll be using the American Digest System, which acts like a subject matter index. Each volume of court report has such a "subject matter index," which in the West Company scheme of things is a breakdown of law into minute "Key Numbers." You'll learn a great deal about Key Numbers in later chapters. For now, just learn that each volume of court report has a subject matter index, which classifies law into a system divided into Key Numbers.

Of vital importance, please learn that in the court reports the Key Number system appears at the *back* of bound volumes and the *front* of advance sheets.

§ 4.2 Official Court Reports

§ 4.2(a) State Cases

About half of the fifty states publish the opinions of their courts officially. Remember that most states have three-level court systems so that opinions are issued by intermediate courts of appeal and by the supreme courts of the states. Significantly, a state usually publishes a separate set of reports for its supreme court and another separate set of reports for its intermediate courts. The reports of the highest courts of virtually all of the states are abbreviated by the abbreviation of the state standing by itself (State Abbreviation Standing by Itself Means the Highest Court). The reports of the intermediate courts, on the other hand, are abbreviated by the state abbreviation plus something else (State Abbreviation Plus Something Else Means the Intermediate Court). This "something else" might be App. (Appellate), Ct. App. (Court of Appeals), Ch. (Chancery), or a host of other possibilities.

Thus, in legal research, when you see a citation to "123 Va. 618, 132 S.E.2d 402," you know that the opinion came from the highest court in Virginia. But when you see a citation to "69 Va. App. 143, 123 S.E.2d 324," you know that the opinion is from some lower court in Virginia, usually the intermediate court of appeals. Knowing this vital information will help you follow Good's Rule of Research #1, which bears repeating here:

GOOD'S RULE OF RESEARCH #1:

Woe be unto the legal researcher who fails to notice the status of the court deciding the case.

Another point on official state reports must be covered. Some states have published their reports in "series." California, for example, published the reports of its supreme court in the *California Reports* (abbreviated "Cal."). It then discontinued the *California Reports* and picked up with the *California Reports, Second Series* (abbreviated "Cal. 2d"). It then discontinued the *California Reports, Second Series* and picked up with the *California Reports, Third Series* (abbreviated "Cal. 3d"). Recently, it discontinued the *California Reports, Third Series* and picked up with the *California Reports, Fourth Series* (abbreviated "Cal. 4th"). For now, you should remember that these "2d's," "3d's," and "4th's" do not constitute the "something else" in the State Abbreviation Plus Something Else Rule. A citation to 23 Cal. 3d 482 is a citation to a case from the highest court of California. The State Abbreviation Standing by Itself Rule still applies.

You should also know that many of the fifty states do not even officially publish the opinions of their courts. Either they have never published their case law, or they have stopped the practice of publishing cases officially. Instead of publishing their cases, these states just rely on the West Company to make their decisions available to the public in its "National Reporter System" (fully discussed below).

Thus, in legal research, you will often encounter citations that look like this: Jones v. Smith, 342 So. 2d 198 (Fla. 1972), a citation that does not even have a citation to an official court report. When you see such a citation, it typically means that the state has stopped publishing its cases officially and relies solely on the West Publishing Company to make its cases available in the National Reporter System.[5] In the above citation the "Fla." in the parentheses alerts you that the case was decided by the highest court in that state. Now consider this citation: Jones v. Jackson, 321 So. 2d 980 (Fla. Dist. Ct. App. 1968). Here the "Fla. Dist. Ct. App.," i.e., the state abbreviation plus something else, alerts you that the court deciding the case was *not* the highest court but some lower court, usually the intermediate court of appeals.

§ 4.2(b) Federal Cases

Few of the federal courts have official reports. Of the courts we've discussed—Supreme Court, courts of appeal, and district courts—only the Supreme Court of the United States officially reports its cases. Most of the courts of appeal (the "circuits") and all of the district courts (the "districts") do not have official reports.

The Supreme Court began publishing its official reports in 1790. Until 1875 these reports bore the individual names of the Supreme Court "reporter," the official at the Court in charge of publishing the opinions. These reports, and many in the older state court report systems, are called "nominative" reports. Thus, the first four volumes of the official reports of the Supreme Court were named after Mr. Dallas and were called the *Dallas Reports*. They would be cited, for example, 1 Dall. 201.

In 1875 the first 90 volumes of the official reports of Supreme Court opinions were renamed the *United States Reports*. Even though these 90 volumes were renamed, they continue to be cited partially to the official U.S. citation and partially to the older nominative report citation. Thus, you will see older Supreme Court cases cited to 26 U.S. (1 Pet.) 344, that is, volume 26 of the renamed *United States Reports*, which is also volume 1 of the older *Peters Reports*, page 344. The following table shows the relationship between these older nominative reports and the official reports:

[5]Please note that the new Harvard *Bluebook* has abolished the "parallel citation rule" for most legal documents. Thus, you will encounter more and more citations omitting the official court report. The parenthetical abbreviation of the court, therefore, becomes the source of "court identity" information. Please see Chapter 6 in *Citing & Typing the Law* (LEL Enterprises 1992) for a complete explanation.

The Relationship between Nominative and U.S. Reports

Reporter	Nominative Citation	U.S. Reports	Dates Covered
Dallas	1 - 4 Dall.	1 - 4 U.S.	1790-1800
Cranch	1 - 9 Cranch	5 - 13 U.S.	1801-1815
Wheaton	1 - 12 Wheat.	14 - 25 U.S.	1816-1827
Peters	1 - 16 Pet.	26 - 41 U.S.	1828-1842
Howard	1 - 24 How.	42 - 65 U.S.	1843-1860
Black	1 - 2 Black	66 - 67 U.S.	1861-1862
Wallace	1 - 23 Wall.	68 - 90 U.S.	1863-1874
U.S. Reports		91 - date	1875-date

§ 4.2(c) Other Federal Courts

The above discussion of the federal court system did not include certain other federal courts that handle special kinds of cases. You should know about these courts, and I introduce them here because some do have official reports.

The following courts are special courts of the United States that handle particular types of cases. The table shows the name of the court, the correct abbreviation of the official report, and the dates of coverage of the reports.

Court	Report	Dates Covered
U.S. Claims Court	Cl. Ct.	1982-date
(formerly U.S. Court of Claims)	Ct. Cl.	1956-1982
U.S. Court of Appeals for the Federal Circuit	No official report	
(formerly Court of Customs and Patent Appeals)	C.C.P.A.	1929-1982
Court of International Trade	Ct. Int'l Trade	1980-date
(formerly Customs Court)	Cust. B. & Dec.	1980-date
	Cust. Ct.	1938-1980

One other type of frequently encountered court is the United States Bankruptcy Court. They do not have official reports, their opinions appearing in a West Company publication, *Bankruptcy Reporter*. I should mention that other federal courts do exist, e.g., the Tax Court, Board of Tax Appeals, Court of Military Appeals, Judicial Panel on Multidistrict Litigation. A listing of these and other federal courts, and the names and abbreviations of reports publishing their decisions, can be found in the Harvard *Bluebook* on pages 165-67.

§ 4.2(d) Summary of Official Reports

Most of the state courts and some of the federal courts publish their court opinions officially. As a general rule, each court report publishes the decisions of only one court so that a citation to a particular court report not only tells the reader "where to go" but "which court" decided the case. Also, for state opinions, the official court report of the highest court in a state is abbreviated by the "state abbreviation standing by itself." Lower state court reports are abbreviated by the "state abbreviation plus something else." Thus, the name of the court report not only can tell us "where to go" but "which court" decided the case.

These chronological reports of case law satisfied the need for speed. But they created havoc for the legal researcher who wanted to find cases on point. After all, no one would want to search through the subject matter indexes of thousands of separate volumes of court reports to locate a case somewhere in the United States.

A need for "location" thus conflicted with the need for "speed." Legal researchers needed access to the opinions quickly, so publishers printed them chronologically. But legal researchers also needed to have a way to *find* case law by *subject matter.* Thus, they needed these cases *rearranged by subject matter.* Imagine, however, trying to rearrange the full text of all cases and reprinting them in a subject matter arrangement.[6] How, for example, would we handle the cases that deal with more than one subject matter, as most do? Do we print the full text of each opinion as many times as needed to classify each case to each legal subject matter it concerned?

No, reprinting the full text of case law in a subject matter arrangement was not the answer. But someone had to develop a subject matter system to enable attorneys to find cases on point, state or federal cases, cases anywhere in the entire country. If such a system could not be developed, then stare decisis might be a forgotten doctrine, for there is no way to "let the decision stand" if we cannot *find* the decision in the first place. Such a system was also needed to promote uniformity among state case law. If the attorneys and courts of one state could not find the decisions of another state, they would be stuck with their own, provincial approach to case law. New ideas, new case law tried in another state could not possibly influence new trends in other states if attorneys in those other states could not find the law from all states.

What this big drum roll is all about, of course, is the introduction of "unofficial reports," the National Reporter System, and some preliminary mention of subject matter classification of American case law, the American Digest System, both created by the West Publishing Company. I'll deal extensively with the National Reporter System because a working knowledge of it is vital if you're ever to become an Ace Legal Researcher. The American Digest System, by the same token, will become the central focus of your research strategy and will be described in detail in Chapter 8.

[6]You'll find out that publishers do precisely that when printing legislative law. For example, they publish federal statutes chronologically in the *Statutes at Large* and then turn around and reprint them again in a subject matter arrangement called the *United States Code.*

§ 4.3 Unofficial Court Reports: National Reporter System

§ 4.3(a) The West Company

In the late 1800s numerous problems existed in the official reporting of case law. In the states, publication was quite slow, often for good reason. The judicial "output" during a given year might not warrant the publication of an entire bound volume, so the court would wait until enough cases accumulated to justify bound volume publication. Also, attorneys wanting to locate opinions in other states would face the ordeals of purchasing other sets of reports and confronting different research systems.

The problems in the federal area were even more severe. Only the Supreme Court had official reports of its opinions. The lower federal court opinions were published by as many as 200 private publishing companies, extremely localized operations. Even federal judges did not have access to all federal case law decided by all federal courts.

The time was ripe for a national and uniform system that would publish the opinions of all courts—state and federal—throughout the United States. The West Publishing Company succeeded in this competition by producing the National Reporter System and the American Digest System.

The National Reporter System publishes the decisions of all state supreme and intermediate appellate courts; some state trial courts; all federal Supreme, circuit, district, and bankruptcy courts; and some special federal courts. For most courts, West publishes these opinions in advance sheet form every week; the *Supreme Court Reporter* advance sheets, however, appear semimonthly. Each part of the National Reporter System uses a standard format of publishing the opinions, contains standard finding aids, and classifies the legal issues of every case to the standard American Digest System.

The National Reporter System now numbers nearly 10,000 volumes. Each volume contains an average of 1,200 pages. Thus, the West Company has printed nearly 12,000,000 pages of American case law. To become an Ace Legal Researcher, you must thoroughly understand the arrangement of the National Reporter System. I'll guide you through a tour of the West reporters, taking the state courts first followed by the federal courts. Then I'll urge you to take your own tour in a real law library so that these books "come alive."

§ 4.3(b) State Case Law: Regional Reporters

When the West Publishing Company started its National Reporter System, it well knew the economics of the publishing industry. In order to create a successful and profitable system of court reports, West needed to attain a certain volume of sales. It realized it could not profitably support a *separate* publication of a single state's cases. There were not enough attorneys in a single state to support such an approach. Consequently, West created a series of seven "regional reporters," each of which would publish the cases of several states. Thus, in the late 1800s, if an attorney in Virginia wanted Virginia cases from the West Company, he would have to subscribe to the *South Eastern Reporter* and receive cases from Georgia, North Carolina, South Carolina, and West Virginia as well.

West divided the country into seven "geographic" regions: Northeast, Southeast, Northwest, Southwest, Atlantic, Pacific, and Southern. As you can see in the table below, these regional reporters might bear "regional" names, but some states included in particular regional reporters are not generally thought of as being from that geographic region of the country. After all, how many people do you know from Ohio who say they're from the "northeast"? Apparently, West was not mistaking its geography but was trying to group those states having similar economic and agricultural interests.

The Regional Reporters of the National Reporter System

Regional Reporter	Cite	States Covered
Atlantic and Atlantic 2d	A. A.2d	Conn., Del., D.C., Me., Md., N.H., N.J., Pa., R.I., Vt.
North Eastern and North Eastern 2d	N.E. N.E.2d	Ill., Ind., Mass., N.Y., Ohio
North Western and North Western 2d	N.W. N.W.2d	Iowa, Mich., Minn., Neb., N.D., S.D., Wis.
Pacific and Pacific 2d	P. P.2d	Alaska, Ariz., Cal., Colo., Haw., Idaho, Kan., Mont., Nev., N.M., Okla., Or., Utah, Wash., Wyo.
South Eastern and South Eastern 2d	S.E. S.E.2d	Ga., N.C., S.C., Va., W. Va.
South Western and South Western 2d	S.W. S.W.2d	Ark., Ky., Mo., Tenn., Tex.
Southern and Southern 2d	So. So. 2d	Ala., Fla., La., Miss.

These seven regional reporters publish the decisions of all state supreme courts and all state intermediate courts. (The sole exceptions are the intermediate courts of California and New York, which are now excluded from P.2d and N.E.2d.) By subscribing to all seven of these reporters, attorneys in the late 1800s could receive state case law from all states. Even if lawyers subscribed only to the regional reporter covering their state, they would get the case law from nearby states. Certainly the development of this system has prompted trends toward uniformity in state case law.

Please note that all seven regional reporters are currently in their "second series." Sometime between 1920 and 1940, West divided the regional reporters into two series. After this decision was made, West waited until each regional reporter reached the next hundred volume number. So when the *North Western Reporter* reached volume 300, West numbered the next volume as volume 1 of the *North Western Reporter, Second Series*. You can readily see how important it is to include the "2d" in the citation to a second series West regional reporter. If you intend to cite 187 N.W.2d 511 and mistakenly omit the "2d," you have sent your reader to 187 N.W. 511. You have sent your reader to volume 187 of the *North Western Reporter*, page 511, not to volume 187 of the *North Western Reporter, Second Series*, page 511.

This "2d" business will help you in the legal research process. You will soon learn that legal publishers made a gigantic mistake when they began to publish legal research sources: they would cite lots of cases but omit the dates from those citations. Thus, when you research and uncover cases on point, the bum publishing companies don't always tell you when those cases were decided.

But remember your calendar! Remember that each unit of the National Reporter System has its own internal calendar and that a single volume and page number marks a precise *week* in time. Also remember that the old first series ended roughly between 1920 and 1940. Thus, the "2d" in a citation marks a case as a fairly modern decision, not one of those old ancient decisions requiring you to plow through cobwebs in the law library to get your hands on it and inevitably evoking paroxysms of sneezing as you open its dust-encrusted pages in the gloomy light of the stacks in the bowels of the law library. Isn't this fun?

§ 4.3(c) State Case Law: Two Special State Reporters

In the late 1800s one state did have enough attorneys to support the publication of a single state court report: New York. Thus, the West Company published the *New York Supplement* (N.Y.S.), which reported the cases of the highest court of New York and many lower courts. This report, too, is now in its second series, *New York Supplement, Second Series* (N.Y.S.2d).

Thus, New York cases would be published in three places: (1) official court reports, (2) West regional reporter (N.E., N.E.2d), and (3) the *New York Supplement* (N.Y.S., N.Y.S.2d).

When the *New York Supplement, Second Series* was published, the West Company decided to remove the New York lower court cases from N.E.2d and publish them only in N.Y.S.2d. These lower court cases are published in two places: (1) official court reports and (2) N.Y.S.2d.

A second state now receives similar treatment: California. West's *California Reporter* began in the late 1950s to publish the opinions of the California courts. West removed the lower California courts from P.2d. The California Supreme Court, however, is published in three places: (1) official court reports, (2) West regional reporter (P., P.2d), and (3) the *California Reporter* (Cal. Rptr., Cal. Rptr. 2d). Lower California courts appear in two places: (1) official reports and (2) the *California Reporter*. In the fall of 1991, the *California Reporter* ended with volume 286, the next volume appearing as volume 1 of the new *California Reporter, Second Series* (Cal. Rptr. 2d).

§ 4.3(d) Federal Case Law

§ 4.3(d)(i) Supreme Court

West publishes the decisions of the Supreme Court in the *Supreme Court Reporter* (S. Ct.). The big competitor to West, Lawyers Cooperative Publishing Company, also publishes Supreme Court opinions in *Lawyers Edition* and *Lawyers Edition, Second Series* (L. Ed. and L. Ed. 2d). A fourth publication, published by the Bureau of National Affairs, reports Supreme Court opinions on a weekly basis in *United States Law Week* (U.S.L.W.).

Thus, Supreme Court opinions appear in four places, one official and three unofficial:

Report	Cite
United States Reports (official)	U.S.
Supreme Court Reporter (West)	S. Ct.
Lawyers Edition (Lawyers Co-op) *Lawyers Edition, Second Series*	L. Ed. L. Ed. 2d
United States Law Week (BNA)	U.S.L.W.

§ 4.3(d)(ii) Lower Federal Courts

In the late 1800s over 200 separate reports published the cases of the lower federal courts. To realize its vision of a single, uniform system of publishing all cases in the United States, West devised a single report to publish lower federal court cases.

To provide a permanent resting place for those cases already in existence, West arranged all lower federal court cases alphabetically and published what is perhaps the only alphabetical arrangement of cases in a source called *Federal Cases*. In the publication, these alphabetically arranged cases are given sequential numbers so that they are cited not only by volume and page number but by case number as well. Only rarely in modern law practice do attorneys find the need to research these older federal cases. We thus turn our attention to the sources West developed for the ongoing publication of federal case law.

After alphabetically arranging and publishing all then-existing lower federal court cases in *Federal Cases*, West introduced its *Federal Reporter* (F.) to report lower trial and appellate federal court opinions. The *Federal Reporter* continued until 1929 when West stopped the first series and introduced the *Federal Reporter, Second*

Series (F.2d). Until 1932, these two reports published all lower federal court case law (circuit and district).

In 1932, West decided to publish the courts of appeals and the trial courts separately, so it created the *Federal Supplement* (F. Supp.). To this day, you will find the circuits published in F.2d and the districts published in F. Supp.[7]

I should point out that many of the "other" federal courts also appear in F.2d or F. Supp. Those appellate in nature appear in F.2d. Those that are trial courts appear in F. Supp. The United States Court of Claims, for example, appeared in F. Supp. from 1932 to 1960. In 1960, when appeals from the Court of Claims were allowed to go directly to the Supreme Court, West changed the publication of its cases from F. Supp. to F.2d since the Court of Claims was more on the level with the courts of appeals. The Court of Claims was recently renamed the United States Claims Court. Its opinions are officially reported in the *Claims Court Reports* (Cl. Ct.) but no longer appear in F. Supp. or F.2d.

To round out its system of federal court reports, West publishes cases involving the federal rules of procedure in *Federal Rules Decisions* (F.R.D.). As a legal researcher, you should also know that F.R.D. publishes articles analyzing the federal rules and can therefore serve as an excellent background source when researching problems dealing with the federal rules of procedure. Finally, West publishes cases from the Bankruptcy Courts in the *Bankruptcy Reporter* (B.R.).

The following table shows the unofficial reports of the federal courts, the abbreviations of their cites, and the courts they cover:

[7]As this book goes to press in late 1992, the *Federal Reporter, Second Series*, "F.2d," is approaching its 1000th volume. The legal profession quakes with anticipation as it wonders whether the volume numbers will continue beyond 1000 or *Federal Reporter, Third Series* will make its debut on the shelf. If the latter, then "F.2d" and "F.3d" will mark a case as a federal circuit court opinion.

Unofficial Federal Court Reports

Report	Cite	Courts Covered
Supreme Court Reporter	S. Ct.	U.S. Supreme Court
Lawyers Edition	L. Ed.	U.S. Supreme Court
Lawyers Edition 2d	L. Ed. 2d	U.S. Supreme Court
United States Law Week	U.S.L.W.	U.S. Supreme Court and other state and federal courts
Federal Cases	F. Cas.	Circuits and Districts until 1880
Federal Reporter	F.	Courts of Appeals, District Courts and special trial and appellate courts until 1929
Federal Reporter 2d	F.2d[8]	Courts of Appeals and special appellate courts, 1929-present
Federal Supplement	F. Supp.	District Courts and other special trial courts, 1932-present
Federal Rules Decisions	F.R.D.	Federal cases involving the federal rules of procedure, 1938-present
Bankruptcy Reporter	B.R.	Bankruptcy Courts and other federal courts, 1975-present

§ 4.4 Summary of Official and Unofficial Reports

As you can see (twice), many court opinions appear in two places: in the official court report and in the West court report. This multiple publication takes place in those states that continue to report their cases officially and in the Supreme Court of the United States, which has its cases published in four places (U.S., S. Ct., L. Ed. 2d, U.S.L.W.).

We've discussed the judicial process in America. We've learned what court opinions are, why attorneys want to find and cite them, and where they are published. Now it's almost time to see how to find cases on point, cases governing any legal

[8]Again, "F.3d" might appear after F.2d reaches volume 1000.

research topic imaginable. But first you will understand the systems of official and unofficial court reporting much better if you complete the following library exercises.

§ 4.5 Library Exercises

Find a fully equipped law library, either in your own firm or in a law school, government agency, court, or bar association. When you arrive at the law library, ask the librarian where the National Reporter System is shelved. Take a tour through all the court reports we've discussed and complete the chart below. You are asked to locate the volume numbers of the last volumes of any "first series" West reports, the volume numbers of the latest bound volumes of the current West reports, and the volume numbers of the latest advance sheets of the current West reports. When you fill in this information in the chart, you can then calculate the total number of West reports to see just how big the National Reporter System is. After you complete the chart, then follow the instructions for some additional library exercises.

§ 4.5(a) Library Exercise: National Reporter System

Instructions: Complete the following chart by visiting the National Reporter System in a well-equipped law library. Fill in the volume numbers indicated for each reporter. The West reports are designated by their proper abbreviations. If you do not recognize them, then review the above discussion of the National Reporter System.

Reporter	First Series Last Volume No.	Current Series, Latest Bound Volume No.	Latest Advance Sheet Volume No.
A.	_____		
A.2d		_____	_____
P.	_____		
P.2d		_____	_____
N.E.	_____		
N.E.2d		_____	_____
S.E.	_____		
S.E.2d		_____	_____
N.W.	_____		
N.W.2d		_____	_____
S.W.	_____		
S.W.2d		_____	_____
So.	_____		
So. 2d		_____	_____
N.Y.S.	_____		
N.Y.S.2d		_____	_____
Cal. Rptr.	_____		
Cal. Rptr. 2d		_____	_____
F.	_____		
F.2d[9]		_____	_____
F. Supp.		_____	_____
F.R.D.		_____	_____
S. Ct.		_____	_____
B.R.		_____	_____
TOTALS	(First) _____	(Current)	_____

GRAND TOTAL First ________ + Current ________ = ______________

Note: A chart completed as of September 16, 1991, appears at the end of this chapter.

[9]If F.3d has arrived by the time you attempt to complete this chart, please add the necessary lines to accommodate its "latest bound volume number" and "latest advance sheet volume number." If it does appear, F.2d, of course, will not have a "latest advance sheet volume number" but will have closed out its bound volumes with 1000.

§ 4.5(b) Library Exercise: Flowers v. District of Columbia

So that you can see what a court opinion is like, and so that you can actually read a court opinion, locate the following case in the A.2d Reporter:

Flowers v. District of Columbia, 478 A.2d 1073 (D.C. 1983)

Have the case photocopied and take it home with you. It involves the liability of a surgeon for a negligent sterilization operation that caused (er, helped to cause) the birth of plaintiff's healthy but unwanted child.

§ 4.6 Picking *Flowers*

First, I picked *Flowers* so I could come up with the terrible pun to which you have just been subjected. Second, I picked *Flowers* because it's on point to Wally and Mipsie's case. And third, I picked *Flowers* because it represents *any case* and can serve as a learning tool just as well as any other case.

If you neglected to complete the library exercise in section 4.5(b) above, I have reproduced the title page of *Flowers* on pages 44 and 45. To become an Ace Legal Researcher, you must learn the features of the title page of a case published by the West Publishing Company, features that play a vital role in the overall legal research process.

§ 4.7 The Title Page of a Case

At the top of the title page of *Flowers* you see what's called the "running head": "Flowers v. District of Columbia." You may use the running head as a "guide" to citing the case name, but you should become accustomed right off the bat to citing case names correctly according to the system of citation found in the Harvard *Bluebook*. So don't be suckered by the running head into citing and abbreviating the case name incorrectly. Here, "Flowers v. District of Columbia" happens to be the correct way to cite the case name, but many running heads incorrectly abbreviate case names.

Below the running head you'll find the following: "Cite as 478 A.2d 1073 (D.C.App. 1984)." Now immediately before this word, right there on your photocopy of *Flowers* or right here in this book you should write this word: "DON'T." That's right: "DON'T Cite as." That's the West Company's way of citing the case; it's not the Harvard *Bluebook* way: 478 A.2d 1073 (D.C. 1984). (The *Bluebook* would identify the highest court of a jurisdiction by the abbreviation of that jurisdiction—D.C.—standing all by itself. "D.C.App." is thus incorrect. And even if "D.C.App." were correct it would still be incorrect; a space must appear before any multiletter abbreviation, *viz.* "D.C. App.")

In the right column at the top of the page you'll find the "caption" of the case: "Geraldine Flowers, Appellant v. District of Columbia, Appellee." From this information, you can immediately see who won and who lost. The appellant is the loser "below," i.e., at trial or at a lower appellate court; the appellee is the winner below.

Below the caption you'll find "No. 82-133," the docket number in the court rendering the decision. Then you'll find the dates when the case was argued and the ultimate date when the case was decided. It is the "decision date" that appears in the parentheses of a legal citation.

Then you'll find a terribly written paragraph with endless sentences and a horrible legal style characterized primarily by the omission of all articles (a, an, the). This is the "prefatory statement" describing the case and the holding of the court. It is written by an editor at the West Publishing Company who has the misfortune of never having read my book, *Mightier than the Sword—Powerful Writing in the Legal Profession* (LEL Enterprises 1988).

In the legal research process, the prefatory statement should serve as a "case eliminator." By quickly reading the prefatory statement, you can often see that the case does not merit your time and attention. Or, by the same token, you can see that the case is right on point and should demand some of your time and attention.

Below the prefatory statement you will find a word that causes great stress to first-time legal researchers and cite checkers. In the *Flowers* case you'll see the word "Affirmed" at the end of the prefatory statement. That word means that the opinion *you are about to read* "affirmed" the case in the court below. That word does *not* mean that *Flowers* was affirmed by some later court higher up in the court system. A moment's thought would reveal the impossibility of such an occurrence: when *Flowers* was decided, the West Company immediately printed it; the loser in *Flowers* would be simultaneously trying to appeal, a process that would take quite some time; thus, it would be impossible for West to print "Affirmed" on the title page of *Flowers* if that meant that *Flowers* itself had been *later* affirmed by some higher court.

So don't let that word "Affirmed" lead you to believe that *Flowers* has what is called "subsequent case history," which should appear in a citation to *Flowers*. Only rarely will such case history appear on the title page of a case itself, and that case history typically is a denial of certiorari by the Supreme Court. If such case history has occurred in time for the West Company to include it on the title page, you will find that information right below the date of decision. *You will not find it at the end of the prefatory statement. Those words are telling you what this case—the one you are about to read—did to the lower court from which the case came.*

§ 4.7(a) Headnotes

Following the prefatory statement you'll find a series of terribly written paragraphs called "headnotes." These headnotes are also products of the editors at the West Company. Note that each headnote has a name, such as "Damages" or "Physicians and Surgeons." Note also that each headnote then has a "Key Number" as shown by the little key symbol.

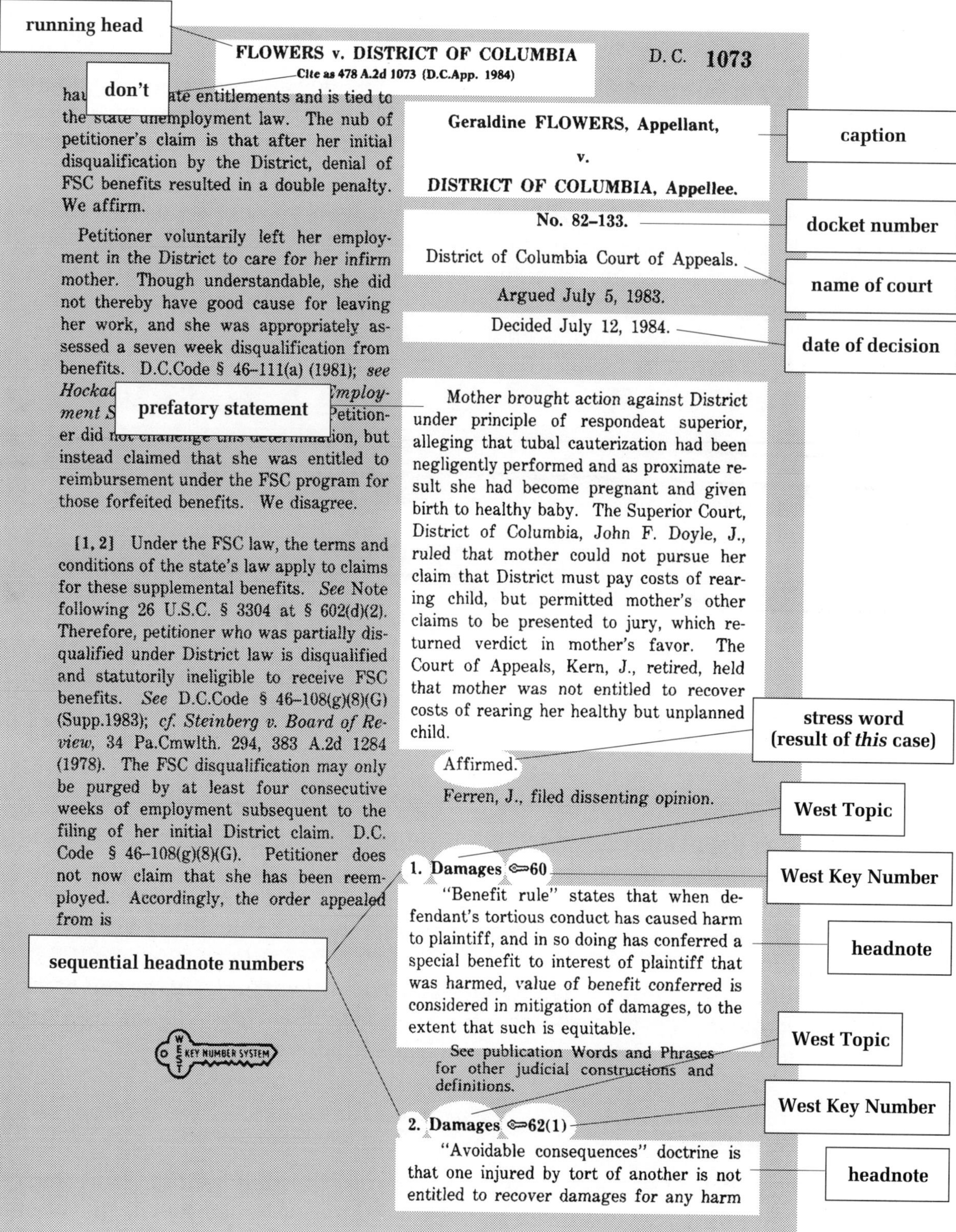

FLOWERS v. DISTRICT OF COLUMBIA D.C. 1073
Cite as 478 A.2d 1073 (D.C.App. 1984)

ha[...]ate entitlements and is tied to the [...]mployment law. The nub of petitioner's claim is that after her initial disqualification by the District, denial of FSC benefits resulted in a double penalty. We affirm.

Petitioner voluntarily left her employment in the District to care for her infirm mother. Though understandable, she did not thereby have good cause for leaving her work, and she was appropriately assessed a seven week disqualification from benefits. D.C.Code § 46–111(a) (1981); *see Hockad[...]mploy-ment S[...]* Petitioner did [...]ion, but instead claimed that she was entitled to reimbursement under the FSC program for those forfeited benefits. We disagree.

[1, 2] Under the FSC law, the terms and conditions of the state's law apply to claims for these supplemental benefits. *See* Note following 26 U.S.C. § 3304 at § 602(d)(2). Therefore, petitioner who was partially disqualified under District law is disqualified and statutorily ineligible to receive FSC benefits. *See* D.C.Code § 46–108(g)(8)(G) (Supp.1983); *cf. Steinberg v. Board of Review*, 34 Pa.Cmwlth. 294, 383 A.2d 1284 (1978). The FSC disqualification may only be purged by at least four consecutive weeks of employment subsequent to the filing of her initial District claim. D.C. Code § 46–108(g)(8)(G). Petitioner does not now claim that she has been reemployed. Accordingly, the order appealed from is

Geraldine FLOWERS, Appellant,

v.

DISTRICT OF COLUMBIA, Appellee.

No. 82–133.

District of Columbia Court of Appeals.

Argued July 5, 1983.

Decided July 12, 1984.

Mother brought action against District under principle of respondeat superior, alleging that tubal cauterization had been negligently performed and as proximate result she had become pregnant and given birth to healthy baby. The Superior Court, District of Columbia, John F. Doyle, J., ruled that mother could not pursue her claim that District must pay costs of rearing child, but permitted mother's other claims to be presented to jury, which returned verdict in mother's favor. The Court of Appeals, Kern, J., retired, held that mother was not entitled to recover costs of rearing her healthy but unplanned child.

Affirmed.

Ferren, J., filed dissenting opinion.

1. Damages ⚷60

"Benefit rule" states that when defendant's tortious conduct has caused harm to plaintiff, and in so doing has conferred a special benefit to interest of plaintiff that was harmed, value of benefit conferred is considered in mitigation of damages, to the extent that such is equitable.

See publication Words and Phrases for other judicial constructions and definitions.

2. Damages ⚷62(1)

"Avoidable consequences" doctrine is that one injured by tort of another is not entitled to recover damages for any harm

1074 D.C. **478 ATLANTIC REPORTER, 2d SERIES**

that he could have avoided by use of reasonable effort.

See publication Words and Phrases for other judicial constructions and definitions.

sequential headnote number

West Topic

West Key Number

3. Physicians and Surgeons ⚷18.12

Permitting parents to bring "wrongful birth" action alleging negligent performance of sterilization to force third person to rear financially their child would have potentially destabilizing effect on families, thereby implicating statutory public policy emphasizing importance of stable home environment and a secure family relationship for children. D.C.Code 1981, § 16–4501.

sequential headnote number

West Topic

West Key Number

4. Physicians and Surgeons ⚷18.110

Mother who alleged that negligent performance of tubal cauterization proximately caused her to become pregnant and give birth to child was not entitled to recover cost of rearing her healthy but unplanned child.

Barry H. Gottfried, Washington, D.C., for appellant.

Leo N. Gorman, Asst. Corp. Counsel, Washington, D.C., with whom Judith W. Rogers, Corp. Counsel, Washington, D.C., at the time the brief was filed, and Charles L. Reischel, Deputy Corp. Counsel, Washington, D.C., were on the brief, for appellee.

John Lewis Smith III, Lee T. Ellis, Jr., Jeffrey S. Holik, and Andrew O. Eshelman, Washington, D.C., filed a brief for amicus curiae, The Medical Society of the District of Columbia.

beginning of court's opinion

Before FERREN, Associate Judge, and PAIR and KERN,* Associate Judges, Retired.

KERN, Associate Judge, Retired:

This appeal comes to the court upon an Agreed Statement in lieu of the Record on Appeal pursuant to DCCA Rule 10(k). According to the agreed statement of facts, after the birth of appellant's third child, appellant and the father of two of her children determined that they could not afford additional children. Therefore, on May 9, 1978, appellant underwent a laparoscopic cauterization to prevent her from becoming pregnant in the future. This surgery w**headnote**y Dr. Marsha Berkeley, as[...]chard Peters, both of whom [...] the District.

In October 1980, appellant filed suit against the District of Columbia under the principle of respondeat superior, alleging that the tubal cauterization had been negligently performed and as a proximate result she had become pregnant and given birth to a h[...]June 30, 1980.

headnote

App[...] the trial court compensation [...] District of Columbia for: her medical expenses, her pain and suffering, and her lost wages, all incurred during her pregnancy;

—the wages she lost after the birth of her child until she could return to work;

—the cost of a properly performed tubal ligation she might undergo in the future; and,

—all costs of rearing her healthy baby until the child reached the age of 18.

The trial court ruled that appellant may not pursue her claim that the District, as a result of its doctors' negligence, must pay the costs of rearing her child. Otherwise, the court permitted appellant's other claims for relief to be presented to the jury and the jury returned a verdict in appellant's favor in the amount of $11,000.

Appellant only challenges the trial court's ruling *in limine* that her claim for child-rearing costs from the doctors might not be pursued. Appellant contends on appeal (Brief at 4), that

> when she negligently failed to perform an effective tubal cauterization, Dr. Mar-

* Judge Kern was an Associate Judge of the court at the time of argument. His status changed to Associate Judge, Retired, on May 25, 1984.

§ 4.7(b) Key Numbers

This Key Number corresponds to the subject matter classification of the law in this case to the American Digest System. *These are the Key Numbers you will use when you launch a search for every case ever decided on the same point of law throughout the United States.* I will not deal with Key Numbers at this point, postponing instead a discussion of the American Digest System to Chapter 8.

After you read only a few headnotes, you'll see that they don't represent the cutting edge of effective legal prose and legal style. In fact, their style represents the worst of legal writing. So, along with the prefatory statement, the headnotes give rise to Good's Rule of Research #2:

> GOOD'S RULE OF RESEARCH #2:
>
> **Never quote or paraphrase a prefatory statement or a headnote in any of your written work.**

§ 4.7(c) Sequential Headnote Numbers

Note that each headnote not only has a Key Number but another number as well, a sequential number. *Flowers*, for example, has four headnotes, numbered 1, 2, 3, and 4. These sequential headnote numbers serve two functions in the research process.

First, the sequential headnote number serves as a table of contents to the opinion itself. In the body of the opinion, you will find a paragraph beginning with a bracketed number. Like this: [1] or [1,2]. That number means that the ensuing paragraph or paragraphs represent that part of the court's opinion that prompted the West Company editor to write the first [1] or first and second [1,2] headnotes (or whatever other number appears in the brackets). This feature can be quite helpful when you unearth an opinion with 87 headnotes and you're only interested in headnote number 79. To read the part of the court's opinion dealing with that legal topic, simply flip over in the opinion until you find a paragraph beginning with "[79]."

Second, the sequential headnote number plays a crucial role in Shepardizing cases. When you encounter the material on Shepard's Citators in a later chapter, I will harken back to this material and have you recall the "sequential headnote number." Your lights will then, no doubt, shine more brightly.

§ 4.8 Conclusion

Now you know what cases are and where they are published. You know that cases are chronologically published and that these systems of chronological court reports create a legal research calendar that helps us keep track of legal research time. You know that the West Company publishes all the law worth having in the National Reporter System, even though many of the states have already published the same law in official court reports, which you never really use in the law library, but they're there anyway so that you can see everything twice. Or, in the case of New York and California, thrice.

You also now know that the total number of cases in the law library roughly approximates the total of the federal budget deficit. Just look at those shelves, those shelves without end. Somewhere in that massive pile of case law sit the cases on point. Somewhere in that pile of stuff are the cases you want, the cases involving the damages that Wally and Mipsie might recover from our client, Dr. Cynthia Schwartz.

So go ahead. Dive right in. Look around. Randomly. You know that cases on point exist. Your common sense tells you that at some point in human history, or at least at some point in American human history, somebody somewhere has experienced a sterilization operation that didn't work. Somebody, somewhere had a child they hadn't planned on and couldn't afford. Somebody, somewhere got the bright idea to:

> SUE THE DOCTOR FOR MEDICAL MALPRACTICE FOR ZILLIONS OF DOLLARS AND RETIRE TO THE RIVIERA.

So there has to be at least one case on point. It's up to you to find it. To find them all. No later than this Friday. At midnight.

§ 4.9 Library Exercise Chart

Note: The chart on the following page was filled out on September 16, 1991. Your numbers for all current West reports will necessarily be greater than those shown. It might be interesting to compare the differences between your numbers and the chart to see how fast the West system grows. Between December 29, 1986, and September 16, 1991, it grew from 8470 volumes to 9483, a 12% increase in less than five years.

Reporter	First Series Last Volume No.	Current Series, Latest Bound Volume No.	Latest Advance Sheet Volume No.
A.	200		
A.2d		589	593
P.	300		
P.2d		809	813
N.E.	200		
N.E.2d		570	575
S.E.	200		
S.E.2d		403	406
N.W.	300		
N.W.2d		468	472
S.W.	300		
S.W.2d		807	811
So.	200		
So. 2d		577	582
N.Y.S.	300		
N.Y.S.2d		557	572
Cal. Rptr.		275	283[10]
F.	300		
F.2d		931	936
F. Supp.		761	765
F.R.D.		134	137
S. Ct.		107	110
B.R.		125	128
TOTALS	(First) 2300	(Current)	7183

GRAND TOTAL First 2300 + Current 7183 = 9483

[10]The *California Reporter* ended its first series at the end of 1991 with bound volume 286.

CHAPTER 5

GETTING STARTED

§ 5.1 The Time Has Come

You are now ready to dive into that rather imposing pile of case law, rummage around, and see if you can find some cases on point so that you can write your Memorandum of Law no later than this Friday. At midnight.

Your legal research professors have failed—actually they're diabolically clever—to specify a state[1] governing your topic, so you must research the entire country and find any and all cases on the recoverability of damages in suits against negligent surgeons whose botched sterilization operations cause the birth of unwanted and unplanned-for children across the globe. Your common sense tells you that the body of American case law undoubtedly includes some, perhaps quite a few, such cases. After all, do people in America get their tubes tied? Do you suppose that somebody's came untied, resulting in the birth of a baby? Do you suppose that somebody just might have decided to sue a doctor? Of course. Thus, it's now your job to plow through all of American case law and find those the boss must have in order to advise the client properly and completely.

Now you can approach this daunting task in two ways: (1) the wrong way or (2) the right way. The wrong way would entail your engaging immediately in *case location*, that is, using the West Key System or, one day, a computer system to locate cases first. This wrong-way approach has one serious drawback.

If you attempt to find cases first, you'll locate them in no particular order. Nothing will make some cases stand out over others, nothing will compartmentalize them into sub-theories or arrange them in an analytically rigorous way, nothing will flag the leading cases over the ho-hum cases, and absolutely nothing will clue you in to the historical way the law has developed. You'll just come up with a list of case citations to look up in no particular order of importance.

But suppose someone walked up to you in the law library with an article analyzing *all* negligent sterilization cases since the beginning of time, arranging them

[1]Actually, some gentle and caring legal research professors do specify a state or federal circuit for first-time projects so that your sanity and time can be preserved. The day will come, however, when national research is required. The techniques you'll learn in this book will apply either to limited research projects or to those national in scope.

in a logical way, pointing out the issues important in an overall analysis, identifying the leading cases, and projecting likely trends the law will take in the future. Suppose the author of that article had done all the dirty work, retrieving all cases on point and thereby identifying the ones you should spend some time with and read. Suppose that article was fairly up to date so that you would only have to worry about finding recent cases decided and published *after* the article was prepared.

Any takers? Sure. You'd look over your shoulder, make certain you weren't about to engage in some mammoth honor code violation, grab the article, and run.

So I've convinced you to use approach #2: the right way. That right way consists, quite simply, of locating sources known as background authority, also known as secondary authority, using the research contained in those sources, borrowing and perhaps improving upon the ideas found in those sources, and then updating the research reflected by those sources to the present day. In a nutshell, so to speak, that's it. That's legal research. Class dismissed. Book over.

Well, maybe not yet.

§ 5.2 Meet Wilbur: the Author of All Secondary Authority

The world of legal publishing is dominated by one indefatigable drone I'll name Wilbur. Wilbur is the world's best researcher and the world's worst writer. He works 24 hours per day, is thoroughly neat and tidy, never met a sentence he thought should end, and always gives 110%. Wilbur is so dominant in the legal publishing world that he works for every publishing company, he writes all their copy, he serves as the assistant for every law professor who's ever penned treatise or article, and he does an incredible amount of research. He does so much research that you can rest assured he has performed hundreds of hours of research into the recoverability of the costs of rearing a child in an action brought against a negligent physician whose messed-up sterilization operation causes the birth of a healthy but unwanted child.

Wilbur, then, is your very own research assistant on virtually every research assignment you will ever undertake. If he's done the dirty work, then there's no reason why you should redo what Wilbur's already done. After all, why replow turf that Wilbur's already plowed. If Wilbur's already located all possible cases dating all the way back to the days of Moses and up to, oh, just a year or so ago, then is there any rational reason why you should cover the same ground that Wilbur has already covered? If you do, then I can tell you what you will find: the *same cases* you've already found in the background sources Wilbur worked so diligently to prepare.

Wilbur has written two broad types of sources: general background sources and specific background sources. The general background sources include the two major encyclopedias in American law, *Corpus Juris Secundum* (C.J.S.) and *American Jurisprudence Second* (Am. Jur. 2d), and the unique and indispensable annotated report known as *American Law Reports* (A.L.R.). Wilbur also penned all specific background sources, which include treatises, legal periodicals, and Restatements of the Law. As the research method unfolds in the following chapters, I will share with you all the bibliographic information you need to use these sources strategically, intelligently, and methodically.

§ 5.3 Your Basic, Four-Part Strategy

Though you will learn to vary your research method with the type of assignment, the urgency of the deadline, and the availability of sources, your basic legal research strategy breaks down into four steps:

> ***Step One:*** Find *general background sources* covering your topic and read those sources (1) to gain an overview of the area of law and (2) to begin to collect cases on point.
>
> ***Step Two:*** Find *specific background sources* covering your topic and read those sources (1) to obtain more critical analysis of your topic, (2) to find even more cases on point, (3) to obtain some ideas for arguments favoring your client's position, and (4) to obtain some secondary authority you can and should cite in your memo or brief.
>
> ***Step Three:*** Figure out where your background authorities stopped researching (because they had to go to press) and then start researching at that point to bring your case law research up to date.
>
> ***Step Four:*** Shepardize the cases you will use in your memo or brief (1) to make certain each case is still good law, (2) to locate citable case history, and (3) to obtain any necessary parallel case citations.

Now I fully realize that questions are swirling around your brain at an incredible rate of speed: general background sources? specific background sources? Shepardize? parallel case citations? citable case history?

Well, you're supposed to be confused. Indeed, you're supposed to be terrified. After all, you're about to dive into a pile of 12,000,000 pages of case law with only a vague hope of bumping into one or two that just might apply to your set of facts. So hold onto those swirling questions. They will be answered, all in good time.

Your strategy, then, in 25 words or fewer, is best described in:

GOOD'S RULE OF RESEARCH #3:

Find research someone else has already done, use it, rely on it, borrow from it, and update it to the present day.

§ 5.4 How to Arrange the Universe

When you enter the law library, those books do indeed smirk at you and dare you to make a fool of yourself in front of God, fellow students, and the acquisitions librarian. As you glance around paranoically, lawyers and law students—those in the know—seem to be engaged in all sorts of complex research maneuvers. "They must be using some sources I'll never learn about," you think to yourself. "They must be looking up incredibly detailed law, and like wow, they must be finding *legal precedents* just like they do between sex scenes on *L.A. Law*. It all looks so complicated, so sophisticated, so intellectually stimulating. How can I possibly fit in?" you wonder.

To make you feel incredibly at ease, let me introduce you to one of the universal truths about the law library. Let me reveal a professional secret . . . now, if this ever hits the mass media . . . if those lowly *laymen* (also known as "nonlawyers") ever find this out . . . well, it will drive legal fees well below those charged by journeymen plumbers (we'll still be rich!).

Here's the secret: when you look at all those intent and knowledgeable legal researchers in the law library, well, what would you do if I told you they were only doing one of *three things*?

That's right. If they're not reading—that is, if they're just looking—that is, if they're *researching*—they are only doing one of three things. And they are doing one of these three things because of:

GOOD'S RULE OF RESEARCH #4:

There are only three things you can do to a lawbook other than cuss at it:
(1) the Analytical Approach,
(2) the Index Approach, and
(3) the Tabular Approach.

Think about the universe for a moment or two.

Finished?

Good.

Now think about *information* in the universe. How could you *arrange* information in the universe, or in the law library, or, say, in a lawbook? There are only about five or six possible ways to arrange things:

1. *Chronologically by time*: Of course, law's already arranged chronologically. That's what's causing all the trouble. Cases are arranged chronologically on never-ending shelves in a massive system of publication called the National Reporter System. So "chronology" serves to satisfy the need

for *speed*, but it creates huge problems of *location*.

2. *Geographically by state or region*: Once again, case law is already arranged geographically in official state reports and in the West Regional Reporters. Case law is also arranged by type of court in federal reporters (federal cases) and regional reporters (state cases). So while "geography" or "type of court" brings some order out of chaos, it does precious little to help you find cases involving somebody's negligently tied tubes.

3. *Visually by color*: This is great for your personal filing system; go ahead and use those little color-coded dooflodgies you stick on your file folders, go ahead and use yellow highlighters in your casebooks, but you won't find much color coding in law libraries, and you'd better not use highlighter marks in lawbooks or the librarian will have you bound, gagged, and shot.

These first three ways of arranging stuff in the universe are distinctly unhelpful to the legal researcher who wants to find cases on point. The researcher, instead, must rely on the next three ways that information is arranged, which, not surprisingly, constitute the three things you can do to a lawbook other than cuss at it: (1) the Index Approach, (2) the Analytical Approach, and (3) the Tabular Approach. So when you see all the diligent researchers in the law library, you can rest assured that, if they aren't reading (or cussing), they are looking up words in an *index*, figuring out topics in an *analysis*, or looking up words or numbers in a *table*.

Stripped to the bare essentials, there are only two things that lawbook publishers can arrange: words and numbers. They can arrange words either logically (Analytical Approach) or alphabetically (Index Approach and Tabular Approach). They can arrange numbers in sequential order (Tabular Approach). That's it. There are no other ways of arranging words or numbers that would help you locate stuff in a law library.

As you hone your research skills, you will probably find that you prefer the Analytical Approach over the Index Approach. The Index Approach relies only on the alphabet for arranging words. And you will soon learn that legal indexers choose the most obscure words to hide away references to your problem. You will also learn that you can't assume that the indexer used a particular word to index your problem. The Index Approach, then, can be the source of considerable frustration, especially in your rookie year.

The Analytical Approach, on the other hand, relies on the old noggin to arrange information. By using logic as the arranging device, the analytical arrangement enables you to eliminate large portions of the arrangement as irrelevant to your inquiry, whereas you cannot eliminate certain chunks of letters in the alphabet to shorten your search in the Index Approach. It wouldn't make much sense to check out an index and say, "Well, today being a cloudy Monday, I'll only check the N through Z words."

As an overview of these arrangements, let's take a simple example. Suppose that you had to retrieve "fruits" from the law library. That's right. Fruits. You're about to engage in "Food Research." Of course, Wilbur has researched food and has found the following: beets, ice cream, hamburger, rice, apples, oranges, steak, milk, hoagie rolls, buns. After finding all that stuff, Wilbur must arrange it in an index and an analysis.

Here's an index:

Foods
- apples
- beets
- buns
- hoagie rolls
- hamburger
- ice cream
- milk
- oranges
- rice
- steak

Here's an analysis:

§ 1.0 Food Groups
- § 1.1 Vegetables
  - § 1.1(a) beets
  - § 1.1(b) rice
- § 1.2 Breads
  - § 1.2(a) buns
  - § 1.2(b) hoagie rolls
- § 1.3 Fruits
  - § 1.3(a) apples
  - § 1.3(b) oranges
- § 1.4 Dairy Products
  - § 1.4(a) milk
  - § 1.4(b) ice cream

In the analysis, you can immediately see that § 1.3 contains precisely the stuff you seek. But in the index, you must search the entire list to discover that "apples" and "oranges" are your, er, cases on point.

Let's look at each of these arrangement devices a bit more closely.

§ 5.4(a) The Analytical Approach

Much of law is broken down into analytical arrangements. An analytical arrangement orders information by subject matter. A large topic will be broken down into subtopics, which will be further broken down into subsubtopics, which will be further broken down into subsubsubtopics, and so on. Each final division of subject matter will then be given a number, usually a "section number," which is then used to arrange text or other blocks of information.

Lawbooks call these analytical breakdowns "analyses," but they are really nothing more than "tables of contents." You will find that treatises (books about the law) and legal encyclopedias (C.J.S. and Am. Jur. 2d) are broken down into sections, which represent a detailed, *subject matter, analytical* arrangement of information.

The largest analytical arrangement of all is the West Key System. In Chapter 8, you will learn that *all American case law* is broken down into more than 400 subject headings called "topics," which are further broken down *analytically* into the tens of thousands of subsubsubtopics called "Key Numbers," which are then numerically arranged to print the headnotes you find on the title pages of all cases published by the West Company.

For now, just learn that the Analytical Approach is one of the three things you can do to a lawbook, that it relies on the use of a *table of contents*, and that this *table of contents* or *analysis* can be found in the *front* of an entire book or in the *front* of a topic within a book. All you need to know right now is that the Analytical Approach relies on logic for its arrangement, not on a sequencing of letters (index) or numbers (table).

§ 5.4(b) The Index Approach

The law library is chock full of indexes, and all you can do in your legal career is to learn to cope with them. For they will drive you stark raving mad, foaming at the mouth, and might even prompt you to consider opening the window, going out on the ledge, and, well, ending it all right there.

To help you cope, I'll share some insight into these legal indexes, some bibliographic information, and some strategies for efficient use. First of all, you should realize that "legal indexers," the actual people who write these things, are just one step above paramecia on the life scale; they are (this is scientific fact) the genetic cousins of map-folders and instruction-writers (try refolding a map on the interstate or assembling a red wagon on Christmas eve and you'll appreciate the rage that legal indexers can engender).

Second, and more important, legal indexes are "hierarchical indexes." That is, indexes will alphabetically list words ("main words"), but most main words will be further broken down into "subwords," which are alphabetically arranged under the main words. In the above "fruit" example, the word "Foods" is a main word, while "oranges," "rice," and "hoagie rolls" are subwords.

Third, as you move ever closer to that coveted status of Ace Legal Researcher, you will find that efficient researchers always follow:

GOOD'S RULE OF RESEARCH #5:
When you use an index, always consult the narrowest word first.

Let's use Wally and Mipsie's case as an example of this vital research strategy. As we'll see below, the first step in the legal research process is to come up with words you can then look up in lawbooks (I hate to burst your bubble, folks, but really, that's all there is to it). So you might come up with the words "medical malpractice" and "sterilization" and "vasectomy." You can readily see that the broadest word is "medical malpractice," that "sterilization" is the next broadest, and that "vasectomy" is the narrowest. As the narrowest word, "vasectomy" would be the first word you'd check in a legal index.

Why?

To save your fingernail. That's why.

When you become an Ace Legal Researcher, you'll find that using legal indexes entails the highly sophisticated approach of legal research known in academic circles as the "nope-nope-nope" approach. Suppose you're trying to find "high-quality meat" in our food research example. Now you might think you could come up with all possible words describing high-quality meat and just check those words, but you couldn't be sure you hadn't missed some. Thus, you'd use the nope-nope-nope approach by placing the fingernail of your index finger[2] at the top of the list so that you could work your way down as follows:

Foods

apples	NOPE
beets	NOPE
buns	NOPE
hoagie rolls	NOPE
hamburger	NOPE (cheap meat)
ice cream	NOPE
milk	NOPE
oranges	NOPE
rice	NOPE
steak	YEP = EUREKA

[2]See! *That's* why they call it an *index* finger!

Quite seriously, when using an index, you must beware: you don't know what words the indexer used, you must check them all, and the nope-nope-nope approach is the only way to go. As you increase your experience in the field of legal research, you will also begin to notice a phenomenon at work, an inexplicable rule of nature known as:

GOOD'S RULE OF RESEARCH #6:

When you start an index search at the top of the list, the answer is always found at the bottom. Try to trick it by starting at the bottom? The answer's at the top.

Thus, to summarize, always choose the narrowest word first. You'll find that these narrow "main words" have fewer "subwords," thereby preserving your fingernail when you nope-nope-nope your way down the list. In Wally and Mipsie's case, for example, the list of subwords under "Medical Malpractice" will stretch on page after page after page. The list of subwords under "Vasectomy," however, is likely to be quite short, thereby saving your fingernail and shortening your research time. Of course, when you find a list of subwords requiring the nope-nope-nope approach, mark *my* words that when you start at the top, the answer's at the bottom. And vice versa.

So much for strategy. You also need some bibliography.

In lawbooks you will find two types of indexes: General Indexes and Volume Indexes. Multivolume sets of books—such as encyclopedias, treatises, Restatements, and legislative codes—will have both types. Multivolume sets will have a General Index *indexing the entire set of books*; this General Index might have many volumes within the General Index itself, the first containing the "A" words, the last ending with the "Z" words. Multivolume sets will also have separate Volume Indexes *in each volume*. These Volume Indexes might index an entire volume or *separate topics or titles within each volume*. A one-volume lawbook, of course, will simply have one index at the back.

Indexes have been known to cause some researchers to cross a time warp into that other time dimension in the law library where you'll find many strange things: odd socks (the ones missing from your wash), the date you couldn't get last weekend, and yet another losing lottery ticket. In this time warp, you can get caught in a perpetual loop when you look up the word "malpractice" and it tells you to "see Medical Malpractice, this index," which, when you check it, tells you to "see Malpractice, this index." When you get caught in such a loop, it's wise to remember:

GOOD'S RULE OF RESEARCH #7:

Use a General Index as a "volume finder" and the Volume Index as a "page finder."

A bit of explanation is in order. As a general rule, don't waste a lot of time in a General Index. Use it as a broad finger pointer, pointing you to the right volume within the larger set of books. Once you locate your correct volume, you'll find that the Volume Index, or better, the Analytical Approach, is a much more efficient way to zero in on the precise page or pages you should read.

Now I realize that all of this is highly theoretical at this point. But if you will pay attention to the basics, it will all fall into place as you begin your own research on your own topic. Also, we'll actually perform some real research, right in the Visual Aids booklet that accompanies this text, on Wally and Mipsie's case and show you how the techniques and the Rules of Research apply in the real world of research.

Let's move on to the Tabular Approach.

§ 5.4(c) The Tabular Approach

The law is not only full of words, which can be alphabetically arranged in indexes or logically arranged in analyses. The law is full of numbers as well, which can be sequentially arranged in tables. Numerical sections of the United States Code, for example, can be arranged sequentially in a table with cross-references to the pages within the source where each particular section of the Code is discussed. Numerical citations to cases, for example, can be sequenced in a source called Shepard's Citators with cross-references to other cases that have cited the cases listed in the table. Numerical sections of the United States Code or sections of the Code of Federal Regulations can be sequentially arranged in an updating table with cross-references to recently enacted statutes or recently promulgated regulations amending or repealing the section listed in the table.

You are going to find tables galore in the law library. Be of good cheer, for the Tabular Approach is the most efficient legal research approach of all. The Tabular Approach entails looking up *known* information (the section in the Code) to find *unknown* information (the page where discussion appears). In the Index Approach or the Analytical Approach, on the other hand, you are looking for *unknown* words to cross-reference you to *unknown pages* or *unknown cases*.

Tables primarily list numbers, but many will list cases as well. For example, perhaps in Wally and Mipsie's case you've discovered that *Flowers v. District of Columbia* is a case on point. Suppose you consult a medical malpractice treatise. You can use its back-of-the-book Index Approach (and play interminable word games with your ragged fingernail), its front-of-the-book Analytical Approach, or, if it has the feature, its Tabular Approach. If the treatise has a "Table of Cases," it's very easy to look up a *known* case name for a cross-reference to the page where that case, and hence its subject matter in general, is discussed.

§ 5.4(d) That's It

That's it. Those are the only three things you can do to lawbooks. Those are the three things that all those intent legal researchers are doing with all those lawbooks in the law library. If they're not reading them or cussing at them, they are using analyses, indexes, or tables. There is nothing else to do.

So throw your fear away. Stare back at those intimidating-looking lawbooks. They're only fooling you. They do not represent the ultimate in sophistication. They do not constitute extreme complexity. Contrary to their appearance, their feel, and, indeed, their smell, they do not deserve your fear and trepidation. Because the bottom line is this:

GOOD'S RULE OF RESEARCH #4:

There are only three things you can do to a lawbook other than cuss at it:
(1) the Analytical Approach,
(2) the Index Approach, and
(3) the Tabular Approach.

§ 5.4(e) Time for a Picture

I thought you'd appreciate a picture of your first set of lawbooks. Let's suppose you're walking up to use C.J.S. or Am. Jur. 2d for the first time (you'll learn all about them in the next chapter). So there you are, standing in front of a set a books numbering 101 volumes (C.J.S.) or 86 volumes (Am. Jur. 2d). The first obvious problem is to figure out which book contains a discussion of botched sterilization operations causing the birth of healthy but unplanned-for children. So, as cleverly shown in the picture below, you use the General Index as a "volume finder." Then you confidently pull that volume off the shelf and use the Analytical Approach (front of the topic) and/or the Index Approach (back of the book) as a "page finder." Then you settle back, giving off the appearance that you know *exactly* what you're doing, for some serious reading and notetaking.[3]

[3]But no highlighting!

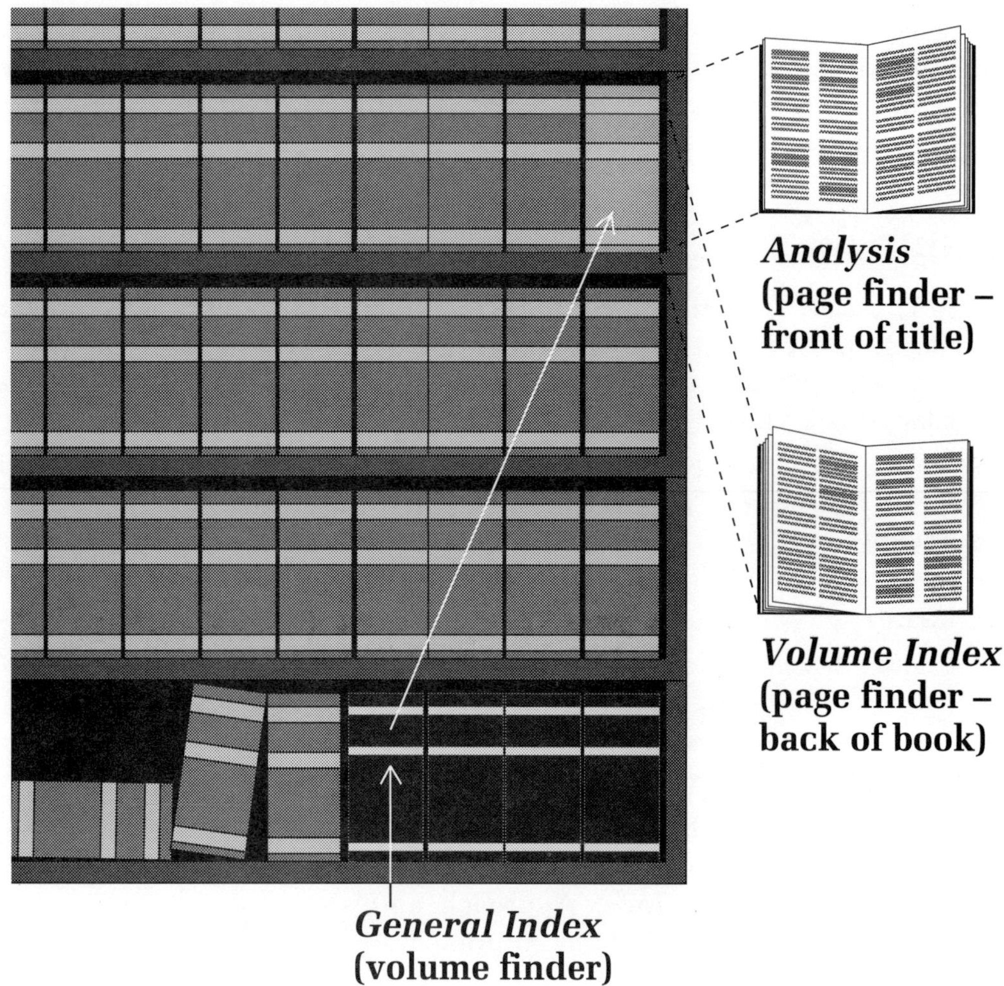

Figure 4
Location Devices

That's it. Those are the only two things you could possibly do to either of these multivolume legal encyclopedias.[4] More, much more, about the ins and outs of using these sources appears in the next chapter.

§ 5.5 Word Games

To use either the Analytical Approach or the Index Approach, you must first come up with words describing concepts, ideas, issues, or theories about your own legal research problem. Broadly, there are two types of words you will discover: fact words and legal words. The former—fact words—present few problems, and in your formative years, will be the words you'll most frequently think of and use in

[4]The third approach, the Tabular Approach, is not applicable to Wally and Mipsie's case, for no statute applies to this type of lawsuit.

preliminary legal research. The reason for this is simple: at this stage of the game you don't know a whole slew of legal words.

Suppose I told you that the words "wrongful birth" or "wrongful conception" or "wrongful pregnancy" were some legal words directly on point to your case. Suppose I said that the "benefits rule" plays a huge part in analyzing Wally and Mipsie's case. These are legal words—causes of action or damages rules—that you are not likely to think of off the top of your head.

§ 5.5(a) The TARP Rule

Legal indexers, despite their tendency to pick the most obscure word imaginable to hide material from you, do use a system in picking words to include in their legal indexes. This system is commonly referred to as the "TARP" rule, an acronym guiding your choice of words in the preliminary legal research process.

T = Thing: What thing or things are involved in your set of facts? Thinking about the "T" or "Things" in your fact situation leads you to a list of fact words. Brainstorm it:

birth control (which is a form of)

contraception (which can be achieved by)

sterilization (on a man it's called a)

vasectomy (on a woman a)

tubal ligation (also achievable by)

birth control pills (which are a form of)

drugs (which are dispensed by a)

prescription (which you don't need to buy a)

condom (for a man or, as recently announced on the news, a)

condom (for a woman)

And on and on you go, jotting down possible words that the legal indexer might have used to cross-reference you to the right book, the right section, and ultimately the right page containing a discussion of the liability of a doctor for a bum sterilization operation that wreaked havoc on unsuspecting parents who are now quite unreasonably seeking a jillion dollars from your poor, put-upon client, Dr. Schwartz.

A = Action: What legal action might be filed in your situation? What defenses might the defendant raise? What legal theories might either party put forth? Brainstorm it in a law office with an attorney, in school with a professor, or in the law library with an upperclass student:

medical malpractice

wrongful birth

wrongful life

wrongful conception
wrongful pregnancy
benefits rule
tort
warranty
contributory negligence
comparative negligence

R = Relief: What legal relief is the plaintiff seeking? How might the defendant avoid or reduce that amount? Brainstorm it, again with someone with legal experience:

damages
compensatory damages
punitive damages
benefits rule
mitigation of damages
duty to abort to mitigate damages?

P = Parties: What people might be involved in this or a similar situation? Whose negligence might cause a similar injury? Here you can shine, for "P" or "Parties" in the TARP rule is asking for fact words. Brainstorm it:

child
baby
mother
father
parents
doctor
physician
surgeon
urologist
gynecologist
druggist
condom manufacturer

Your objective in this preliminary word game is quite simply to come up with the same words that the legal indexer used to index your problem in the wide variety of lawbooks you will use in Step One (General Background Sources) and Step Two (Specific Background Sources).

Your objective also is to identify *concepts* that might have been used in an *analytical arrangement* of law governing this particular problem. Only by conceiving of some words can you launch the legal research process, because of the well-known, highly scientific:

> **GOOD'S RULE OF RESEARCH #8:**
>
> **All preliminary legal research is a word game. Nothing else.**

§ 5.5(b) Brainstorming with a Lawyer

When an attorney gives you a research assignment, do not be afraid to ask questions. Especially in your rookie season, you are not expected to know all the law governing your topic; indeed, that's what you hope to learn when you research the stupid thing in the law library. So here are some suggested questions you should ask the attorney assigning the problem:

1. Does state or federal law govern the problem?
2. Are there any statutes or administrative regulations that might be involved? If so, do you know the name of the statute?
3. Do I research the law of a given state or federal circuit? If not, do you want a national survey, or should I focus on just nearby states or particular federal circuits?
4. What legal theories are involved? What is the plaintiff likely to claim? What are the defendant's defenses?
5. As you see it right now, what are the main legal issues that must be resolved in the fact situation?
6. Do you know the names of any on-point cases I should be on the lookout for or can use to help launch the research process?
7. Do you know the names of any treatises commonly used in this area of the law? What about the names of any nationally recognized authorities or law professors?
8. Would any of the Restatements of the Law be of help in resolving the issues presented?
9. When would you like the results of my research?

No later than Friday. At midnight.

§ 5.6 Conclusion

Whether you know it or not, you've learned 10 important things in this chapter:

1. The best way to do legal research is to cash in on the legal research that some other poor schmuck has already done.
2. The poor schmuck is Wilbur, author of all background authority.
3. There are only three things you can do to lawbooks.
4. One of those things is called the Index Approach in a General Index (volume finder) and then in a Volume Index (page finder).
5. Another of those things is called the Analytical Approach in analyses, which appear at the front of books or at the front of topics within books.
6. The final of those things is called the Tabular Approach, which doesn't really involve Wally and Mipsie right now so we'll talk about it much more when we get to statutes.
7. All preliminary legal research is a word game, which the icky legal indexer always wins.
8. One good way to dream up words is to play the TARP game and look for things, actions, relief, and parties running around your fact situation.
9. Pick the brain of the attorney assigning the problem.
10. Your research is due this Friday night.

Now let's learn how to do it. Step by step.

CHAPTER 6

STEP ONE: GENERAL BACKGROUND SOURCES

§ 6.1 A Personal Anecdote

When I was a first-year law student, I remember hearing a law professor describe C.J.S. this way: "Oh, that's just some legal encyclopedia. I wouldn't bother with it." Now that sage advice wisely counsels the law student worried about writing a law review note or a moot court brief, for C.J.S. is not the sort of thing that should show up in the footnotes to a law review note or an Index to Authorities in an appellate brief.

So I didn't bother with it. Until the second semester of my second year, when I was doing some very real-world research for a real-world lawyer paying me some very real money to do some legal research. I had been researching (rather inefficiently as I look back on it now) for about six to seven hours, trying to find out about the liability of a surety bond company that had taken over a construction project of its defaulting contractor (some legal research projects really sizzle!). In any event, I had looked and looked for a case, any case, remotely on point. And I had come up empty.

Wandering haphazardly through the law library, I came upon C.J.S., paused, looked at it, flailed around awhile figuring out how to use it, found some stuff that looked relevant, began to read in earnest, and located in 10 minutes flat *the only two cases in the country that were precisely on point with my fact situation.*

So much for "not bothering with it."

§ 6.2 Three General Background Sources

In this chapter, you will learn about three sets of lawbooks: C.J.S., Am. Jur. 2d, and A.L.R. These sources, I must tell you, are pooh-poohed in academic circles, but, as the above story amply illustrates, can be godsends in the real-world practice of law. They are "general" background sources because they treat virtually every legal issue that has ever arisen in American case law, do not focus on a single jurisdiction, do not cite other secondary authority such as treatises and periodicals, and do not attempt to analyze the law critically or deeply.

They are sources that will help you gain an overview of your legal area. They will help you spot issues in your facts that you otherwise might miss. They will provide for you, please note, few if any "quotable passages" to include in your own writing. But most importantly, they will help you begin to locate cases on point, from all across the country, from the dawn of time to the previous calendar year.

Two of these sets, C.J.S. and Am. Jur. 2d, are virtually identical to one another. Each is a major legal encyclopedia that attempts to cover the entirety of American law. C.J.S. is published by our good friends at the West Publishing Company, Am. Jur. 2d by the major competitor to West, the Lawyers Cooperative Publishing Company, a.k.a. Lawyers Co-op.

The other set, A.L.R., also published by Lawyers Co-op, dramatically differs from the encyclopedias and offers a potential gold mine of legal research information.

§ 6.3 The Three Phases of Research

Before we get to their actual use, let's pause a moment and consider:

> GOOD'S RULE OF RESEARCH #9:
>
> **Using any lawbook consists of three phases: (1) finding, (2) using, and (3) updating.**

§ 6.3(a) The Finding Phase

When you approach any source in the library, you immediately go into the "finding mode." Your goal might be to locate one on-point law review article out of the 3,539,203,798 articles already published, or you might want to find the correct title-section-page-footnote in C.J.S. discussing Wally and Mipsie's case.

Of course, you already know, in general, how to make your way successfully through the finding phase, for you have, no doubt, committed all of Good's Rules of Research either to memory or to the tattoo parlor's ink for instant retrieval from the inside of your wrist. For the infinitesimal percentage of those readers who have forgotten these vital rules, here's the one that will guide you through the finding phase:

GOOD'S RULE OF RESEARCH #4:

There are only three things you can do to a lawbook other than cuss at it:
(1) the Analytical Approach,
(2) the Index Approach, and
(3) the Tabular Approach.

Thus, when you take your first tentative steps toward your first lawbook, you now know, by looking at the inside of your wrist, that you'll find some sort of index, which leads you to some sort of analysis, which leads you to some pages to read and read and read.

As we approach various books, book by book, I'll acquaint you with the various "finding features" so that you can go straight to the right place and at least look like you know what you're doing. In the law library, image is everything.

§ 6.3(b) The Use Phase

Proper use of each individual source, of course, depends totally on your knowledge of the bibliographic features of the book. So, for each source we visit, I'll provide all the information you need to use the source correctly and efficiently. You'll learn all about each source's general indexes, volume or title indexes, tables of statutes or table of cases, various analyses and sub-analyses, page layout, footnote arrangement, case arrangement within footnote, and other bibliographic quirks.

As you read these titillating descriptions, don't worry about remembering everything. Your familiarity with all these sources will grow over time. Indeed, seasoned researchers can gain valuable insight by reviewing these bibliographic descriptions to learn of features they didn't realize even existed.

§ 6.3(c) The Updating Phase

Pity the poor legal publishing company.

Think about this: the instant a legal publishing company publishes a book, it's out of date. The very second that the book rolls off the press and hits the shipping department, some court somewhere is writing an opinion of law affecting footnote 101.12 in section 1.34(a)(1)(iii)(z) on page 4,345 in volume 98.

So the book on your shelf—yes, that one right there, the one you're about to pick up—is out of date. It's old news. A has-been. Obsolete. Practically an antique.

Fear not, however. The book publishers relish this built-in obsolescence, for it opened a gigantic market for:

POCKET PARTS!

Now I realize that "pocket parts" sounds vaguely obscene, but I promised you a weird world filled with peculiar time zones and bizarre characters. So why not "pocket parts"?

To keep their books up to date, lawbook publishers love to publish some form of supplementations, which are sent automatically to the book buyer, along with an invoice (suitable for framing). The most popular form of supplementation is a "pocket part." This pocket part comes in a flimsy paperback with a cardboard back, which is then inserted into a sleeve found in the inside back cover of the book.

When researchers find some on-point material in the outdated hardbound volume, they then simply turn to the pocket part and consult the same title, same section, and same footnote number to find references to cases decided *after* the hardbound volume was published and shipped from the Shipping Department. Of course, the instant the *pocket part* rolls off the press and hits the Shipping Department, some court somewhere is deciding a case that affects footnote 101.12 in section 1.34(a)(1)(iii)(z) on page 4,345 in volume 98. This phenomenon of obsolescing the supplementation device that was designed to keep the bound volume from obsolescing delighted the lawbook publishers, for it gave rise to a gigantic market of:

CUMULATIVE ANNUAL POCKET PARTS!

Yes, friends, one pocket part is definitely not enough. To truly satisfy the needs of lawbook buyers, book publishers are primarily in the business of sending out invoices *forever*!

So each and every year, your pocket part will "cumulate." That is, the lawbook publisher will reprint your pocket part, retaining the stuff already there and adding new stuff decided during the year. Naturally, the pocket part gets a bit thicker each and every year, growing ever so slightly until it begins to split the spine of the hardbound volume where it lives until one day the lawbook publisher realizes to its great glee that the hardbound book must be:

REWRITTEN AND SPLIT INTO TWO HARDBOUND VOLUMES!

So out come more hardbound volumes, each with its own invoice, each with its own new Cumulative Annual Pocket Part, which gets larger year by year until . . . until . . . until the entire world is filled with nothing but lawbooks and . . . pocket parts.

What a business to be in! What an incredible source of revenue! What a scam! If car manufacturers built in such instantaneous obsolescence, there'd be a public outcry for some federal agency somewhere to "do something!"

Of course, when you consult a bound volume and update it with a pocket part, your research will not be completely up to date. Your research will be "good" only up to the end of the preceding calendar year. Meanwhile, thousands of cases all over the country have been in the pipeline, coming off the judges' wordprocessors, being sent to West, having their headnotes written, getting set in type, going to press, hitting the Shipping Department, and finally coming to rest on your shelf . . . sitting quietly, perhaps unnoticed, definitely sneering at you, all alone there in the dreaded:

NO ZONE.

As you will discover, proper legal research requires updating "beyond the supplement." You will learn all about the dangerous NO ZONE that awaits you there and how to traverse it when we get to Step Three.

So those are the three phases of lawbook use: (1) finding, (2) using, and (3) updating. As we study each legal research book, I'll point out various features of the book that help you with each of the three phases.

Ready? Go.

§ 6.4 The Nitty-Gritty

Now it's time to get down to the real nitty-gritty and acquaint you with some actual lawbooks. To bring you up to speed in the shortest amount of time with the smallest amount of pain and the loss of only part of your mind, I plan to follow a set, four-part approach for each source covered throughout this book:

First, I will briefly give you necessary *bibliographic information* about the source to familiarize you with its scope, coverage, and publication format, and the research function the source will serve.

Second, I will then take you through the *finding* phase, showing you the specific finding devices the source has, where you can find them, and how you can efficiently use them.

Third, I will review the *use* phase of consulting the source, showing you some tricks of actually reading the source and using the information you find there.

Fourth, I will teach you the *updating* phase of using the source, showing you how the source is updated to the present day. *Most importantly of all, I will begin to show you how each source relates to the overall research process and how you can interrelate the various sources so that you reduce "chronological case research" to the bare minimum.*

Here we go. Here are the first three sources you should learn about. In my overall scheme of things—in your rookie year—you will use one or more of these sources as *Step One.* When you advance toward the status of Ace Legal Researcher, you'll find that your Step One will vary with the type of research problem you confront. Indeed, as you become really good, you might find that you skip over Step One and go straight to Step Two. For now, however, just realize that the true Ace Legal Researcher knows all about these Step One sources and knows they can help tremendously in certain types of research projects (like Wally and Mipsie's case).

§ 6.5 The Visual Aids

As explained in the Preface, the Visual Aids accompanying this text contain some of the pages you would encounter when researching Wally and Mipsie's lawsuit against your client, Dr. Schwartz. In the following text and in the margins, you will find notations that look like this: {4}. The number refers to a page number in the Visual Aids

example
{4}

booklet. Thus, as you read the text, you can refer to the correct page in the Visual Aids and actually see the page or pages I'm referring to in the text. Having these pages available in a collateral booklet, you won't be bothered with flipping back and forth in this book.

As you review the Visual Aids pages and begin to compare them with the actual pages existing in your law library at the time when you read this book, please understand that the Visual Aids pages were put together in the summer of 1992. Some of the actual pages in your law library right now will necessarily have changed.

In the boxes on the Visual Aids pages you'll find my commentary explaining what the source is doing for you and how the source fits in with your overall strategy.

§ 6.6 C.J.S.

§ 6.6(a) C.J.S.: Bibliographic Information

Published by the West Publishing Company, C.J.S. is a giant legal encyclopedia, much like the *World Book* or the *Encyclopedia Britannica.* C.J.S. stands for *Corpus Juris Secundum*, which, in the Latin, means "body of the law, second edition." As its name suggests, C.J.S. superseded the older C.J. (*Corpus Juris*).

C.J.S. appears in 101 volumes and contains encyclopedic discussion of hundreds of legal subject matter areas called "titles." Such a discussion might stretch on for hundreds or even thousands of pages. The titles are arranged alphabetically throughout the 101 volumes from "Abandoned Property" in the first volume to "Zoning" in the 101st. The titles might be quite broad ("Constitutional Law") or quite narrow ("Flags" or "Dead Bodies").

The text of each title is *analytically* arranged into "sections," which are listed in
{2} a broad *analysis* {2} at the front of each title and then specifically broken down in a
{2,3,4} *subanalysis* {2,3,4} following the *analysis*. Thus, the Analytical Approach is readily
available and, indeed, constitutes one of the most efficient approaches to finding on-point discussions in C.J.S.

{1} Other finding aids include a General Index {1}, which indexes the entire
{5} encyclopedia and is best used as a *volume finder* or *title finder*, and Title Indexes {5}
for each of the 400+ titles in C.J.S. Some long titles stretch over two volumes, so the Title Index resides in the volume concluding the title. The Title Indexes are best used as *page finders*.

The Tabular Approach is not available in most C.J.S. volumes. In very recent, recompiled volumes, however, you will find a Table of Statutes and Regulations Cited immediately following the *analysis* at the front of the title.

{6} The text in C.J.S. {6}, unfortunately, ranks among the worst-written examples of prose in the language of the law. After you fight through the layers of nouny abstractions, however, you'll find substantive coverage of virtually every conceivable legal issue ever litigated in American law. For that reason, a visit to C.J.S. can be worth the pain and suffering experienced when actually reading the text.

The text is then copiously footnoted, the footnotes {6,7} containing citations to cases from state and federal courts all across the nation. As noted below, C.J.S. used to cite *every* case on each point of law but now includes "selected authority." Even under the new "selective authority" approach, C.J.S. is notorious for loading up its footnotes with scads of case citations. **{6,7}**

These bloated footnotes provide for the researcher both good news and bad news. The good news is that the more cases you find via C.J.S. the fewer you'll have to find by other means. The bad news is that, because West cites so many cases in the footnote part of the page, it can only list most of the cases, having no room left over to "blurb" the cases, that is, briefly discuss them so that you'll know what they're about.

§ 6.6(b) C.J.S.: The Finding Phase

When you approach C.J.S. to shake hands for the first time, your task is to pinpoint the precise *title* containing textual discussion of your research problem. In Wally and Mipsie's case, potential words that come to mind include Negligence, Medical Malpractice, Torts, Contracts, Damages, and the list goes on. Many rookie researchers make the terrible mistake of trying to second-guess C.J.S. by concluding that "it's got to be 'Damages'" and running off stark raving mad, foaming at the mouth in search of the "D" volume.

There is a better way: the Index Approach.

§ 6.6(b)(i) *C.J.S. Step One*

Locate the *General Indexes* {1} at the end of the entire set of C.J.S. volumes. Using the TARP rule, pick some narrow words describing your factual or legal situation. "Sterilization" and "Vasectomy" come to mind. As you peruse the General Index, you should sit back and ponder: **{1}**

GOOD'S RULE OF RESEARCH #10:

Do not search forever in a General Index for the *precise page* or *section* containing on-point text. Instead, use the General Index to identify the *title* or *topic* and then find that volume to continue the search for the *precise page* or *section*.

When you review the *General Index*, you'll notice that it stretches over quite a few volumes. All the "A," "B," and perhaps part of the "C" words will appear in the first volume and so on to the "Z" words in the last volume.

Having found a potential title, or several potential titles, you now proceed to get the volume containing your title and commence *C.J.S. Step Two.* But first, you sit back and muse about:

> **GOOD'S RULE OF RESEARCH #11:**
>
> **The first thing you do when taking a lawbook off the shelf is to consult its copyright date.**

Now that pearl of wisdom requires a few comments. Often in the legal research process, you'll have a choice among sources. Indeed, in the real world, you would not necessarily check *both* C.J.S. and Am. Jur. 2d. One way to zero in on one source and ignore another is by simply choosing the more up-to-date source. If the coverage of your problem in C.J.S. appears in a 1962 volume, you'll do a heckuva lot better in an Am. Jur. 2d volume published in 1991.

So on you go. On to *C.J.S. Step Two.*

§ 6.6(b)(ii) *C.J.S. Step Two*

{5} In the volume containing your title, look in the back for the *title index* {5}. Remember to look for *narrow words first.* Here, the index is far more detailed, so some serious looking can pay dividends in finding the precise sections of text you should read.

§ 6.6(b)(ii) *C.J.S. Step Two*

No, you haven't found a typo. This is *C.J.S. Step Two* just like the *C.J.S. Step Two* above is *C.J.S. Step Two.* There are two *C.J.S. Steps Two.* You can use either or both. Personally, I prefer this *C.J.S. Step Two,* the Analytical Approach. After finding a potential title and the volume containing that title, look at the front of the title. There
{2} you will find an "Analysis" {2}, broadly breaking your title down into Roman Numerals and Alphabetical Letters, not unlike an ordinary outline. Here you can eliminate broad chunks of the coverage as totally inapplicable to your research problem, a feat not possible in an alphabetical index where you must destroy your fingernail with the nope-nope-nope approach. The Analytical Approach enables you to see how the information is arranged and to quickly narrow your search down to information relevant to your problem.

{2,3,4} Following the "Analysis," you'll find a "Subanalysis" {2,3,4}, enabling you to pinpoint precise sections applicable to your problem and to find cross-references to the pages where text appears.

You have now successfully traversed the Finding Phase in C.J.S. Turn your attention, please, to the Use Phase.

§ 6.6(c) C.J.S.: The Use Phase

In C.J.S., you'll find two different page layouts: (1) the older volumes used a two-column text layout and a three-column footnote layout, but (2) the newer volumes use a two-column layout for both text and footnotes.

At the beginning of each section, you'll find a bold-faced statement of a rule of law followed by several paragraphs or several pages of text developing that rule of law and showing how the various states differ in their application of the particular rule or in their adoption of completely different rules {6,7}. **{6,7}**

As you begin reading the first bit of law in your young career as lawyer or paralegal, you should roll up your sleeve, get out the tattoo kit, and add:

GOOD'S RULE OF RESEARCH #12:

When reading lawbooks, don't jerk your head up and down looking at *every single footnote*. Instead, wait for the "*heart palpitation footnote*."

You can go crazy reading the text of most legal writing in encyclopedias, treatises, law reviews, and other sources. Every word, sometimes, bears its own footnote, and if you nod down to the footnote part of the page each time a footnote appears, two bad things will happen: (1) you'll fail to ingest what the writer has to say and (2) you'll get an incurable case of whiplash. Thus, follow the above Rule of Research and "wait for the *heart palpitation footnote*." This is the footnote accompanying text that absolutely nails your legal research problem, text that describes your facts to a "T," text that appears to have been written just for you {7}. {7}

In the C.J.S. scheme of things, footnotes begin in section 1 of a title with footnote #1. Nothing strange about that. Then the footnote numbers go up to #100. Then they start all over again at footnote #1. The West Company will make certain that no single section of text has more than 100 footnotes. If the text of such a section should require more than 100 footnotes, then the West Company will use decimal numbers as footnote numbers, again making certain that each footnote number within a section is a *unique number.* In other words, § 440 of a title cannot have two footnote numbers bearing the same number. The reason will become clear in the Updating Phase, described below.

The footnotes in C.J.S. cite primarily cases and other primary authority, not other legal material, not other encyclopedias, not treatises, not law review articles. Just cases. And, as noted above, because it cites so many cases, it has little room left over to "blurb" many of the cases.

To arrange these cases within a single footnote, the West Company follows a system of arrangement it uses throughout all of its publications, including the massive American Digest System, also known as the West Key Number System. Cases are arranged as follows: (1) U.S. Supreme Court cases, (2) federal circuit course cases arranged alphabetically by the states from which the cases arose (a word on that below), (3) federal district court cases alphabetically by state, (4) state court cases alphabetically by state and by hierarchy of court within state.

The above system makes eminently good sense with one huge exception: arranging federal circuit court cases alphabetically by the states from which the cases arose instead of *numerically by circuit* makes zero sense. Who cares that a Ninth Circuit case arose in Alaska or California or Washington? Nobody. The researcher wants to know what the Ninth Circuit or the Second Circuit has to say on an issue, and it's bloody inconvenient to have to memorize exactly which state is in which circuit.

So the hands-down winner of the Boo of the Century Award is the West Publishing Company for devising this silly approach to arranging cases in C.J.S. footnotes (and headnotes in the Digest System).[1]

Another complaint: when West cites cases in footnotes, it, like most other publishing companies, fails to include the date of decision in the citation. Boo! Hiss! The researcher, then, is left to wonder about how old the case is and whether it's too old to bother with. You can, however, gain some insight by following:

GOOD'S RULE OF RESEARCH #13:

When jotting down case citations found in the footnotes of background sources, notice the "2d" in their citations and the volume numbers. If "2d" is present and the volume number is high, the case is relatively recent. If "2d" is missing, the case is old and might not be worth retrieving.

If you've followed the Use Phase to this point, you are sitting there right now in the middle of the law library with a volume of C.J.S. propped open before you, reading some of the most riveting prose on the face of the globe. As you read, you gain an

[1]Oh well, there goes the West Company as a potential publisher of this sizzling bestseller. Please note, however, that in the current volumes of the American Digest System, the West Company has finally changed its system by providing the circuit number; it still insists, though, on arranging the federal circuit court cases alphabetically by state, not numerically by circuit.

appreciation of the issues confronting your client, you spot issues you might not have otherwise seen, and, perhaps most importantly, you begin to *find cases.* You begin to jot down citations to cases that might or might not merit your careful attention. Then you hightail it over to the National Reporter System and begin to read those cases yourself.

Strategically, you must keep at the front of your mind a crucial fact: *Wilbur found all these cases cited in the footnotes; Wilbur worked diligently for hundreds of hours researching all case law in existence from the dawn of time to the time when the book you're reading was published; Wilbur is sharing his research notes with you and saving you an enormous amount of time.*

When you realize that you're cashing in on Wilbur's research, you realize another important fact of life: *Wilbur had to stop researching; he had to put his pencil down when the editor screamed over the intercom: "Wilbur, dadburnit, hurry up with that revised volume of C.J.S., we've got to go to press; put it to bed, now!"*

You thus enter the third phase of lawbook use, and as you do, you check your wrist and find:

GOOD'S RULE OF RESEARCH #14:

Never put a lawbook back on the shelf without checking its pocket part.

§ 6.6(d) C.J.S.: The Updating Phase

As mentioned above, most lawbooks have some sort of built-in updating feature. The most widely used is the Cumulative Annual Pocket Part {8}, which updates the bound **{8}**
volume text from the copyright date of that volume to the previous December. You'll find pocket parts in C.J.S., Am. Jur. 2d, A.L.R., some treatises, the federal codes (U.S.C.A. and U.S.C.S.), and other sources.

Updating C.J.S. with its pocket part is relatively easy. First, you must jot down the title and sections and footnotes containing on-point cases. Then, in the pocket part, you locate the *same title, same sections,* and *same footnotes* in order to obtain cases decided since the bound volume was published.

Right away you'll notice that most of the pocket part consists of mere listings of cases and not very much, if any, additional text. Thus, if significant legal changes have occurred, you won't find many detailed explanations of those changes in a C.J.S. pocket part.

So in the pocket part you will find additional cases decided since the publication of the bound volume. Though the pocket part theoretically cuts off at the previous December, it collects cases that were being put on the shelf during the previous autumn—at the time when Wilbur was completing his research to collect the cases to include in the pocket part.

§ 6.6(d)(i) Two Important Questions

Two strategic questions inevitably arise about the coverage of C.J.S. pocket parts: (1) does C.J.S. include *all* cases on any given point of law? and (2) how far in the case law publication system did C.J.S. get in listing cases in the pocket part?

The first question has two answers. First, C.J.S. used to include *all* cases on any given point of law. That is, C.J.S. stated, as a matter of editorial policy, that it included every case in the footnotes to C.J.S. text and in C.J.S. pocket parts. Thus, as recently as the 1980s, one could rely on C.J.S. as providing an inclusive listing of cases on a point of law. Hence, legal researchers could use C.J.S., and if they located a "heart palpitation footnote," they could rely on the cases cited in that footnote as being an exhaustive listing of cases such that the researchers would then only have to update "beyond the supplement."

Now the answer is different. The pocket part of C.J.S. now states that it includes "selective supplementary materials." That's another way of saying that some cases are listed and some cases aren't. These days, therefore, you cannot rely on C.J.S. as providing a *complete* list of *every* on-point case. Thus, you will use the cases you locate in C.J.S. as contributing to an overall list that *all* background research will uncover.

Now to the second question: how far in the case law publication system did C.J.S. get in listing cases in the pocket part? You can ask the same question another way: where and when did Wilbur stop researching? Where did Wilbur put his research pencil down when the editor was squawking at him over the intercom?

Think of it this way: the writers at West (collectively known as Wilbur) had to *research* in order to find those cases listed in the C.J.S. pocket part. They didn't just find these cases randomly on the shelves. No, to retrieve them, they had to "run West Key Numbers" in the American Digest System. And they had to stop at some *point in time.*

§ 6.6(d)(ii) Marking Judicial Time

In an earlier chapter, you learned all about the National Reporter System. You learned that the seven current Regional Reporters (A.2d, So. 2d, P.2d, N.E.2d, S.E.2d, N.W.2d, S.W.2d), that the two state reporters (Cal. Rptr. 2d, N.Y.S.2d), and that the two major federal reporters (F.2d, F. Supp.) all hit the shelves in advance sheet form *once each week.* You also learned that the spines of these advance sheets have sequential numbers corresponding to the weeks of the year. And finally you learned, I hope, that any given court report acts much like a calendar: *the volume and page number of any given court report marks a precise week in time when that court report hit the shelves of America's law libraries.*

Thus, 434 F.2d 101 is a more recent event than 433 F.2d 1072. Or 434 F.2d 101 is an older event than 435 F.2d 1.

So consider this:

GOOD'S RULE OF RESEARCH #15:

If you know the volume and page number of a court report marking the point where some other researcher *stopped* researching, then you know where to *start* researching.

Think about it this way: suppose *you* are researching a case and you finish researching *all the way to the present day*; to keep track of where *you* stop, you jot down the *volume* and *page* number of the *latest* volume of *any* court report on the shelf. You might jot down 936 F.2d 101 or 765 F. Supp. 1209; *either one marks the same moment in time*, because both of those volumes hit the shelves during the same week.

A month later you ask your assistant or your roommate to update your research. "Like how far'dja get?" asks your roommate (roommates tend to use that word "like" a lot). Saying you stopped "last month" doesn't help. But if you say you got as far as 765 F. Supp. 1209, then that bit of information marks a precise moment in time *because that book hit the shelf during a given week of the year.*

§ 6.6(d)(iii) Pay Attention to This Section

So wouldn't it be great if C.J.S. or any other lawbook told you exactly where it stopped collecting cases? Wouldn't it be great if you could call Wilbur on the phone and say, "Hey, Wilbur, where'd you stop researching when you wrote that pocket part collecting those cases involving the liability of a surgeon for a negligent sterilization operation?" And wouldn't it be great if Wilbur responded, "Like 765 F. Supp. 1209" (Wilbur, after all, is *somebody's* roommate).

Well, Wilbur has done just that on:

THE SECOND MOST IMPORTANT PAGE IN ALL OF LEGAL RESEARCH {9}. **{9}**

If you will turn to the *front* of any C.J.S. pocket part, you will find what I call *the second most important page in all of legal research.* On that page you'll find a table listing the volume and page numbers of all court reports where the pocket part *stopped* collecting cases. I call these citations "Stop Cites," for they show the exact point in each court report where the background source stopped collecting cases. Of course, each Stop Cite marks the *identical point in time.* All Wilbur did to obtain the Stop Cites was to write down the citation of the last book on each shelf at the time he stopped researching.

It is crucial at this stage of your legal research career that you understand the importance of this page and the meaning of the information appearing on it. Take my word for it, this page, which appears elsewhere in a variety of legal research sources, serves a vital role in the legal research process. In fact, not surprisingly, it serves the *second most important* function in legal research.

The page, simply put, tells you where Wilbur put his research pencil down. It tells you exactly where Wilbur stopped locating new cases for inclusion in the pocket part. The information on the page, simply put, acts as a marker on the time line, on all time lines, on all court reports, where Wilbur put his pencil down. The incredibly clever graphic on the opposite page depicts this vital research concept.

So think fleetingly about it: if you know where Wilbur *stopped* researching, doesn't that give you a tip on where you should *start* researching? In other words, if Wilbur has collected all cases to the *left*, i.e., in the past, of the point where he stopped researching, then isn't it your task to collect cases to the *right*, i.e., from that point to RIGHT NOW? Yes indeed. That, precisely, is your task.

How to do it? Stay tuned. We'll pick up with the overall updating process when we get to Step Three. For now, just know that part of effective research strategy requires your understanding a few facts of life: (1) Wilbur had to stop somewhere, (2) you'll be starting where Wilbur stopped, and (3) if you fail to comprehend what I'm trying to tell you, you are in for some real heartache.

§ 6.6(e) C.J.S.: Summary

Now you know how to use C.J.S. as one of the first sources you consult in the legal research process. In a nutshell, you go to the *General Index* to find the right volume and then switch to the Volume Index or the Analysis to locate the right section or sections. You then read and read and jot down citations to on-point cases. You then supplement by checking the pocket part under the same title, same section, same footnotes to locate more recent cases. You conclude by checking the *second most important page in all of legal research* and jotting down a Stop Cite, that is, just one citation of a volume and page number of just one court report as a marker to show where the pocket part stopped collecting cases.

On page 80, for your convenience, is a Research Roadmap for C.J.S.

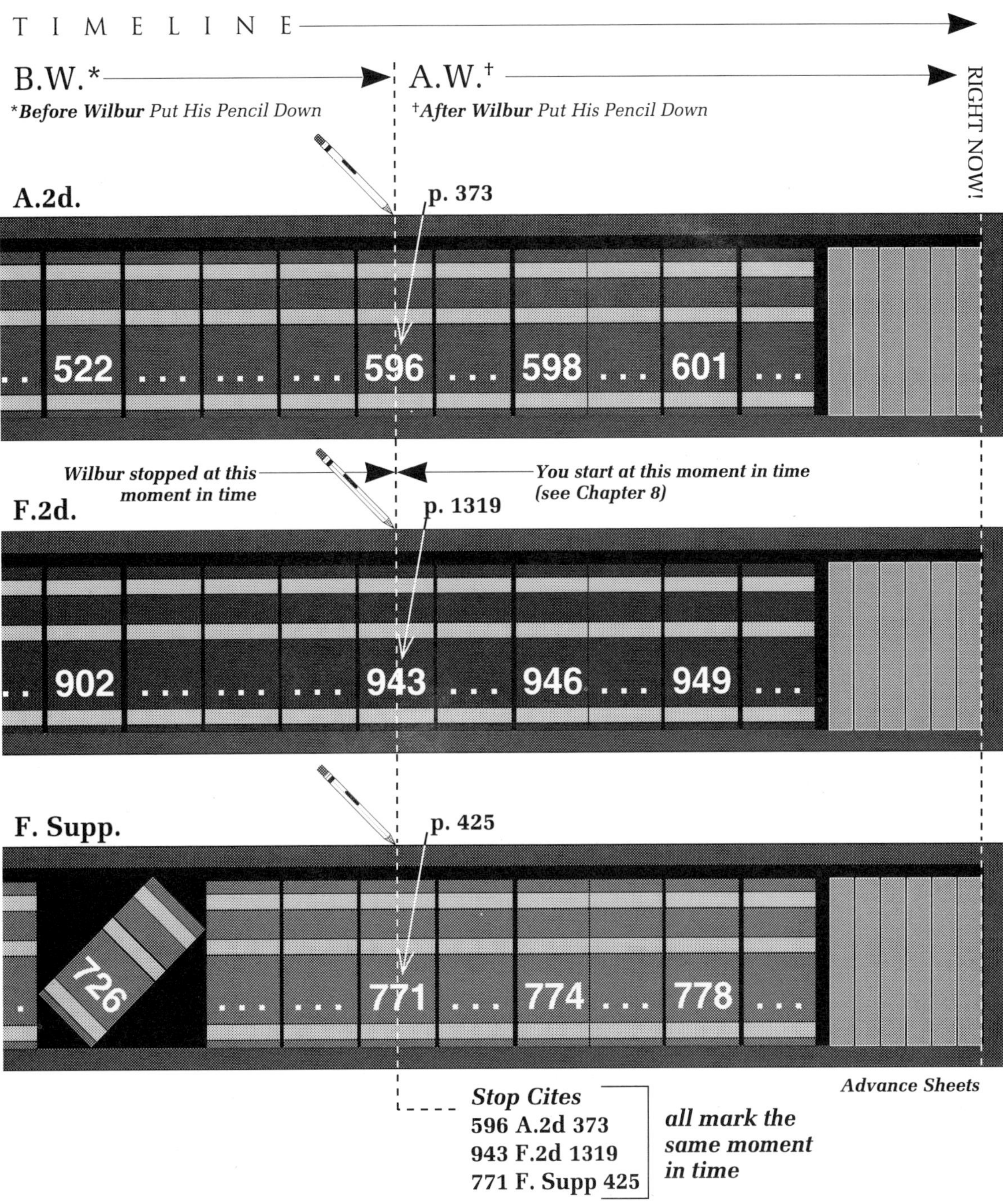

Figure 5

Stop Cites: Where Wilbur Stopped Researching

§ 6.6(f) C.J.S.: A Roadmap for Research

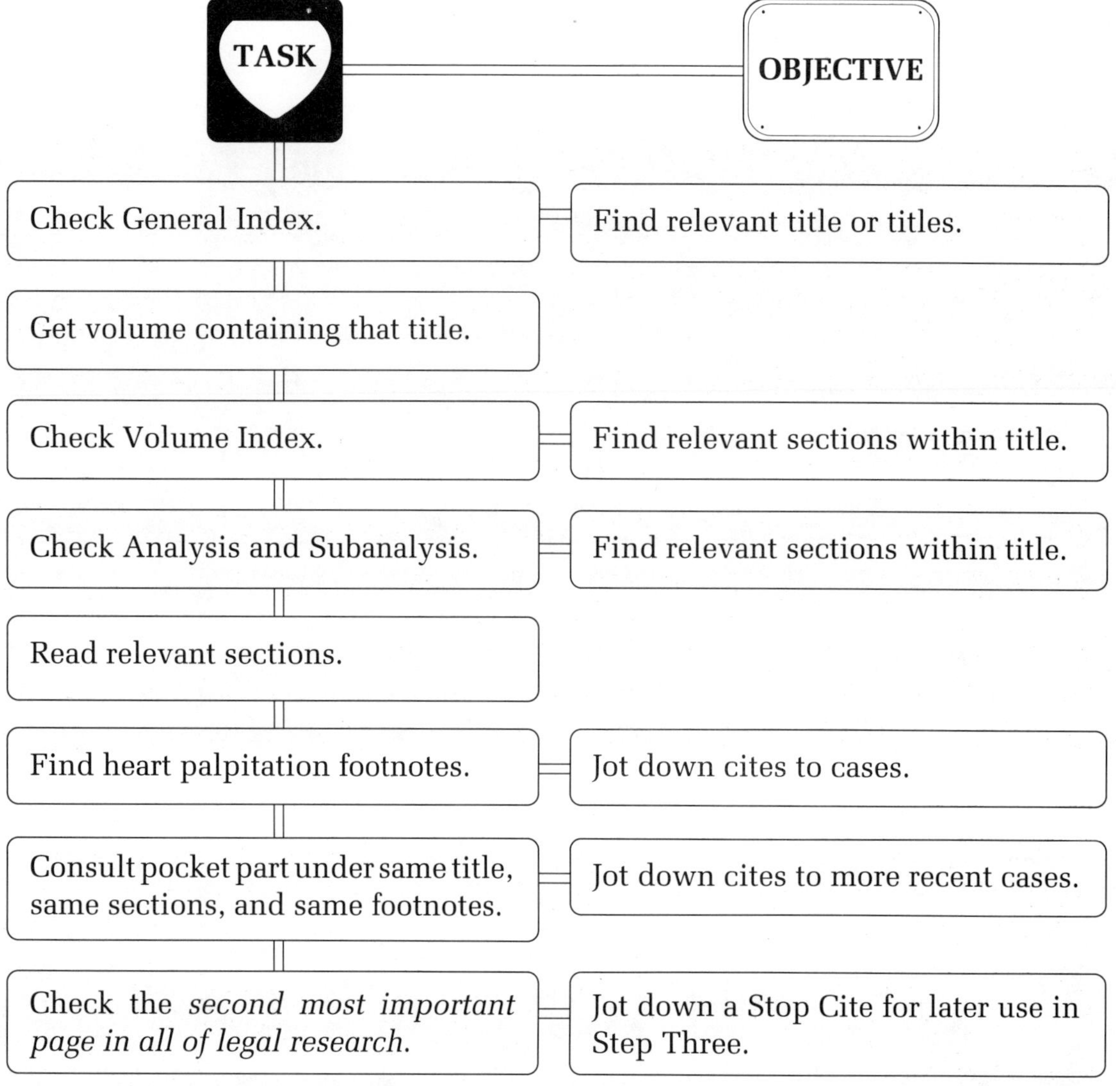

{1-9} § 6.6(g) C.J.S.: Visual Aids {1-9}

In the Visual Aids booklet, I have reproduced selected pages from C.J.S. that you would encounter in researching Wally and Mipsie's case. On each page, in the box, you'll find my commentary showing exactly what the researcher is doing and how the source is supplying the information the researcher seeks.

Please note that these pages are selective. In the real world of legal research, you would consult many more pages, especially during the Finding Phase. You would, most likely, go down lots of dead ends, locating irrelevant information, getting frustrated, and, yes, perhaps even *losing your mind.*

But if you'll follow the above instructions, step by step, and study the Visual Aids, page by page, you'll begin to learn how to do legal research *without losing your mind.*

§ 6.7 Am. Jur. 2d

§ 6.7(a) Am. Jur. 2d: Bibliographic Information

One of the great plots weaving through the fabric of legal publishing (if anything can beat "pocket parts") is the Cain and Abel relationship between big brother West Publishing Company and little brother Lawyers Cooperative Publishing Company. Count on it: whatever big brother West does or tries, little brother Lawyers Co-op will come along and try the same thing—only better (it hopes) and different.

Thus, when big brother West published the old, original *Corpus Juris* (C.J.), little brother Lawyers Co-op cranked up *American Jurisprudence* (Am. Jur.). No sooner did little brother Lawyers Co-op finish Am. Jur. than big brother West one-upped Lawyers Co-op (big brothers are like that) and came out with *Corpus Juris Secundum.* Lawyers Co-op, of course, was insanely jealous and immediately set about writing the second edition of its encyclopedia and produced Am. Jur. 2d.

Am. Jur. 2d is quite similar to C.J.S. It too is a legal encyclopedia treating virtually every issue cropping up in American law. Whereas C.J.S. appears in 101 volumes, Am. Jur. 2d has 86. Both encyclopedias are divided into 400+ subject matter areas. As noted above, C.J.S. calls these subject matter discussions "titles." Am. Jur. 2d calls them "topics." And though C.J.S. *used to* include *all cases* in its footnotes, Am. Jur. 2d as a matter of editorial policy has always included only selective cases, i.e., those it thinks are important.

This "selective authority" philosophy permeates nearly all Lawyers Co-op publications. You'll find, for example, a similar approach in its federal code, *United States Code Service* (U.S.C.S.). Lawyers Co-op's approach also cuts both ways. On the one hand, the researcher cannot rely on Am. Jur. 2d as providing a *complete* list of *all* on-point cases. On the other hand, because Am. Jur. 2d does not cite every case, it does have room available for "blurbing" the cases cited, especially in the pocket parts.

As with C.J.S., the text of each topic in Am. Jur. 2d is *analytically* arranged into
"sections," which are listed in a broad *outline* {11} at the front of each topic and then **{11}**
specifically broken down in a *detailed outline* {12, 13} after the broad *outline*. Thus, **{12,13}**
the Analytical Approach is readily available and, indeed, constitutes one of the most efficient approaches to finding on-point discussions in Am. Jur. 2d.

Other finding aids include a *General Index* {10}, which indexes the entire **{10}**
encyclopedia and is best used as a *volume finder* or *topic finder*, and Topic Indexes for each of the 400+ topics in Am. Jur. 2d. Some long topics stretch over two volumes, so the Topic Index resides in the volume concluding the topic. The Topic Indexes are best used as *page finders.*

While the Tabular Approach is not available in most C.J.S. volumes, Am. Jur. 2d does include a Table of Statutes Cited. These tables appear in two places: (1) at the end of the entire set, you'll find volumes entitled *Table of Statutes Cited*; these tables sequentially list all titles and all sections of the entire United States Code[2] and cross-reference you to the topics and sections where each legislative provision is discussed in the entire encyclopedia; (2) at the front of each volume, you'll find a separate Table of Statutes Cited providing similar cross-references to U.S. Code provisions discussed in that individual volume. Thus, little brother Am. Jur. 2d has one-upped big brother C.J.S. by providing the Tabular Approach, which probably prompted the West Company to include the Table of Statutes and Regulations Cited in recent, recompiled volumes. As a result, Am. Jur. 2d would have to rank as the favored source to use in any legal research problem involving federal law, rules of procedure, or uniform laws.

{14} The text in Am. Jur. 2d {14}, as a rule, is a bit more captivating than the drivel in C.J.S. Somehow the writers at Am. Jur. 2d have managed to downplay the legalese just a bit so that ordinary people can read the stuff without falling into a deep coma. Though it won't win a PEN award, Am. Jur. 2d does write about virtually every conceivable legal issue ever litigated in American law. For that reason, a visit to Am. Jur. 2d will mark most of your legal research quests.

The text in Am. Jur. 2d is less copiously footnoted than that in C.J.S., the footnotes containing citations to selected cases from state and federal courts all across the nation. As mentioned earlier, this "selective authority" approach frees up footnote space so that some of the cases can be "blurbed."

The Am. Jur. 2d encyclopedia contains one feature missing from C.J.S. When new areas of the law arise, Am. Jur. 2d will create a new topic to accommodate it, write a brand new topic, and publish it in a feature called the *New Topic Service*. You'll find this feature located at the end of the entire encyclopedia, and it's a good idea to check it periodically.

§ 6.7(a)(i) Crucial Cross-References

The footnotes of Am. Jur. 2d contain one other vital reference. In the footnotes of Am. Jur. 2d you'll find cross-references to *A.L.R. Annotations*, one of the best background sources of all. Thus, when researching a topic in Am. Jur. 2d, you'll frequently notice an "Annotation" reference in the footnotes, which means that the annotation so referenced concerns the identical subject matter as the text supported by that footnote.

§ 6.7(b) Am. Jur. 2d: the Finding Phase

The Finding Phase of researching with Am. Jur. 2d is virtually identical to the Finding
{10} Phase of researching with C.J.S. Basically, you should use the *General Index* {10} to locate a potential topic or topics. When you identify a topic that appears to discuss the

[2]The tables also list court rules, federal regulations, and uniform laws such as the Uniform Commercial Code, and provide cross-references to Am. Jur. 2d text discussing each provision or rule.

legal issues in your statement of facts, you should fetch that volume and immediately shift to the Analytical Approach {11,12,13} or the volume Index Approach {omitted **{11,12,13}**
from Visual Aids}. Also in the Finding Phase, remember that Am. Jur. 2d does provide the Tabular Approach, with the separate volume entitled *Table of Statutes Cited* (covering the entire encyclopedia) or the separate table in each volume (covering that particular volume). Again, this Tabular Approach helps only when your topic concerns law found in a federal statute, rule of procedure, or uniform law.

§ 6.7(c) Am. Jur. 2d: the Use Phase

The Use Phase of researching with Am. Jur. 2d is identical to the Use Phase of C.J.S. When either the Index Approach, the Analytical Approach, or, in federal topics, the Tabular Approach yields some sections for your reading, you proceed as usual, reading and reading and reading the text {14} without jerking your head down at each **{14}**
and every footnote. When you find that heart palpitation footnote, you proceed to jot down citations to cases. And in all events, you remain ever vigilant for any footnote references whatsoever to A.L.R. Annotations, for, as we shall see below, A.L.R. is a gold mine of information for the frazzled legal researcher.

§ 6.7(d) Am. Jur. 2d: the Updating Phase

The Updating Phase, too, is almost identical to the Updating Phase of C.J.S. Each volume of Am. Jur. 2d includes a Cumulative Annual Pocket Part {15}. There you will **{15}**
find that the philosophy of "selective citation of authority" pays some dividends, for virtually every case cited in an Am. Jur. 2d pocket part is blurbed so that you can immediately determine whether the case is sufficiently on point to merit your retrieving it and reading it and writing about it in your memorandum or brief. That same philosophy, of course, has its drawbacks as well. You cannot rely on the cases in Am. Jur. 2d as constituting a complete list of every case ever decided on that particular point of law. You must undertake additional research in other sources to assemble such a list.

The Updating Phase of Am. Jur. 2d differs from C.J.S. in one important respect. Am. Jur. 2d does not contain *the second most important page in all of legal research.* Nowhere does the pocket part inform you about the precise mark on the shelf where Wilbur stopped collecting cases. Of course, such information would not help very much anyway, for Am. Jur. 2d does not pretend to cite every case. So you could not use Am. Jur. 2d as an *inclusive* background source. It would be nice, however, if every lawbook would contain *the second most important page in all of legal research* to clue you in about the precise point where they ceased legal research. As an aside, you'll find that Lawyers Co-op does provide this vital information in its federal code, *United States Code Service* (U.S.C.S.).

§ 6.7(e) Am. Jur. 2d: Summary

Now you know how to use Am. Jur. 2d as one of the first sources to consult in the legal research process. Quite simply, you go to the *General Index* to find the right volume and then switch to the Volume Index (Index Approach) or the Outline (Analytical Approach) to locate the right section or sections. If you have a federal problem, you can use the separate volume entitled *Table of Statutes Cited* or in each encyclopedia volume the feature at the front entitled "Table of Statutes Cited" (Tabular Approach) as well. You then read and read and jot down citations to on-point cases. You then supplement by checking the pocket part under the same topic, same section, same footnotes to locate more recent cases. In the supplementation process, you'll be able to eliminate some of the cases by reading the blurbs provided.

Here, for your convenience, is a Research Roadmap for Am. Jur. 2d.

§ 6.7(f) Am. Jur. 2d: A Roadmap for Research

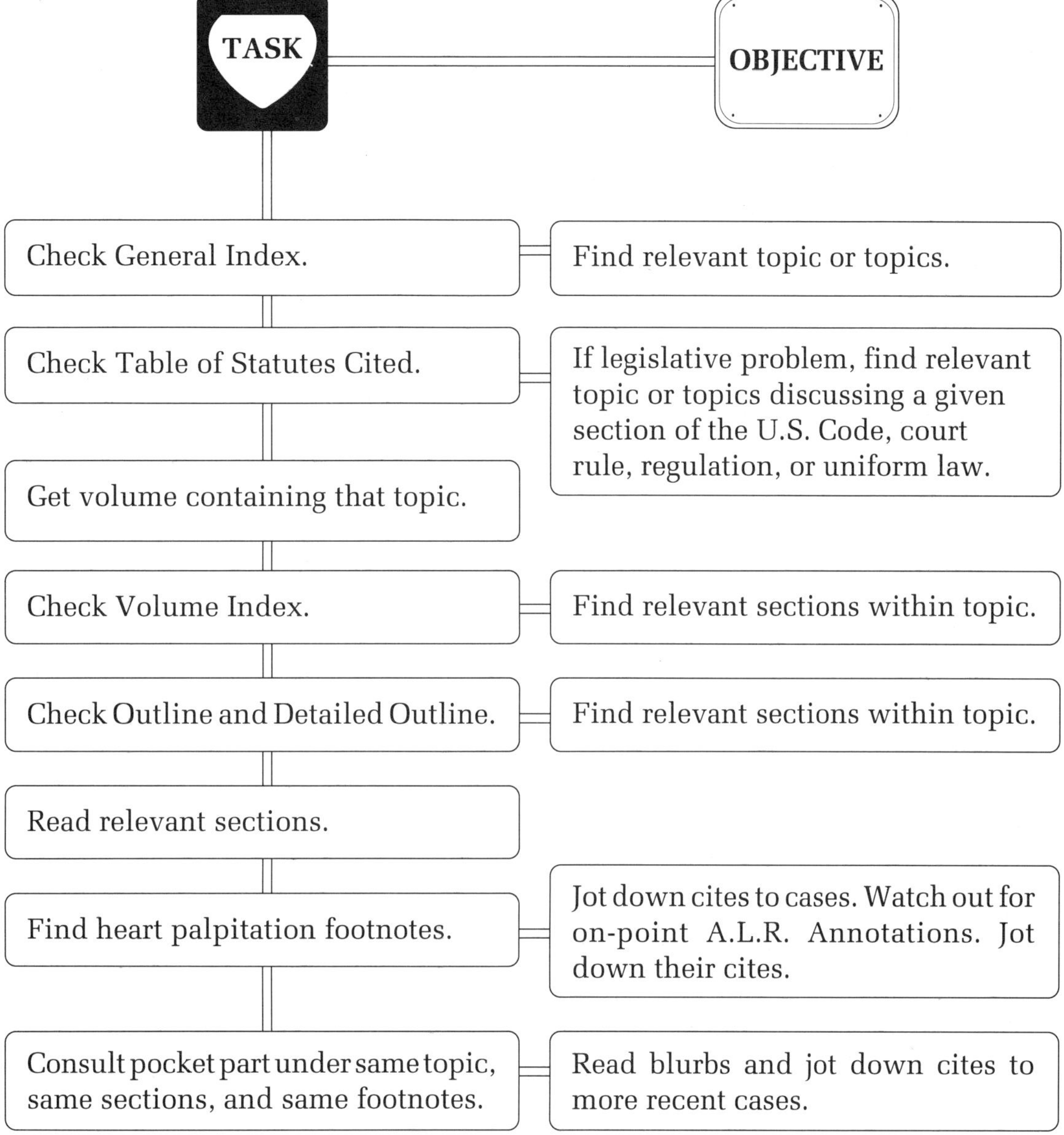

§ 6.7(g) Am. Jur. 2d: Visual Aids {10-15}

In the Visual Aids booklet, I have reproduced selected pages from Am. Jur. 2d that you would encounter in researching Wally and Mipsie's case. On each page, in the box, you'll find my commentary showing exactly what the researcher is doing and how the source is supplying the information the researcher seeks.

Please note that these pages are selective. In the real world of legal research, you would consult many more pages, especially during the Finding Phase. You would, most likely, go down lots of dead ends, locating irrelevant information, getting frustrated, and, yes, perhaps even *losing your mind*.

But if you'll follow the above instructions, step by step, and study the Visual Aids, page by page, you'll begin to learn how to do legal research *without losing your mind*.

§ 6.8 A.L.R.

§ 6.8(a) A.L.R.: Bibliographic Information

As your research skills increase, you will find that you tend to favor certain sources over others. In many legal areas, particularly the more academic ones, you'll find that you don't even use the first two sources we've discussed, C.J.S. and Am. Jur. 2d. But I think you'll agree, as you become an Ace Legal Researcher, that one *indispensable* source in any legal research problem requiring the location of on-point cases, i.e., almost all legal research problems, is *American Law Reports*, also known as A.L.R.

A.L.R. stands as a unique legal research tool. It came about, no doubt, as a direct result of Lawyers Co-op's sibling rivalry with its big brother, the West Publishing Company. Green with envy, little brother Lawyers Co-op was watching big brother West succeed with its National Reporter System. So Lawyers Co-op figured that it needed to publish a court report as well. Fortunately, reason prevailed at Lawyers Co-op, and they didn't take West head on and try to put out another court report system publishing all opinions of all state and federal courts nationwide.

Instead, Lawyers Co-op took a radically different approach: instead of publishing all court opinions, they would just publish the full text of *important* court opinions, cases likely to become *leading cases*, or cases that represent a significant type of case, or cases that are strange, unique, funny—no one really knows the exact criteria for publication in A.L.R.

The point is that *American Law Reports* is a court report. It does publish the full text of cases the editors think will be of help to the legal profession. Well, if that's all A.L.R. did, I can assure you of one thing: nobody in his or her right mind would buy the doggone thing. Lawyers don't want some editorial board at Lawyers Co-op dictating to them about what cases are important and what cases are not. The lawyers, quite rightly, want access to *all* case law, and you know who already provides that in the National Reporter System: big brother West.

§ 6.8(a)(i) What Is an A.L.R. *Annotation*?

But publishing the full text of these selected opinions is not all that A.L.R. does. In addition, immediately after the full text of the opinion, A.L.R. publishes an A.L.R. *annotation*, and an A.L.R. annotation is worth its weight in platinum. An A.L.R. annotation is a complete article analyzing the point of law found in the reported case. Thus, in a single volume of A.L.R., the first case might involve the liability of a taxicab company for discharging a passenger on the wrong side of the cab, and it would be followed by a complete annotation analyzing all similar taxicab cases. The very next case might involve landlord-tenant law and lease provisions concerning the keeping of cats in an apartment, and it would be followed by a complete annotation analyzing all similar cats-in-apartments cases.

You can readily see, then, that A.L.R. is not an encyclopedia, not a treatise, not anything but A.L.R. It's not the kind of source you'd use to browse away a rainy afternoon in the law library boning up on Constitutional Law. But it is the kind of source you should use from now on in your entire legal career. It's that good.

Why is it so good? Certainly not because of its writing style, which ranks as *the worst* in all of legal literature (average sentence length is, oh, about 140 words per sentence). What makes it so good is the narrowness of the topics annotated: I was not kidding in the preceding paragraph; there is indeed an A.L.R. annotatation entitled "Lease Provisions with respect to the Keeping of Cats."[3] Can you imagine having to research "cats-in-apartments lease law" in a treatise or encyclopedia? Or consider the factual narrowness of this recent A.L.R. Annotation: "Liability for Injury or Death Allegedly Caused by Foreign Substance in Beverage."

A.L.R., therefore, usually is the first step I take in virtually any case-law research problem (legislative problems begin elsewhere). Recently I purchased some property and was having a bit of a squabble over the boundary lines of the lot. To check out my legal status, I went straight to A.L.R. You guessed it. Here's the annotation title: "Boundary Line Adjustments in Contracts for the Sale of Real Property."

§ 6.8(a)(ii) The Structure of A.L.R.

A.L.R. appears in six series. The following table shows their names, their beginning dates, their ending dates, and the number of their volumes as of August 1992:

Name	Begin	End	No. Volumes
A.L.R.	1919	1948	175
A.L.R.2d	1948	1965	100
A.L.R.3d	1965	1980	100
A.L.R. 4th	1980	1991	90
A.L.R. 5th	1991	present	4 (as of August 1992)
A.L.R. Fed.	1969	present	108 (as of August 1992)

From the above table, you can readily see that the old A.L.R. is ancient history, and quite frankly, not very useful in modern legal research. The others, however, should become part of your research routine as you strive toward the status of Ace Legal Researcher. In addition, A.L.R. Fed, which began in 1969, became the sole source for federal legal issues from that point forward. Before that time, however, you'll find federal issues intermingled with state issues in A.L.R.3d and A.L.R.2d.

[3]See? I told you lawyers like that fancy-sounding compound preposition *with respect to.* Henry Fowler in *Fowler's Modern English Usage* calls these structures the "compost of our language."

§ 6.8(a)(iii) Supplementation of A.L.R.: Various Experiments

For some reason the editors at Lawyers Co-op couldn't seem to decide on a set way to supplement A.L.R. and have tried out differing approaches over the years. Though you will rarely use A.L.R. (the old, first series), you should know that the annotations appearing there are supplemented in the *Blue Books of Supplemental Decisions* (not to be confused with the notorious Harvard *Bluebook*). This is a collateral *set* of books, appearing in approximately seven volumes, each picking up the supplementation process where the preceding volume left off. Thus, if you've located an A.L.R. annotation at, say, 64 A.L.R. 101, you'd have to consult that citation in *each one* of the *Blue Books of Supplemental Decisions*. And there you wouldn't find a great deal of help, for the *Blue Books* just cite more recent cases dealing with the subject matter of the annotation. Whoopie-do. That's what you need, a *list* of cases, maybe a hundred or so; terrific, a hundred cases you'll have to look up just to see whether or not they're relevant.

So much for A.L.R., the first series.

When A.L.R.2d came along, the editors wisely changed the supplementing feature. Strangely, they retained the collateral-set-of-books approach to supplementation and devised the *Later Case Service*, which you'll find shelved somewhere close to A.L.R.2d. Unlike the *Blue Books*, however, the *Later Case Service* not only cites more recent on-point cases but summarizes them so that you can decide which ones merit your time and attention and which ones don't. Because such summaries require considerably more pages than the listing approach of the *Blue Books*, you'll find that each individual volume of the *Later Case Service* will cover just several volumes of A.L.R.2d. Also, the bound volume of the *Later Case Service* itself must be supplemented, so in the back you'll find a pocket part—one of the rare "supplements to a supplement" in legal literature.

With the advent of A.L.R.3d, the editors at Lawyers Co-op were struck with an ingenious idea: instead of sending the users of A.L.R. to the other side of the library in search of this other set of books, why not just supplement each individual volume of A.L.R. with a . . . hold on, folks, are you ready for sheer genius? . . . yes, with a pocket part. Right there in the book you want to supplement! Now how on earth did they ever think of *that*? This system of *internal supplementation* worked so well that Lawyers Co-op decided to stick with it in all later series of A.L.R. Thus, A.L.R.3d, A.L.R. 4th, A.L.R. 5th, and A.L.R. Fed. are all internally supplemented with pocket parts.

There was one slight problem, however. What could the editors do when the pocket part started to get too big to fit into the back of the hardbound volume it was supplementing. Easy. They could look in the pocket part, find out which annotation was being deluged with so many recent cases, and tell Wilbur to write

A SUPERSEDING ANNOTATION

if the law had changed such that the original annotation should be rewritten. Or they could tell Wilbur to write

A SUPPLEMENTING ANNOTATION

if the new, more recent cases were merely adding to the cases cited in the original annotation.

Each of these—superseding annotations and supplementing annotations—appears in later volumes of A.L.R. Thus, if the pocket part of an annotation appearing in volume 75 of A.L.R.2d is getting too big for its britches because the subject matter in the annotation appearing at 75 A.L.R.2d 101 is a particularly hot topic generating oodles of new cases, then Wilbur will write a brand-new annotation that either replaces (Superseding) or adds to (Supplementing) the original annotation. This new annotation might appear, for example, at 16 A.L.R. 4th 902.

You can, I hope, see the danger lurking. If you find 75 A.L.R.2d 101 and fail to find its superseding annotation, then all the time spent reading 75 A.L.R.2d 101 is totally wasted. You can avoid this heartache, and consequent loss of your mind, by adding to your growing list of universal truths:

GOOD'S RULE OF RESEARCH #16:

Woe be unto the legal researcher who fails to consult A.L.R.'s "Annotation History Table" *before reading any A.L.R. annotation.*

I alert you to the problem here. You will find crystal clear instructions on the use of the Annotation History Table in the Finding Phase of A.L.R. below.

§ 6.8(a)(iv) A.L.R. 5th: Some Attractive Changes

In the spring of 1992, Lawyers Co-op stopped A.L.R. 4th abruptly at volume 90 and introduced the new A.L.R. 5th. This new series of A.L.R. contains some rather attractive features. First, it provides more cross-references to other research tools:

1. Other A.L.R. Annotations.
2. Am. Jur. 2d and other Lawyers Co-op texts.
3. Practice Aids.
4. Digests and Indexes (actual references to Index words).
5. Auto Cite (a computerized cite-checking service of Lawyers Co-op.

The new A.L.R. 5th also provides research cross-references to treatises and encyclopedias, including that of its competitor: West Company's C.J.S.

Finally, A.L.R. 5th provides cross-references to West Key Numbers. It also provides a neat new feature called "Electronic Search Queries." These are suggested word searches you can perform on LEXIS or WESTLAW, the two leading computer-assisted legal research services. These two new features—Electronic Search Queries and West Digest Key Numbers—already appear in a separate paperback edition for A.L.R. 4th and will appear regularly in all pocket parts to A.L.R. 4th.

These new features represent a major development in legal publishing. Publishing companies are recognizing the value of giving references to their competitors' sources; by providing such references they help the people who really count: the legal researchers of the world.

§ 6.8(a)(v) A.L.R.: Catch Your Breath

I realize your mind is spinning right now. Let's face it, A.L.R. is the most complicated source we've encountered so far, and I haven't even told you how to go through the three phases of finding, using, and supplementing yet. It is a complicated source, but I cannot stress too strongly its value. On many occasions, an on-point A.L.R. annotation has saved me hours and hours of research, and I didn't even learn about it until my second year in law school when I was haphazardly researching my moot court topic.

So find yourself a law library, locate A.L.R. in all its series, study the discussions above and the instructions below, and get to know this vital legal research tool. You'll be very glad you did. Despite its terrible writing style.

§ 6.8(b) A.L.R.: the Finding Phase

§ 6.8(b)(i) A.L.R.'s *Index to Annotations*

You've already learned one way to locate an on-point A.L.R. annotation: the footnotes in Am. Jur. 2d contain cross-references to A.L.R. annotations. Often, however, you will not have used Am. Jur. 2d and will prefer A.L.R. as the *first* source you consult. So you need to learn the Finding Phase of using A.L.R.

A.L.R. has one of the best indexes in all of legal literature. Its *Index to Annotations*
{16} {16} (currently a grotesque pink-colored affair appearing in several volumes) provides the Index Approach to locating on-point A.L.R. annotations. A few comments about the *Index to Annotations* are in order. First of all, it indexes all A.L.R. series *except* A.L.R., the first series. But as noted above this source rarely helps in the legal research process, so you won't be missing much, if anything, by not finding any A.L.R. (1st) annotations.

Second, the *Index to Annotations* provides a unique indexing device most helpful in rescuing your fingernail when you must engage in the nope-nope-nope approach. Please recall that the inherent difficulty of the Index Approach is the researcher's inability to psych out the legal indexer and eliminate large chunks of material; you can't exactly refuse to check subwords beginning with M through Z. So, when you face a broad index word having page after page of alphabetically arranged subwords, you're pretty much stuck with the nope-nope-nope approach, running your fingernail from the top of the list, only to find what you're looking for at the very bottom.

Well, A.L.R. decided to combine the Index Approach and the Analytical Approach in its *Index to Annotations*. When you find a particularly broad index word, having scores and scores of alphabetically arranged subwords, you'll also find that A.L.R. has *analytically divided the subwords*. Let me illustrate the method using my "food research" example in Chapter 5.

Here's a standard alphabetical index entry:

Foods

apples
beets
buns
hoagie rolls
hamburger
ice cream
milk
oranges
rice
steak

Here's what A.L.R.'s *Index to Annotations* would do with the same list:

Foods

§ 1 Fruits
§ 2 Vegetables
§ 3 Other Foods
§ 1 Fruits
apples
oranges
§ 2 Vegetables
beets
rice
§ 3 Other Foods
buns
hamburger
hoagie rolls
ice cream
milk
steak

Naturally, if you were looking for "fruits," you could ignore the other *analytical* subdivisions of the *index*. Clever.

After checking the *Index to Annotations*, you must then check the pocket part {17} **{17}**
of the Index. There you'll find index references to annotations published since the bound volume of the Index was published.

§ 6.8(b)(ii) A.L.R.'s Digest

In its never-ending quest to "be like West," Lawyers Co-op not only decided it needed a court report. That court report would also need a "digest system," like the West Company's American Digest System. So it created a separate digest for A.L.R. and A.L.R.2d, and a combined digest for A.L.R.3d, A.L.R. 4th, and A.L.R. Fed.[4] These digests divide all of law into approximately 400 "titles" and then analytically subdivide each title into minute subclassifications, each bearing a "section number." The section numbers then contain references to A.L.R. annotations, references to Am. Jur. 2d and other Lawyers Co-op publications, and blurbs to selected cases.

The A.L.R. digests, therefore, provide an Analytical Approach to finding A.L.R. annotations, an approach many researchers prefer over the Index Approach.

§ 6.8(b)(iii) The Vital "Annotation History Table"

Please recall the words of that wise sage:

GOOD'S RULE OF RESEARCH #16:

Woe be unto the legal researcher who fails to consult A.L.R.'s "Annotation History Table" *before reading any A.L.R. annotation.*

Once you have located an A.L.R. annotation by any means—from Am. Jur. 2d, from the *Index to Annotations*, from A.L.R.'s digest, or from any other reference—you'll be extraordinarily tempted to race directly to that volume and look up that page to begin to locate cases on point. And you will make a terrible, terrible mistake.

Remember "Superseding Annotations" and "Supplementing Annotations"? When the pocket parts of a single volume get too big, the editors at A.L.R. will instruct Wilbur to write either a brand-new annotation (Superseding) or an additional annotation (Supplementing) so that the case citations and case blurbs taking up so much space in the pocket part can be extracted and moved to a later bound volume and appear as an entirely new A.L.R. annotation.

Inevitably, of course, you've found a citation to the *old* annotation and it has been *superseded*, which means the 3.2 hours you're about to expend reading this 125-page

[4] As this book goes to press, the new A.L.R. 5th had just hit the shelves. It's unclear whether Lawyers Co-op will close out the combined A.L.R.3d, A.L.R. 4th, and A.L.R. Fed. digest and begin a new A.L.R. 5th and A.L.R. Fed. digest. It would not make much sense to have A.L.R. Fed. span two different digests, so perhaps Lawyers Co-op plans to close out A.L.R. Fed. and begin A.L.R. Fed. 2d. If so, then watch for the close-out of the combined A.L.R.3d, A.L.R. 4th, and A.L.R. Fed. digest, i.e, no more pocket parts, and the beginning of a new combined digest for A.L.R. 5th and A.L.R. Fed. 2d. If you'll study the shelf carefully, you'll be able to figure out which way the company decides to go.

monster will all be for naught when you *later* find out that the annotation was replaced.

There is a better way: the Annotation History Table {18}. **{18}**

The Annotation History Table provides a cross-reference from the citation of the annotation you're about to read to the citation of any later *superseding* or *supplementing* annotations. Thus, if our hypothetical 75 A.L.R.2d 101 has been superseded by an annotation published at 16 A.L.R. 4th 902, the Annotation History Table will cross-reference you from 75 A.L.R.2d 101 to 16 A.L.R. 4th 902 and alert you that the later annotation supersedes the earlier one. If you find out that your annotation has been *superseded*, then you read only the later, superseding annotation. If, on the other hand, you find out that your annotation has been supplemented, then you must, of course, read *both* the older and later annotations.

The Annotation History Table appears in two places: (1) in the back of the last
volume {18} of the *Index to Annotations* and (2) in the pocket part of the last **{18}**
volume {19} of the *Index to Annotations*. To use this feature correctly you *must* look **{19}**
up the citation to your annotation in *both* the table appearing in the last bound volume of the Index to Annotations *and* the table appearing in its pocket part.

Then, not finding any superseding or supplementing annotation, you may now race to the shelves in search of your volume of A.L.R. containing your on-point annotation.

§ 6.8(c) A.L.R.: the Use Phase

Keep in mind what an A.L.R. annotation is: a comprehensive article on the same subject matter represented by the case published by A.L.R. Thus, immediately before an A.L.R. annotation, you'll find the full text of a reported court opinion. The "headnotes" of this opinion are the headnotes appearing in the A.L.R. Digest. The same opinion, of course, is published by the West Publishing Company, and you'll find the West citation to the same case printed in A.L.R.

But it's not the case that attracts you to A.L.R. Indeed, there's one very good reason why you should read the case not in A.L.R. but in the West court report: by reading the case in the West report you'll find, on the title page, the headnotes and thus the Key Numbers the West Company uses to classify your legal issue.

It's the annotation {20} that attracts you to A.L.R. An A.L.R. annotation might **{20}**
appear in 10 pages or 200 pages. It collects *all cases* decided on the same point of law or subject area as the case reported by A.L.R. It is likely to treat a very narrow and fact-specific subject area. And though the annotation is terribly written, it does provide a gold mine of legal research information.

Because the annotation itself can be quite long, it provides its own internal "finding phase" location devices. At the front of the annotation you'll find an
"Analysis," {20} providing the Analytical Approach to the annotation itself. Follow- **{20}**
ing the Analysis, you'll find an "Index," {20} providing the Index Approach to the **{20}**
annotation itself. Finally, you'll even find the Tabular Approach in the form of a

{21} "Table of Jurisdictions" {21} (one of the geographic arrangements of information in legal literature). In state law A.L.R. annotations, this table shows you the exact sections of the annotation where cases from any given state are cited. In federal law A.L.R. annotations, the table shows the same information for the federal circuits.

Once you've used one or more of these finding devices to locate sections within the annotation that deal with your problem, you'll be extremely tempted to race off to those sections to begin wading through the thicket of legalese you'll find there. But wait! First read the annotation's § 1(b), entitled "Related Matters." This section will cross-reference you to other potentially relevant A.L.R. annotations *and to some on-point law review articles.*

These research cross-references can be extremely helpful. Many times, I have failed to find a truly on-point annotation in the *Index to Annotations*. But, by finding one related to my inquiry, I can often check out § 1(b) in that annotation and find a cross-reference to a truly on-point annotation elsewhere (which my deficient index search failed to reveal).

Also, the list of law review articles provides an added attraction. Be careful, however. Do not rely on this list of law review articles as an exhaustive list of on-point periodical literature. It isn't. Wilbur is just sharing his research notes with you, and I don't think he intends this list as definitive. So you can't skip over Step Two of the legal research process (Chapter 7) by relying on A.L.R.'s list of law review articles in § 1(b) of an annotation.

Once you've used the finding devices to locate the pertinent parts of the
{22} annotation {22} and checked out § 1(b), you're ready to begin reading some of the worst prose the English language has ever suffered. Here's a sample:

> In Christensen v. Thornby (1934) 192 Minn 123, 255 NW 620, 93 ALR 570, where the court affirmed the sustaining of a demurrer to a complaint alleging deceit on the part of the defendant physician in representing that the vasectomy performed upon the plaintiff would result in sterility, following which the plaintiff's wife conceived, on the ground that there was no showing of fraudulent intent in the making of the representation, the court also stated that because the plaintiff's wife had survived the resulting pregnancy and delivery, and since the purpose of the operation was to save the wife from the hazards to her life which were incident to childbirth, the plaintiff had suffered no damage in that instead of losing his wife the plaintiff had been blessed with the fatherhood of another child.[5]

Nice, huh? One sentence. More than 150 words.

[5]Annotation, *Medical Malpractice, and Measure and Elements of Damages, in Connection with Sterilization or Birth Control Procedures*, 27 A.L.R.3d 906, 916 (1969).

§ 6.8(d) A.L.R.: the Updating Phase

In § 6.8(a) above (the bibliographic description of A.L.R.), I pointed out the various experiments A.L.R. has used over the years to update the various series of A.L.R. Most of your research will occur in A.L.R.3d, A.L.R. 4th, A.L.R. 5th, and A.L.R. Fed, all four of which are updated by a pocket part in the back of each volume.[6]

If you use an A.L.R.2d annotation, you must update it in the collateral set of books, the *Later Case Service*. The spine of each of those volumes will contain the span of volumes of A.L.R.2d updated by that particular volume of *Later Case Service*. To update in that volume of *Later Case Service*, simply look up the citation to your A.L.R.2d annotation and then look up the same sections you used in the annotation. There you'll find more recent cases, all blurbed so that you can eliminate the irrelevant ones. After finding additional cases in the bound volume of the *Later Case Service*, turn to the pocket part in the back of that volume and look up the citation to your annotation. There you'll find cases decided after the bound volume of *Later Case Service* was published.

Finally, if you ever have to use an A.L.R. (1st series) annotation, you'll have to update it in the cumbersome and distinctly unhelpful *Blue Books of Supplemental Decisions*, checking each hardbound volume under the citation to your annotation. Remember, you'll only get a list of cases, not blurbs, which would help you not at all in identifying the truly on-point cases.

When using any supplementation device, you have several questions to consider: (1) does the source cite *all* cases on point or just selected cases? (2) how can I interrelate this source with other legal research sources to reduce the amount of chronological case research (running Key Numbers) I have to do? and (3) is there any way I can supplement "beyond the supplement"?

On the first question, A.L.R., as a matter of policy, does cite every case on point. So you can rely on the cases found in the main annotation and in the supplements as an inclusive collection of cases.

Now the second question concerning the interrelationship among A.L.R. and other research sources. Unfortunately, A.L.R. does not provide the *second most important page in all of legal research*, the one you found at the front of the C.J.S. pocket parts, the one telling you the exact volume number and page number of all West reports where Wilbur *stopped* collecting cases. From that page, please recall, you pick *one* report and jot down the Stop Cite. This Stop Cite will serve as the link between background sources and the West Digest System.

But A.L.R. doesn't provide that information. You have two choices. First, look in the A.L.R. pocket part and find the date of the *latest* case cited. Jot down its West court report citation and use that cite as your Stop Cite. Second, why not just use the C.J.S. Stop Cite as the Stop Cite for all your background research? It seems to me that all the Wilburs are researching and putting together pocket parts at roughly the same time of

[6]A sample page from the pocket part does not appear in the Visual Aids. The A.L.R. 4th Annotation was so recent that a pocket part for that volume had not yet appeared when the Visual Aids were assembled.

the year. So perhaps we could use the C.J.S. Stop Cite as some sort of universal Stop Cite. If time is short, folks, and the boss is screaming for an answer, such an approach might serve you well indeed. (We'll return to discuss this concept at some depth in Chapter 8.)

Now the third question: how can I supplement "beyond the supplement." Well, not to be outdone by Ross Perot and Jerry Brown, A.L.R. has its own . . .

TOLL-FREE NUMBER

Yes, folks, not only can you Dial-A-Perot, Dial-A-Jerry, Dial-A-Joke, or Dial-A-Porn, you can . . . Dial-A-Case. In the pocket parts of A.L.R. you are given this number 1-800-225-7488. By dialing it, you'll gain direct contact with . . . uh . . . Wilbur. Seriously, a real voice does answer. Just give that voice the citation to your annotation, and the voice responds instantaneously with citations to more recent cases. Cases "beyond the supplement." Cases dwelling in the dreaded "NO ZONE." Cases that you find, and, you hope, the opponent doesn't.

§ 6.8(e) A.L.R.: Summary

A.L.R. is unique in all of legal publishing. It's not an encyclopedia. Not a treatise. Not a textbook. It's not even a court report really, even though it claims to be. Nobody is going to purchase A.L.R. because of its *reporting* of cases. All subscribers surely rely upon the West Company for their court report "needs." But smart libraries do buy A.L.R., and smart legal researchers definitely use the source as an indispensable research tool.

It's the annotation that gets everybody so worked up. Though terribly written, the annotation is a veritable gold mine of information for legal researchers. Its most attractive feature has to be the narrowness of its subject areas, the fact-specific nature of its annotation titles:

Lease Provisions with respect to the Keeping of Cats.

That says it all. Not the stuff of high-brow legal treatises or scholarly tomes in *Harvard Law Review.* But definitely the stuff of which ordinary legal research is often made.

It's a good source. Use it.

§ 6.8(f) A.L.R.: A Roadmap for Research

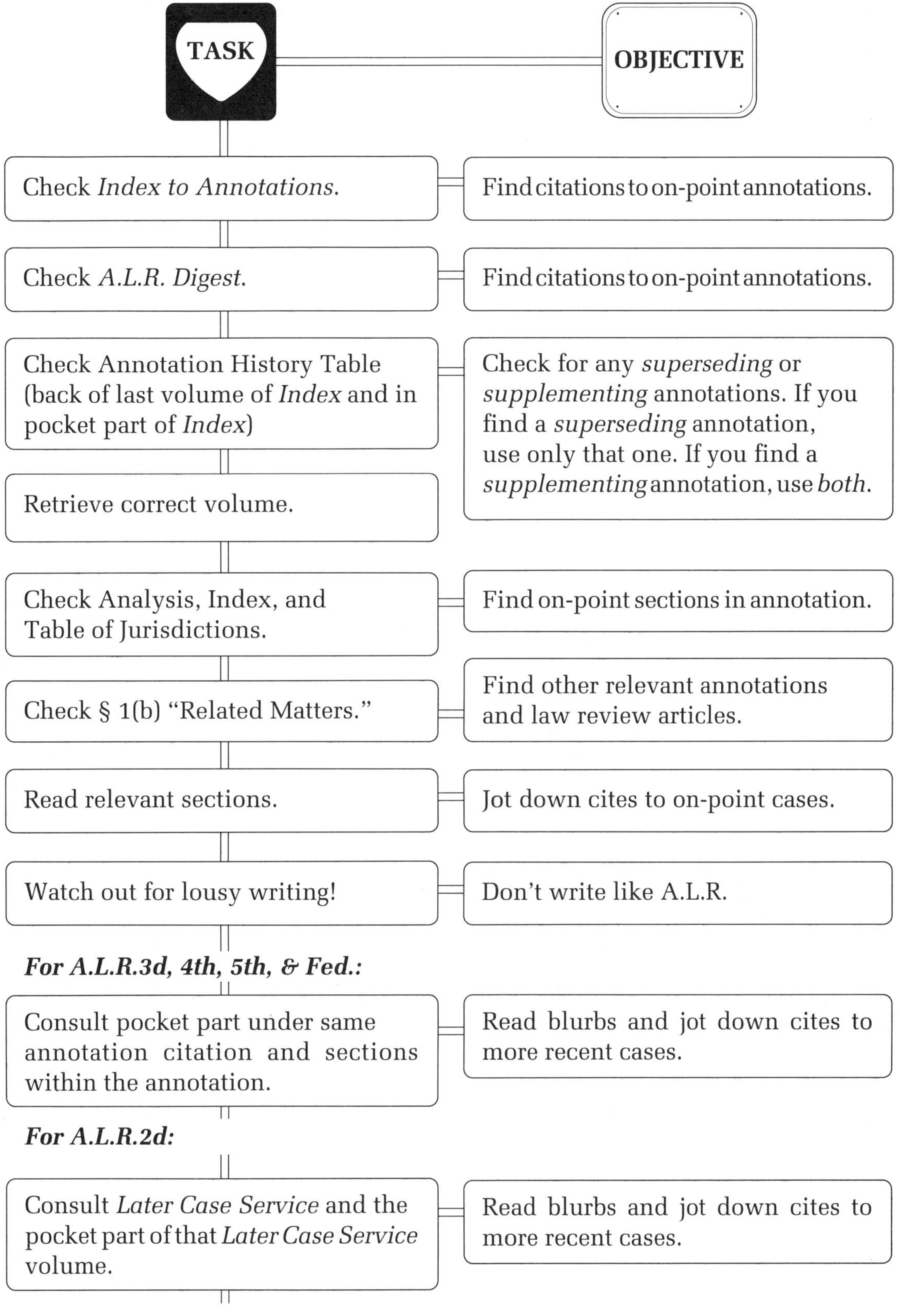

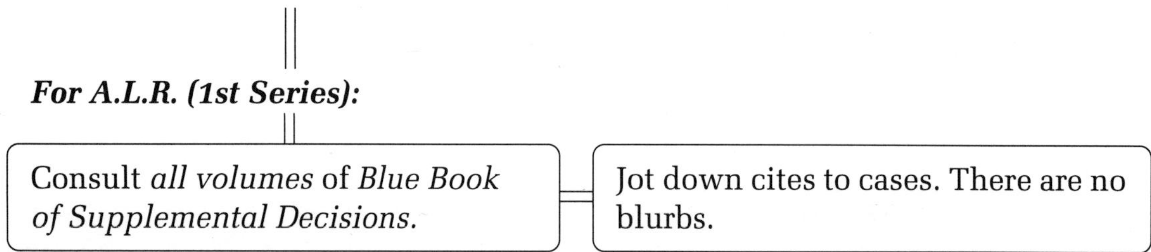

§ 6.8(g) A.L.R.: Visual Aids {16-22}

In the Visual Aids booklet, I have reproduced selected pages from A.L.R. that you would encounter in researching Wally and Mipsie's case. On each page, in the box, you'll find my commentary showing exactly what the researcher is doing and how the source is supplying the information the researcher seeks.

Please note that these pages are selective. In the real world of legal research, you would consult many more pages, especially during the Finding Phase. You would, most likely, go down lots of dead ends, locating irrelevant information, getting frustrated, and, yes, perhaps even *losing your mind.*

But if you'll follow the above instructions, step by step, and study the Visual Aids, page by page, you'll begin to learn how to do legal research *without losing your mind.*

§ 6.9 Conclusion of Step One

In Step One you have located some general background authority on your topic. You have read some real bad writing but gained an appreciation of the issues in your statement of facts, learned about trends in the law, and begun to find on-point cases, which you must, at some point, read in the court reports themselves.

Though Step One has served you well by getting you going in the research process, you have come up short in the "citable authority" category. After all, C.J.S., Am. Jur. 2d, and A.L.R. are not the types of sources that wow the justices of a state supreme court or a sitting federal judge. Indeed, the material found in these background sources is not particularly critical of the law. Neither does it pretend to analyze the law in great depth.

It is time, therefore, to move on to Step Two, the Specific Background sources, which will provide critical insight, detailed analysis, and some quotable quotes to impress your readers.

CHAPTER 7

STEP TWO: SPECIFIC BACKGROUND SOURCES

§ 7.1 Introduction to Step Two

When you finish Step One, you have gained an overview of the law, identified issues in your facts, and begun to collect citations to on-point cases. You lack, however, any deep analysis of your legal issues, criticism of the law, and quotable language you can use in your memo or brief. You turn your attention, then, to Step Two: the Specific Background Sources.

The specific background sources include treatises, legal periodicals, and Restatements of the Law. These three types of sources are highly persuasive to state and federal judges. Indeed, it's the rare court opinion that does not cite treatises, periodicals, and Restatements of the Law. Quotations of passages from these sources, favoring your client's position, therefore, should definitely appear in your memo or brief.

As your research experience increases and you become more aware of the various sources available to you in the law library, you will probably find that some legal research projects *begin* with specific background sources. Suppose, for example, you were to conduct some research on sexual harassment. After consulting the applicable statutes, you'd probably head straight for the legal periodicals, knowing that the issue has been exhaustively treated by America's legal scholars.

My stress on the importance of these Step Two sources should in no way diminish the importance of the Step One sources. The Ace Legal Researcher knows all these sources and how to use them to the best advantage.

Let's look, then, at these three important sources in American legal research: treatises, legal periodicals, and Restatements of the Law. I'll follow the same four-part approach used in Chapter 6: (1) bibliography, (2) finding phase, (3) use phase, and (4) updating phase.

§ 7.2 Treatises

The word "treatise" is just a fancy word for a "book." The authors of treatises—your law professors—don't like to say they "write books" for a living. It's much more exciting and impressive to pick another verb and another noun and say they "author treatises" for a living. Has a certain ring to it.

A treatise is a textbook on a given legal subject matter. The subject matter might be quite broad, such as *Prosser On Torts* (treatise authors like that intriguing preposition "on"). In one volume (a highly entertaining one, I might add) the late, great Professor Prosser of Hastings College of Law in San Francisco wrote a masterpiece on the entirety of tort law. Or the subject matter might be quite narrow, such as Frumer & Friedman's *Products Liability Law.* In Prosser's one-volume treatise on torts, you'd find a broad discussion of the various theories used by courts in disposing of cases brought by injured purchasers of products against the manufacturer or seller of defective products. In Frumer & Friedman, on the other hand, you'd find a detailed analysis of every conceivable issue from all cases ever deciding that particular legal issue.

As alluded to above, treatises might appear as a single volume or as a multivolume work. Multivolume works range from the two-volume treatise by McCarthy on trademark law to the 26-volume *Couch On Insurance* or the 17-volume *Blashfield's Automobile Law and Practice.* And, as you proceed through your legal or paralegal schooling, you'll undoubtedly begin to hear about *Corbin On Contracts* and *Williston On Contracts*, about *Wigmore On Evidence*, and about a host of other nationally recognized experts who gained their reputations (and their tenure!) by penning an "unbelievable work of monumental proportions" (the review on the back cover).

Quite seriously, these works provide a vast reservoir of information for the parched legal researcher. The treatises cite cases and statutes and administrative regulations, indeed all forms of law. They cite legal periodical articles. They cite the Restatements. Many might even cite other treatises. In short, Wilbur (who works as the research assistant of all treatise writers) has provided for you all you might need to know about your legal research problem. Finding an on-point treatise, then, is definitely worth the time.

But treatises provide more than information about your legal research problem. Treatises provide clout. Treatises provide "quotable quotes" for your memo or brief.

Think about it.

Suppose you had spent 20 years as a highly successful criminal defense attorney. After attending scores of $1,000-a-plate dinners for the incumbent president's re-election campaign, you suddenly receive, out of the blue, an appointment to the federal bench. The Senate confirms your appointment. You get your black robes and your gavel. You assume your position. Your first case involves . . . antitrust law, which you can't remember how to spell ("Is it hyphenated?" you muse, as you read the plaintiff's complaint).

Now, when faced with a "motion to dismiss for failure to state a claim upon which relief can be granted," mightn't you be tempted to take a little peek at an exhaustive treatise on antitrust law written by the world's foremost expert on antitrust law? You'd better believe you would. And you'd better believe federal judges, and state judges, do just that: they do read leading treatises and they do rely on what those experts have to say.

It's your job, therefore, to *find* that leading treatise, find material that supports your position, and serve it up to the judge in your "Memorandum of Points and Authorities in Support of Defendant's Motion for Summary Judgment."

§ 7.2(a) Treatises: Bibliographic Information

Basically, there are three types of treatises: (1) expository treatises, (2) interpretative treatises, and (3) critical treatises.

The expository treatises closely resemble C.J.S., Am. Jur. 2d, and A.L.R. They merely state what the law is, making no attempt to analyze the law deeply. Don't shy away from a treatise, however, merely because it fails to interpret or criticize the law. Many times you can find an expository treatise on your exact problem; it's like finding a huge, on-point A.L.R. annotation. You won't be able to use much language to quote in your memo or brief, but you'll find a wealth of information, be able to spot issues in your facts, and begin to collect on-point cases.

The interpretative treatise does analyze the law deeply. The writing you find in an interpretative treatise might closely parallel the writing found in scholarly, periodical writing. The language there, indeed the ideas and insights, provide ample ammunition for use in your memo or brief.

The critical treatise goes a step beyond the interpretative treatise. In addition to analyzing the law deeply, the author takes the next step and says whether the law makes sense, is just, is outdated, or ought to be changed to a more enlightened posture in keeping with the treatise author's views. Here, of course, you can find language that might help a judge decide to strike out on a new course, all because you, the Ace Legal Researcher, took the time to find and read a critical treatise on your legal research problem.

The bibliographic formats of all treatises are virtually the same. You'll find the text topically divided into sections and then copiously footnoted. And, if the treatise succeeds, it might feature some supplementation device. If the treatise is a multivolume work, it will usually contain cumulative annual pocket parts. If it's a one-volume work, it might have a collateral supplement appearing in paperback. Most treatises, however, are one-shot deals: they were written and published but they were not and will never be supplemented. As with any lawbook, therefore, you should pay special attention to the copyright date.

It's difficult to tell whether a treatise cites *all cases* on any given point of law. If the treatise appears in six zillion volumes and treats a minute area of law, then it likely cites all cases on point and enables you to rely on the case law research found in that treatise *as of the cite of the latest case cited in the supplement* or *as of its Stop Cite* (some treatises do contain the *second most important page in all of legal research* at the front of their pocket parts).

Some treatises will alert you to their inclusivity. The text itself might say, "Only two cases in the entire country have treated this issue . . . ." In that situation, you can rely on the statement and update the source "beyond the supplement" (which we'll study in great detail in Chapter 8).

§ 7.2(b) Treatises: the Finding Phase

The finding phase of researching with treatises breaks down into two distinct, and entirely different, parts: (1) finding the treatise itself and (2) finding text within the treatise once you've retrieved it from the shelf.

§ 7.2(b)(i) The Find-the-Treatise Phase

There are several approaches to locating on-point treatises, and, unfortunately, most legal researchers rely on the "happen approach." That is, most legal researchers will use a treatise if they *happen* across one in the law library, or if they *happen* to hear of one in the student lounge, or if they *happen* to see one cited in an on-point case or legal periodical.

I kid you not. Once, back in the dark ages when I attended law school, I was doing some research on the Federal Torts Claim Act. I didn't have the foggiest idea about the Federal Torts Claim Act, so I researched it in C.J.S., A.L.R., and perhaps some law review articles. I don't remember what the topic was, but I do remember that it took me about 20 hours to produce a 12-page memo. As I was leaving the law library late one night (probably a Friday), *after I had finished my research*, I did a triple take when I spotted a book lying on a library table: Professor Jayson's *Federal Torts Claim Act.* Wonderful. What a finely honed research method I had.

Lighting strikes twice. I used to be part owner of the National Legal Research Group, a firm in Charlottesville, Virginia, that does legal research assignments for lawyers all over the world. A lawyer commissioned our company to do a national search of all states' wrongful death acts. The lawyer wanted to know dollar limits of the various acts, statutes of limitations, and other procedural quirks. So we assigned a team to retrieve the actual statutes from the state codes, read all 50 acts, study the differences, and come up with an exhaustive chart and final report. *After the project was complete*, I was walking through the law library and saw, probably on the same table . . . Professor Spieser's *The Wrongful Death Acts of the Fifty States.*

There's a lesson here. Indeed there's:

> **GOOD'S RULE OF RESEARCH #17:**
>
> **Woe be unto the legal researcher who fails to launch an independent search for an on-point treatise.**

To mince no words, it is stupid to be researching in one part of the library when on the treatise shelves a few feet away sits a book on your precise topic, a book that resulted from thousands of hours of legal research, a book whose author (or student assistant) had to do what you are now doing, a book that lays out everything you need to know about your statement of facts. So please take heed and find out whether a treatise exists on your particular legal problem.

Several find-the-treatise approaches come to mind:

1. *The Card Catalogue Approach*

Even if a library has automated its collection, it probably maintains its *hard copy* card catalogue, an approach to research I find excruciatingly painful. As you must know by now, card catalogues are divided into Author, Title, and Subject classifications, two of which are distinctly unhelpful. I mean, I don't have the foggiest notion what the book's title is or who the author is. That's what I'm trying to find out. So I'm stuck with *Subject.* Great. So I look up one subject and it tells me to look somewhere else. Then I finally find the subject and it's as broad as the Mississippi, containing about six drawers of these ancient, dusty cards arranged alphabetically by author, whose name I don't know in the first place. Wonderful. Maybe I should try another career.

The acts of violence committed by wild-eyed card-catalogue looker-uppers with those sharp, short pencils they give you to stab crazily at random passersby somehow prompted the law librarians of the world to computerize the card catalogue systems. The world of legal researchers, now deinstitutionalized, breathed a collective sigh of relief.

2. *The Computerized Card Catalogue Approach*

Several popular computer systems have attracted law librarians to automate their card catalogue systems. In general university libraries, you'll find the NOTIS system, developed by Northwestern University. The law school library might simply hook in to the overall NOTIS system. Most law libraries, however, use a system developed by Innovative Interfaces, Inc. in Berkeley, California.

Computerized systems enable you to search for books by Author, Title, Subject, and, most importantly of all, Keyword. Again, the Author and Title searches help when you know what you're looking for. Usually you don't know, so you now use computerized Subject and Keyword searches. If you plug in a Subject and get 600 "hits," you can limit the search by date or by country.

At libraries having an automated system, you'll usually find detailed instructions available at the computer terminals, which usually can be found next to the old card catalogues. Also, some of these systems have small printers next to the terminals so that you can print out your titles and call numbers and forget about those short, menacing pencils.

Finally, some of these automated card catalogues are accessible by modem. You should ask your librarian for the telephone number so that you can do find-the-treatise research from the comfort of your home.

3. *The Reserved Book List Approach*

Most law school libraries have "reserved book lists." Professors teaching various courses will alert the librarians that certain books pertaining to those courses should be put "on reserve." They might be on a "one-day" reserve or even a "one-hour" reserve. The important point is that the circulation desk will have a big notebook containing pages for each course with books on reserve. Locate the course concerning your subject matter, and you'll get a list of treatises the professor believes are the most important.

Some years ago I got involved in a tradename case. As a plaintiff. Some competitor had stolen my tradename, and I threatened to sue if he didn't stop. He didn't stop. I sued. Instead of having to pay my lawyer's gigantic hourly rate, I did quite a bit of my own research. My *first step* was to consult the reserved book list for the Intellectual Property course. Right there I found *the* leading treatise on trademark and tradename law. I was off and running, having saved scores of hours simply by beginning in the right place. By the way, I won.

4. *The Ask-the-Librarian Approach*

Early in your research career you should cultivate a relationship with your librarians. These people have uncanny memories about *every* lawbook the library owns. Often you can approach a librarian, mention the subject matter of your topic, and get an immediate reference to an on-point treatise. I once mentioned Wally and Mipsie's case to a librarian friend of mine. He said, "Try the *Human Reproduction Law Reporter.*" Bingo.

Once you use one of the four approaches discussed above, you'll then get a "call number." Most law libraries have "open stacks," which means you've got to go to the shelves and find the treatise. Once you get there, you'll find that most collections are shelved alphabetically by author's last name.

§ 7.2(b)(ii) The Find-the-Stuff-in-the-Treatise Phase

Once you've got your hands on the treatise, locating relevant text is a piece of cake. You already know the only three things you can do to a lawbook other than cuss at it: (1) the Index Approach, (2) the Analytical Approach, and (3) the Tabular Approach. You'll usually find all three approaches available in most treatises, certainly in the multivolume works that are regularly supplemented.

If a treatise is a multivolume work, be on the lookout for a *General Index*, indexing the entire set of books. Once you use the TARP rule and look up "thing" words, "action" words, "relief" words, and "parties" words, you'll locate the right volume. Then recall the more detailed Volume Indexes. Also, you'll probably find it best to convert to an Analytical Approach once you find the right volume.

Also, by the time you've gotten to Step Two, you probably have some idea of the leading cases in your area of law. Thus, if the leading case is *Jackson v. Reynolds*, then instead of playing word games with the Index Approach and the Analytical Approach, you could check the Table of Cases in the treatise and find those sections citing *Jackson v. Reynolds*. The Tabular Approach is *always* easier than the Index Approach and the Analytical Approach, for you are always proceeding from the known to the unknown, whereas in the other two approaches you're always proceeding from the unknown (what word do I look up?) to the unknown (what page is it on?).

When you locate a treatise covering your subject matter, you should take a few minutes to look over the treatise. Depending on the subject matter, you're likely to find special finding devices. For example, in the five-volume treatise Louis R. Frumer & Melvin I. Friedman, *Products Liability* (Matthew Bender 1992), you'll find a cumulative table of cases *by product*. Thus, you can look up "comb" or "glue" and find cases dealing with injuries arising from the use of those products.

§ 7.2(c) The Use Phase

When you open your first treatise you'll find pretty much what you found in the Step One sources: endless text copiously footnoted by endless footnotes. As a broad rule, the writing in treatises is better than that found in C.J.S., Am. Jur. 2d, and A.L.R. Also, in the footnotes in treatises you'll find the full array of legal authority cited: federal and state statutes, federal and state cases, administrative regulations, and even secondary authority. Unafraid of the competition, some treatises will even cite competing treatises; most will cite periodical articles and the Restatements of the Law.

§ 7.2(d) The Updating Phase

As mentioned in the bibliography section above, most treatises do not have supplementation devices. They are one-shot deals, written, published, and sent to the shelves by the publishers for users to use. If the treatise succeeds, that is, it sells a boatload of copies, then the publisher and treatise author are predisposed to publish either a new and revised edition or a collateral supplement to the treatise. You should, therefore, be on the lookout for such collateral supplements.

If the treatise is a large multivolume work, then it most likely will have cumulative annual pocket parts supplementing the bound volumes. The pocket parts of some treatises will have *the second most important page in all of legal research*, that page at the *front* of the pocket part, that page that tells you exactly, by volume and page number of all court reports, where Wilbur put his research pencil down and stopped researching. When you use such a treatise, make it a habit to write down a Stop Cite. Simply pick any court report and jot down the volume and page number of that court report where Wilbur *stopped* researching.

After all, wherever Wilbur stopped is exactly where you will *start*.

§ 7.2(e) Treatises: A Roadmap for Research

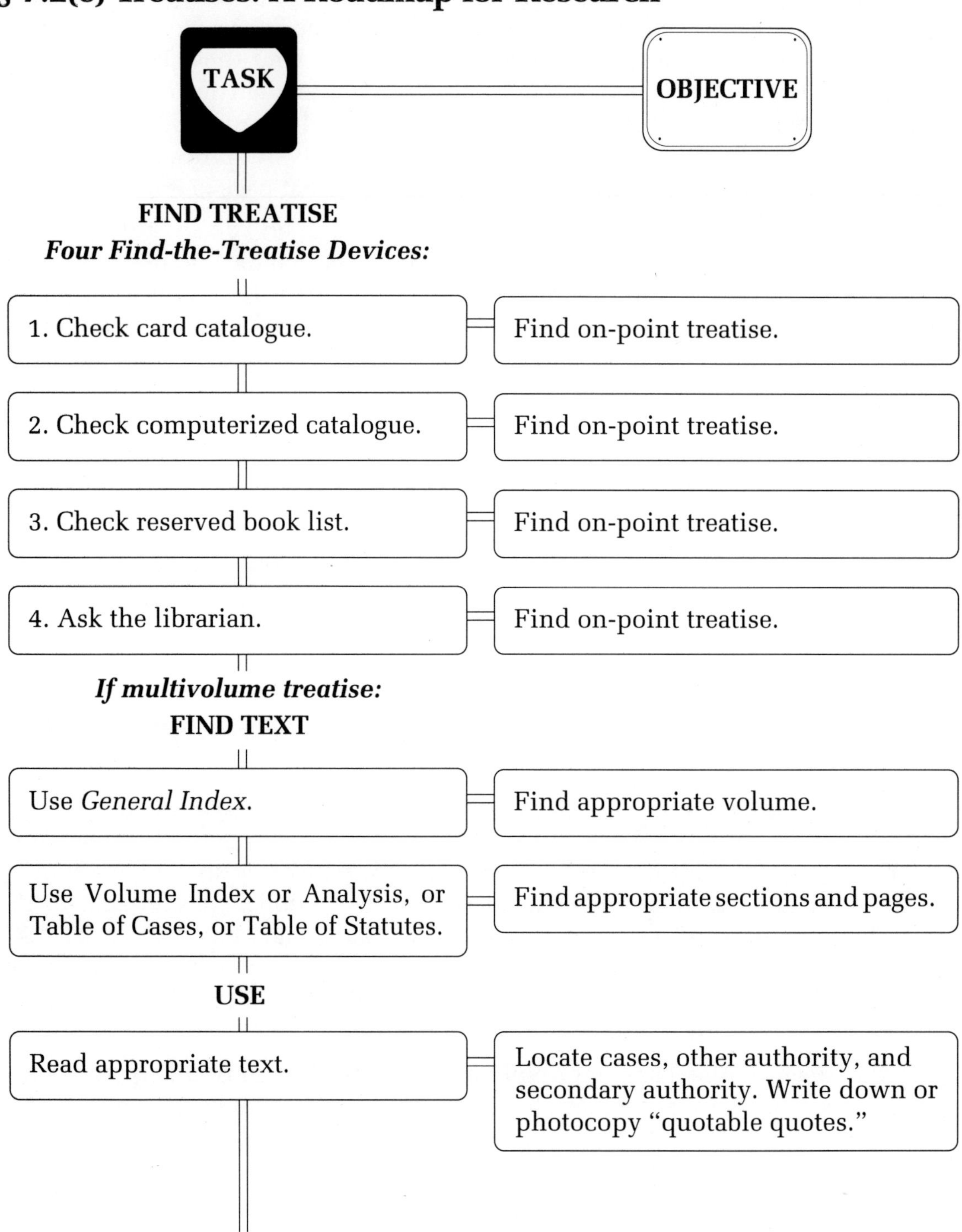

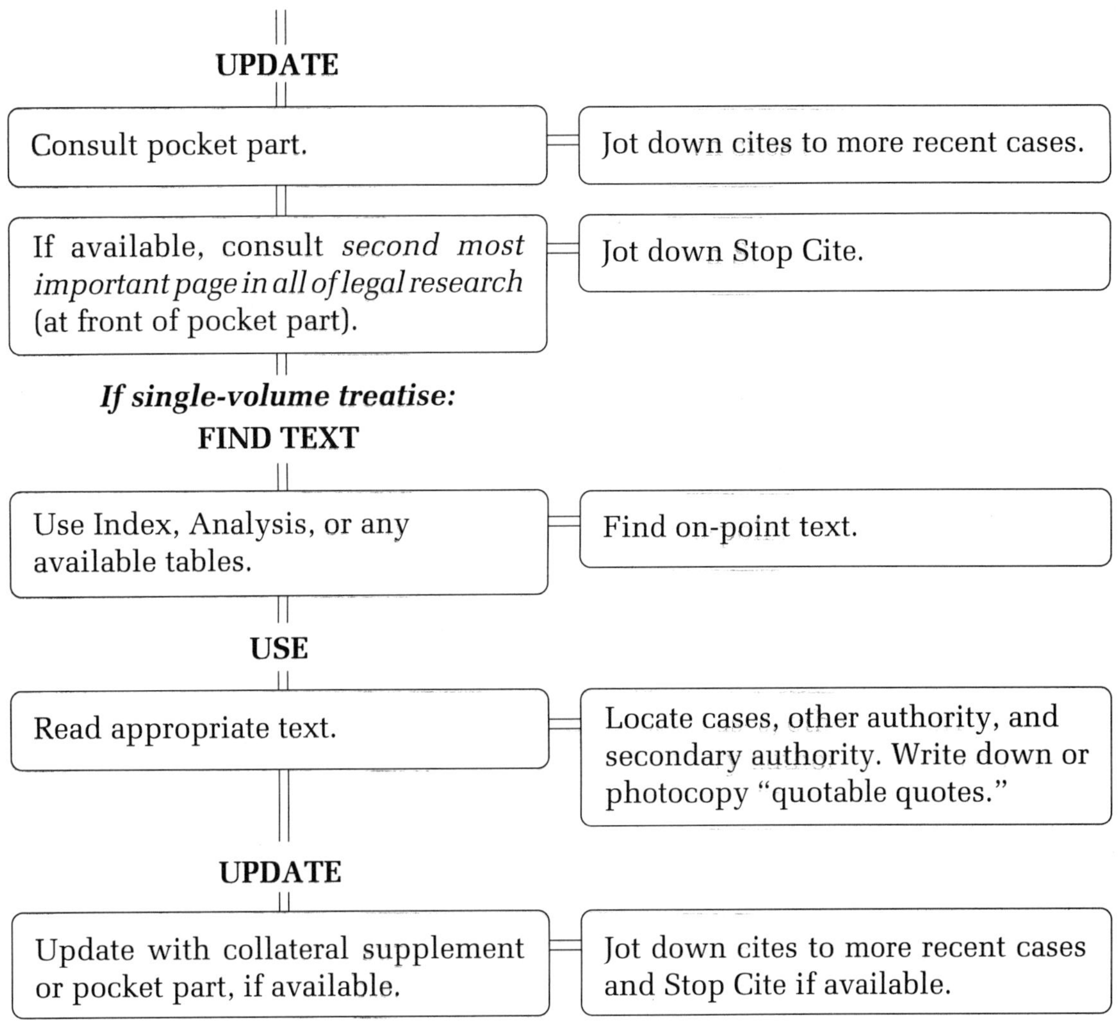

§ 7.2(f) Treatises: Visual Aids

Because space in the Visual Aids booklet is severely limited, I have not included any sample pages from a treatise. Please do not conclude from this omission that treatises are unimportant. On the contrary, they are vital and should become an indispensable step in your research method.

§ 7.3 Legal Periodicals

In the late 1970s I was serving as a Judicial Fellow at the Supreme Court and, for a brief period of time, was detailed to President Carter's Government Reorganization Project (it didn't work). On our team, assigned to study suggestions for change in the federal government's role in the criminal justice system, were law professors, law students, and staff members. I struck up a conversation with a law student, and somehow we got to talking about legal research and how the subject was taught in law school. When we began to discuss research strategy (this was a real humdinger of a conversation), I mentioned the importance of finding persuasive background authority. To which she replied: "Well, I'm a law review student and will be clerking with [a large Washington law firm] this summer and can't imagine having to locate law review articles. After all, that firm mostly does litigation."

A litigator who doesn't feel the need to find law review articles? If so, she won't be much of a litigator.

As you read court opinions, try to notice how many *don't* cite law review articles. Without question, legal periodicals play a major role in shaping the law as decided by state and federal courts. Here's a law review article analyzing the importance of law review articles (they ran out of things to analyze, so they began to analyze themselves):

> Today, periodical writing plays a leading part in the shaping of our law. While law reviews exert some influence over legislation and administration, their greatest impact in the formation of law is through the courts. Although objections to judicial reliance on legal periodicals have erupted in Congress and the press, such writing has generally been accepted now for several years as a central part of the judicial process. In 1941, Mr. Chief Justice Charles Evans Hughes characterized legal periodicals as the "fourth estate" of the law.
>
> . . . .
>
> The growth of legal writing has enlarged the knowledge available to the [Supreme] Court. When they are aware of it, the Justices are compelled to take notice of such writing if they are to base their opinions on the best available knowledge. **This is true whether or not counsel in a case takes notice of such sources.** If the Justices had to be restricted by the **weaknesses of counsel**, in many instances their judgment would be unnecessarily impaired. At the same time, in our adversary system the Court must rely heavily upon counsel for elucidation of the facts and law in a case, **including information about pertinent legal writings**. In this system, able counsel are essential to the maintenance of high standards. Admittedly, this duty imposes a heavy burden on the bar. And **when counsel fail**, their weaknesses may be reflected in judicial opinions. On the other hand, to as great an extent as possible, a Justice may be expected to draw on "all the facts of life" as Mr. Justice Cardozo said, "wherever he can find them . . . . " Today, legal periodicals and other learned journals are principal sources of such information.[1]

Law reviews indeed are important. Just ask Michael Jordan. Jordan makes, oh, about 10 zillion dollars a year selling his picture to Wheaties and Nike. Now he can do that because of . . . you guessed it, a law review article. It seems that back in 1902, the highest court in New York wrote a major court opinion. At the time, of course, the

[1]Chester A. Newland, *The Supreme Court and Legal Writings, Learned Journals as Vehicles of an Anti-Trust Lobby*, 48 Geo. L.J. 105, 126, 142-43 (1959)(citations omitted, emphasis added).

New York justices didn't realize that the opinion would affect Michael's financial situation, so they decided the case wrongly. The court decided the case wrongly because it failed to "take notice" of some very sound reasoning in a law review article.

The case in New York[2] was brought against the Rochester Folding-Box Company by a justifiably distraught woman. It seems the company had used a picture of the plaintiff without the plaintiff's permission. The company used this picture . . . on its boxes of flour. I guess the woman was shopping at her local A&P one morning and, to her dismay, saw her picture prominently displayed for all to see and ogle. By now you know that when people are harmed or even just dismayed, they dash to the nearest pay phone and . . . call their lawyer.

The plaintiff sued for invasion of privacy. The high New York court held that, at common law, the tort of invasion of privacy did not include the appropriation of someone's likeness without that person's consent. Maybe some other tort or implied contract theory might lie, said the court, but not invasion of privacy.

Well, it seems that a man named Louis Brandeis had written a comprehensive law review article in *Harvard Law Review* back in 1890[3] pointing out, through exhaustive common law research into ancient English cases, that the tort of invasion of privacy could include the appropriation of someone's likeness without consent and showing the growing need for protection of privacy because of the scurrilous gossip appearing in the press at the turn of the century (he should take a look today at "infojournalism" on Donahue, Geraldo, Oprah, and the programs of other leading social commentators!).

The New York case was met with an outpouring of criticism in the press and in the New York legislature. The following year, the New York legislature passed a statute granting the right to sue for "invasion of privacy." Three years later, the Georgia Supreme Court, faced with a similar likeness-appropriation case, cited the Brandeis article, rejected the New York court's reasoning, and allowed a plaintiff to recover damages from the appropriator.[4] And as a direct result of that single law review article, courts across the country began to adopt the "appropriation of likeness" segment of the invasion of privacy tort. In states where courts failed to adopt the theory, legislatures passed laws granting the right to sue to people whose pictures appeared on boxes of flour. Or Wheaties.

So today Michael Jordan gladly grants his permission. When the price is right. Which is why his picture doesn't appear on the front cover of this best-selling book on legal research. You were probably wondering why Michael's picture is missing from the cover. Now you know.

So don't let anybody hornswoggle you into believing that periodical literature is not important in the litigation process. It is vitally important, especially in appellate

---

[2]*Roberson v. Rochester Folding-Box Co.*, 171 N.Y. 538, 64 N.E. 442 (1902).

[3]Samuel D. Warren & Louis D. Brandeis, *The Right to Privacy*, 4 Harv. L. Rev. 193 (1890).

[4]*Pavesich v. New England Life Insurance Co.*, 122 Ga. 190, 50 S.E. 68 (1905).

litigation and even more especially in federal court litigation. Referring to the Brandeis article, Professor William Prosser had this to say:

> The recognition and development of the so-called "right of privacy" is perhaps the outstanding illustration of the influence of legal periodicals upon the courts.[5]

In the late 1970s, the Federal Judicial Center (FJC) did a study analyzing the reliance by federal judges on legal periodicals in their court opinions. The FJC found that a significant percentage of federal court opinions cited at least one law review article. The FJC's study went on to find even more remarkable information.

The study ranked the various law reviews by frequency of citation by federal court opinions. You can guess what the #1 law review was: Harvard or Yale. And you can guess what #2 was: Harvard or Yale. And #3 and #4: Columbia, Pennsylvania, or Stanford (I really can't remember). But you'll *never* guess what #5 was. A roll of the drums please: the fifth most frequently cited law review by federal judges across the country was . . .

Georgia Law Review!

Now with all due respect to the state of my birth, the law review at the University of Georgia is not the fifth best in the United States. But it was, in the late 1970s, the fifth most frequently cited by federal judges. How come? Those crackers are no dummies: the University of Georgia Law Review sent complimentary subscriptions to every federal judge in the United States! Federal judges were citing the *Georgia Law Review* simply because *it was there.*

There's a lesson to be learned. Indeed, you guessed it, there's:

GOOD'S RULE OF RESEARCH #18:

Woe be unto the legal researcher who fails to find on-point periodical literature.

§ 7.3(a) Legal Periodicals: Bibliographic Information

Legal periodicals can be classified in several different ways. One way focuses on their pagination: consecutively paginated vs. nonconsecutively paginated. A consecutive paginated periodical such as *Harvard Law Review* comes out in installments, that is "periodically" in paperback editions, the page numbers running consecutively throughout the year until the next bound volume comes along and supersedes the paperback editions. A nonconsecutively paginated periodical such as the *ABA*

[5]William L. Prosser, *The Law of Torts* 802 (4th ed. 1971).

Journal comes out "periodically" in a magazine-like publication, the page numbers running consecutively in that one issue but starting all over at page 1 in the next issue. For legal citation purposes, the Harvard *Bluebook* distinguishes between consecutively paginated periodicals and nonconsecutively paginated periodicals.

Legal researchers are likely to distinguish between periodicals in another way: those affiliated with the nation's law schools vs. those affiliated with other professional groups such as state bar associations. The law school's periodicals are commonly referred to as "law reviews," though the publications of many might bear the name of "law journal." Naturally, roughly 98.654% of all first-year law students are hoping to "make" law review, meaning they either aced out on grades or made it through a legal citation and writing tryout. Unfortunately, only a small portion of these law students will "make" law review, so the others are relegated to buying those highly popular sweatshirts announcing to the world: "Make Love, Not Law Review."

The law reviews of a law school consist of an editorial board, which is responsible for selecting articles for publication, editing those articles, checking the accuracy of citations against the original source in the law library, getting the type set, producing galley for proofing, retaining a printer, keeping the subscription list, balancing the budget, and staying afloat. Strangely enough, these student editorial boards have the power to select or reject an article submitted by a law professor. Indeed, law schools are the only postgraduate institutions that give this vast power over a professor's academic future to student-run organizations.

Until recently. The law school at George Mason University recently took control of its law review so that the students on the editorial board now work for the law school. A committee of professors decides which articles will be published and which rejected. It will be interesting to see whether or not the trend continues at other institutions.

In the legal periodicals themselves, you'll find several different types of articles. "Leading articles" are those written by law professors, lawyers, judges, or experts from other disciplines, e.g., psychiatrists. These articles exhaustively analyze an area of law or even a single case. "Notes" or "Comments" are those written by law students. "Case Comments" are written by students analyzing a single case. Other student pieces include "Recent Developments," "Surveys," and others.

Now, for some strange reason, legal periodical writers (and authors of textbooks on legal research) insist on giving their works clever and cutesy names. One article on wrongful pregnancy, for example, is entitled "Busting the Blessing Balloon." Others, on a variety of topics, include:

Through a Glass Darkly: A Look at State Equal Rights Amendments, 12 Suffolk U. L. Rev. 1282 (1978).

Quick, Before It Melts: Toward Resolution of the Jurisdictional Morass in Antarctica, 10 Cornell L.J. 173 (1976).

Strict Liability: A "Lady in Waiting" for Wrongful Birth Cases, 11 Calif. Western L. Rev. 136 (1974).

Though the clever names might entertain, they create havoc for the legal researcher. Also, with the advent of computerized keyword-search systems, legal periodical authors should become much more descriptive with their titles to ensure that legal researchers, e.g., federal judges, can *find* their articles and cite them, e.g., in federal court opinions. (That's why the name of my book is *Legal Research*. It'll pop right up on the screen when someone keys in the words "legal research.")

In a typical legal periodical article, you'll find a vast array of information. In the footnotes, the author cites cases, statutes, Restatements, treatises, other law review articles, indeed the whole schmeer. Often, a single law review article can provide virtually all the legal information you need (*up to the time when the article was published*), ideas for organizing your memo or brief, and juicy passages of commentary arguing for the precise position your client needs to assert. And to top it all off, the whole thing is written by Professor Zasofgij, the world's foremost expert in tort law.

§ 7.3(b) Legal Periodicals: the Finding Phase

Now for the fun part.

First of all, the English language boasts more than 800 legal periodicals, each published anywhere from one to 12 times each year. Most law school libraries will subscribe to several hundred legal periodicals, typically shelved alphabetically by periodical name. Buried somewhere in that mass of material are some legal periodical articles on point, analyzing your precise legal topic.

Two of the finding approaches are available to you in your search for an on-point article: the Index Approach and the Tabular Approach. These two approaches appear in three different sources: (1) the *Index to Legal Periodicals*, (2) the *Current Law Index*, and (3) the WilsonDisc service. Let's look at each in turn.

§ 7.3(b)(i) *Index to Legal Periodicals*

Remember the *Guide to Periodical Literature* you used in junior high and high school to find magazine articles on your science project about the reproductive habits of mushrooms? Well, that delightful source is published by the H. W. Wilson Company. And guess what? The same company publishes the *Index to Legal Periodicals* (as well as a host of other scholarly indexes). Thought you could escape them, huh?

The *Index to Legal Periodicals* began in 1908, appearing in annual volumes until 1926. In 1926, it switched to triennial volumes until 1980. In 1980, it switched back to annual volumes. To fill in the year, the publisher provides 11 monthly issues running from October through August. (Do not do as I once did as a law student and spend 30 minutes searching for the September edition. It doesn't exist.) These 11 monthly issues are numbered 1 through 11. Numbers 2, 5, 8, and 11 cumulate the preceding one or two issues. Number 2 cumulates all the stuff in 1. Number 5 cumulates 3 and 4. Number 8 cumulates 6 and 7. And number 11 cumulates 9 and 10.

Conducting a search through the *Index to Legal Periodicals* is a painful experience. At the front of any volume you'll find a "List of Subject Headings" {23}, a list **{23}**
totalling more than 1500 entries. The trick, of course, is to find the right heading. Failure to find the right one could result in disaster, for the indexers will list most articles under just one heading. Sometimes they'll use two headings, but usually just one.

Now here's the rub. When you've located a likely heading, you then turn to that heading {24} in the *Index*. Then you discover that the index is not a hierarchical index, **{24}**
i.e., there are no subheadings to guide your search. Instead, the articles are listed alphabetically under the heading by title to the article. At that point, you'll wonder why on earth the authors insisted on being so cutesy in naming their articles "How Many Warranties Can Dance on the Head of a Pin?" If they had begun their titles with obvious subject-related words, they would increase the odds of their article being found by some strung-out legal researcher such as a Supreme Court law clerk working for the Chief Justice.

A complete search of the *Index to Legal Periodicals*, therefore, consists of (1) locating potential headings, (2) consulting those headings in the latest annual volume, (3) deciding which heading or headings are the ones used by the indexers for articles on your topic, (4) consulting those headings in the recent monthly issues of the *Index* (remember that 2, 5, 8, and 11 cumulate), (5) consulting those headings in annual volumes working backwards to 1980, and then (6) consulting triennial volumes working backwards until it makes no sense to continue or until you've got more articles than you can possibly read or until you've gone bonkers.

I should note here that the *Index to Legal Periodicals* also indexes articles by author. From volume 13 to the present, you'll find authors' last names alphabetically intertwined with alphabetized subject headings. Before volume 13, you'll find the authors separately alphabetized. In all volumes up through Volume 22 the author's name will then refer you to the subject matter heading where that author's article is indexed; a parenthetical letter, such as (C), will tell you that the author's article begins with that letter. From Volume 23 to the present, the *Index to Legal Periodicals* began to list the title of the article and its citation under the author's name rather than sending you on a wild goose chase to the subject matter heading in search of the title and citation.

I should also note here that the *Index to Legal Periodicals* contains two kinds of tables. First, in all volumes, at the back, you'll find a Table of Cases, giving you citations to articles analyzing a single case. Please note that many "leading articles" don't analyze a single case; these articles, though they might cite a particular case, are not listed in the Table of Cases. Consequently, I'd use the Table of Cases only when I needed an article analyzing a particular case, not when I needed an area of law thoroughly discussed. Second, in the volumes from 20 to the present, the *Index to Legal Periodicals* includes a "Table of Statutes Commented Upon." Unfortunately, the table is an alphabetical one, listing statutes alphabetically by name. It should be a sequential table, listing statutes sequentially by title and section number. How come? Well, what does the *Index to Legal Periodicals* do with a legal periodical article analyzing a federal statute *that has no name*? Many statutes don't have a name. And many "nameless" federal statutes are analyzed in legal periodical articles.

So plan on spending some time in the *Index to Legal Periodicals*, plan on smashing into several dead ends, and plan on gnashing your teeth at those hateful legal indexers who choose weird subject matter headings, who create alphabetical tables of federal statutes, and who do other major damage to hassle the legal researchers of the world.

§ 7.3(b)(ii) *Current Law Index*

The *Index to Legal Periodicals* has one serious drawback: it's slow. In fact, the law librarians of the world were downright irked with the *Index to Legal Periodicals*, so
{25} they sponsored the creation of a new competing index, the *Current Law Index* {25}.
The *Current Law Index* began in 1980, indexes roughly 100 more periodicals than the *Index to Legal Periodicals*, uses roughly the same number of headings, and apparently publishes its index faster than the *Index to Legal Periodicals*. The *Current Law Index* also breaks up large subject matter headings with hierarchical subheadings, a device that can save your fingernail when you have to nope-nope-nope a huge list of alphabetically arranged article titles.

The *Current Law Index* is published monthly, the March, June, and September issues cumulating the preceding two issues. The twelfth issue each year is the annual edition. The index appears in three sections: the Author/Title Index, the Table of Cases, and the Table of Statutes.

§ 7.3(b)(iii) The WilsonDisc Service

To the great relief of legal researchers across the globe, the H. W. Wilson Company has put its indexes on a CD-ROM computer system. Most larger law libraries will have this service available. At the computer terminal, you'll find an instruction booklet carrying you step-by-step through a computer search for on-point periodical articles. Basically, you can search the database, which consists of the *titles* to legal periodical articles, for subject matter headings or keywords. (This new research tool should definitely prompt the authors of articles to be more descriptive and less humorous when naming their articles.) If your library has this service, you would do well to learn to use it, for it is far more efficient and less frustrating than the hard-copy *Index to Legal Periodicals*.

§ 7.3(c) Legal Periodicals: the Use Phase

Using legal periodicals is not a whole lot different from using any book containing
{26} textual discussions of the law {26}. You will find in the footnotes to legal periodical
articles a broad array of legal authority, including cases, statutes, regulations, Restatements, state and federal law, treatises, and even other legal periodical articles.
{27} So the article itself will provide a wealth of legal research information {27}.

You will also find in legal periodicals "quotable quotes." If a passage from the article nails your legal problem and supports your client, by all means quote the passage in your memo or brief. For a more complete discussion of quoting from secondary sources, see C. Edward Good, *Mightier than the Sword—Powerful Writing in the Legal Profession* (LEL Enterprises 1988) (I love to sneak in these plugs).

§ 7.3(d) Legal Periodicals: the Updating Phase

Legal periodicals have no internal means of supplementation. You will not find pocket parts or collateral paperback supplements. Once a professor or student or judge or lawyer writes and publishes an article, that's it. The writer does not return for annual supplementation.

It would be nice, however, to find out if cases had cited a particular article favorably (or unfavorably). It would also be nice to find out if other articles had cited the article you're about to rely upon in your memo or brief.

Well, there is a way. *Shepard's Law Review Citations* enables you to look up the citation to your article (roughly 200 legal periodicals are covered) and locate any case decided since 1957 citing your article or any article written since 1957 citing your article. In Chapter 9, I will review the ins and outs of Shepardizing. Suffice it to say at this point that any article that is Shepardizable should be Shepardized. Doing so is the only means of supplementing a legal periodical article.

§ 7.3(e) Legal Periodicals: A Roadmap for Research

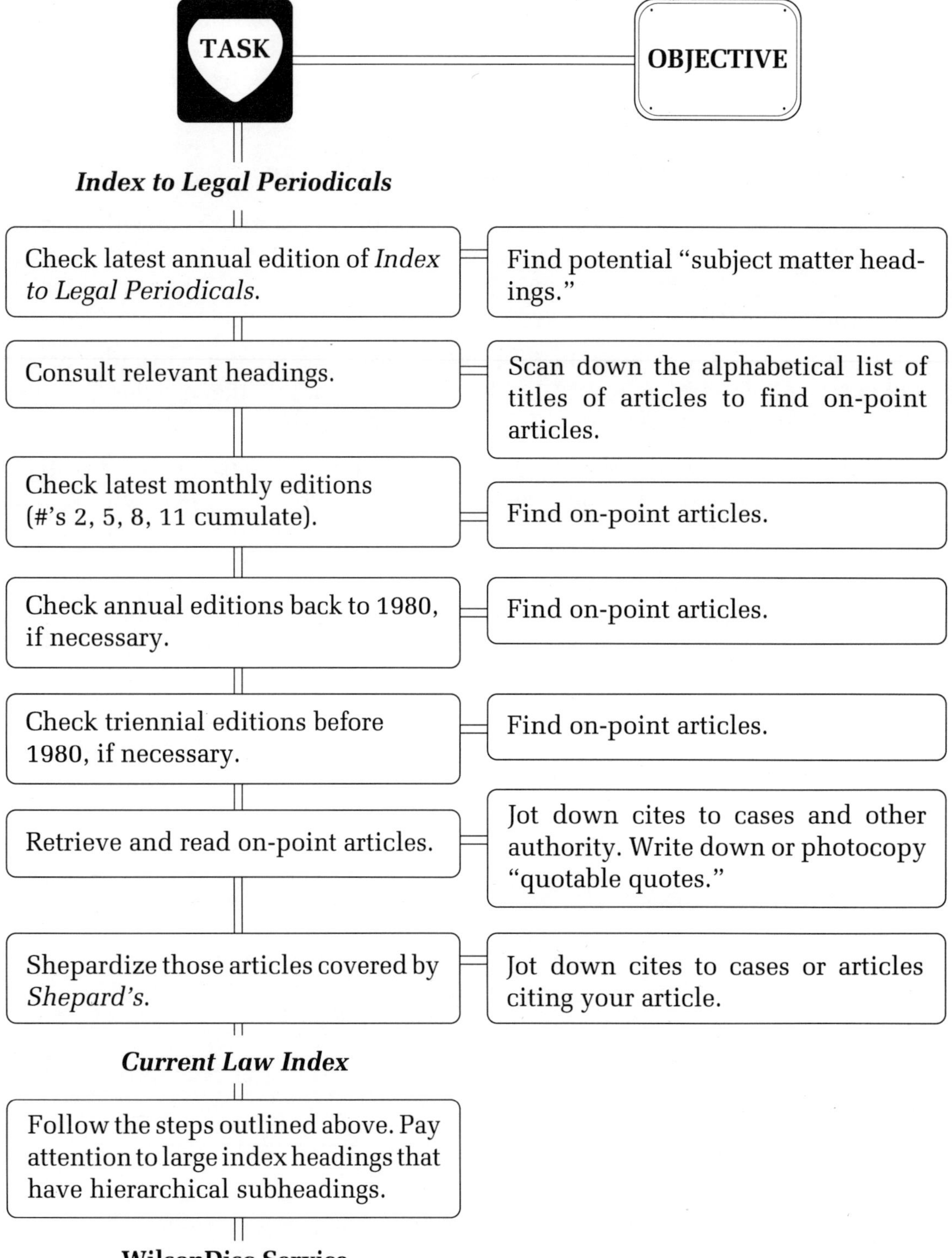

Note: If your library has the WilsonDisc Service, refer to the instruction booklet at the computer terminal. As mentioned in the preface, I will not deal with computerized legal research in this text.

§ 7.3(f) Legal Periodicals: Visual Aids {23-27}

On the Visual Aids pages, I have reproduced selected pages from the *Index to Legal Periodicals* and the *Current Law Index* that you would encounter in researching Wally and Mipsie's case. On each page, in the box, you'll find my commentary showing exactly what the researcher is doing and how these two indexes are supplying the information the researcher seeks. Following the index pages, you'll find some sample pages from a law review article. Sample pages from *Shepard's Law Review Citations* are not included. Please refer to Chapter 9 to see the Shepardizing process unfold.

Please note that these pages are selective. In the real world of legal research, you would consult many more pages, especially during the Finding Phase. You would, most likely, go down lots of dead ends, locating irrelevant information, getting frustrated, and, yes, perhaps even *losing your mind.*

But if you'll follow the above instructions, step by step, and study the Visual Aids, page by page, you'll begin to learn how to do legal research *without losing your mind.*

§ 7.4 Restatements of the Law

One of the most prestigious groups in the legal profession is the American Law Institute (ALI), whose membership includes noted professors, judges, and lawyers. Back in the 1920s, the ALI was concerned about the "litigation explosion." To stem the tide of cases, the ALI proposed to take key areas of the law, study the rules at work in the 50 states, extract the best of those rules, and *restate* those rules in a series of "Restatements of the Law." Presumably, if the ALI could succinctly state the preferred rule of law on all possible points, attorneys would be less inclined to bring so many lawsuits.[6]

The ALI set about its task and completed Restatements in the areas of Agency (2d),[7] Conflicts of Laws (2d), Contracts (2d), Foreign Relations Law of the United States (3d), Judgments (2d), Property (2d), Restitution (1st), Security (1st), Torts (2d), and Trusts (2d).

The committees given this awesome task divided the law analytically into hundreds of key legal questions or circumstances, each having a rule of law governing the question or circumstance. The committee then wrote the rule of law preferred by the majority of states (or preferred by the committee), gave it a section number, and then wrote "Comments" showing how the rule would apply to various situations and stating why the rule was the preferred rule of law.

The Restatements caught on like gangbusters. Attorneys began to cite the Restatement provisions in their briefs, and courts began to rely on them in their opinions of law. But instead of stemming the tide of litigation, the Restatements probably served as a catalyst to litigation over the question of whether a state would

[6]Doesn't sound like any lawyers I know!

[7]The parenthetical number shows whether the particular restatement is a second or third (or just first) restatement of the law.

adopt the Restatement view on a particular issue of law. As courts began to cite the Restatements more and more, attorneys began to rely on them in litigation documents and law professors began to rely on them in their courses. Undoubtedly law students and paralegal students will hear about "the Restatement view" in many of their classes in Torts, Contracts, and Property.

Because the Restatements exert such great influence on the judicial process, it behooves you to become familiar with these sources, to learn how to use them, and to cite their provisions in your finished written work. To familiarize you with a typical Restatement, I'll provide some basic bibliographical information on the *Second Restatement of Torts* and mention the finding aids you can use to locate pertinent Restatement provisions and cases citing those provisions.

§ 7.4(a) The *Second Restatement of Torts*

The *Second Restatement of Torts* evolved over 14 years. Divided into 951 sections, the Restatement published the first 280 sections in 1965, sections 281-503 in 1965, sections 504-707A in 1971, and sections 708-951 in 1979. The entire set appears in four main Restatement volumes and 17 Appendix volumes. The Appendix volumes, each covering a span of Restatement sections over a particular span of time, provide citations to cases citing Restatement provisions.

§ 7.4(b) The Finding Phase

With each Restatement, you'll find the standard finding aids: typically an index and an analytical breakdown of the entire Restatement into sections. Though you can and should independently launch a search for on-point Restatement sections, usually in the legal research process you'll find references to Restatement sections in court opinions, law review articles, and treatises.

§ 7.4(c) The Use Phase

When you've identified on-point Restatement sections, do not just copy quotations to the provisions in court opinions or law review articles. Go to the Restatement itself, read the section, and study the commentary in the "Comments." Here you can find a wealth of information enabling you to construct an entire legal argument to support the Restatement view (if it favors your client).

§ 7.4(d) The Updating Phase

Use the Appendix volumes to locate cases interpreting your Restatement sections. Also, please note that in the *State Shepard's* (not the *Regional Shepard's*) you can "Shepardize" the Restatements and gain citations to state cases citing those Restatement provisions. More about Shepardizing in Chapter 9.

§ 7.4(e) Research Roadmap and Visual Aids

I've described the finding, use, and updating phases above, so a "research roadmap" is not really needed. Also, because space is severely limited in the Visual Aids booklet, I have omitted sample pages of the Restatements. This different treatment should in no way diminish the importance of these sources in your eyes. Quite the contrary, the Restatements are among the most persuasive of all the secondary sources. Unless you visit the shelves and get to know these sources, you'll never be able to claim the status of Ace Legal Researcher.

§ 7.5 Conclusion of Step Two

When you've found treatises, legal periodicals, and Restatement provisions, your background research is at an end. You've cashed in on thousands of hours of research expended by our good friend Wilbur. He has meticulously researched case law in the law library, found all the cases on point, and summarized most of those cases in the many sources you've used. And where did Wilbur find all these cases? Did he trip over them in the aisles? Did they fly off the shelf into his waiting arms? Did he just happen across them in the law library? No. Wilbur found these cases by running Key Numbers in the American Digest System. He also found them by using LEXIS and WESTLAW.

So what are you going to do? Retrace his steps? Redo what he's already done?

No. As an Ace Legal Researcher you will figure out where Wilbur *stopped* his research. At that point you will *start* your research. To learn how, let's move on to the hard part: the American Digest System.

CHAPTER 8

STEP THREE: RUNNING KEY NUMBERS

§ 8.1 Introduction to Step Three

To date, your strategy has sought to reduce the amount of basic chronological case research required to complete your assignment. You figured out, quite rightly, that all the sources we've discussed—C.J.S., Am. Jur. 2d, A.L.R., treatises, legal periodicals, and Restatements—had to find the cases *they* cited. And how did they find all those cases cited in all those footnotes? Easy. They told Wilbur to do it. And how did Wilbur do it? By engaging in basic chronological case research. And what is basic chronological case research?

Simple. Running Key Numbers in the American Digest System.

Simple? Well, not so simple. In fact, grasping all the details of the American Digest System requires patience and a great deal of practice. But it'll be well worth the effort, for the American Digest System provides *the only subject matter rearrangement of all state and federal case law in America.* Mastering the intricacies of "running Key Numbers" in the American Digest System will ensure your ability to find any case on any point of law from 1658, the date of the first reported case in America, to the present day.

Many in the legal profession, for some strange reason, pooh-pooh "running Key Numbers." Once, in the faculty lounge at Virginia Law School, I overheard a nationally known law professor say the following: "I never run Key Numbers in the West System. I get all the cases I need from law review articles."

"And where do the law review articles get 'em from," I thought to myself, repressing the urge to set the professor straight. Believe me, folks, cases do not leap off the shelf into your waiting arms. Somebody has to look for them, and "looking for them" means "running Key Numbers" in the American Digest System.

You will soon learn that "running Key Numbers"[1] is not a whole lot of fun. It's not the kind of thing that makes you click your heels with glee when you find out

[1]From now on I won't use quotation marks. You've got to get used to the term even if it doesn't sound very lawyerly.

you've got to do it. But it is the kind of thing you *must* do in *every* legal research project that requires the location of case law, which is virtually every legal research project.

Fortunately for you, you're reading a book written by an author who hates to run Key Numbers. Consequently, the entire strategy of this book seeks to reduce that burden to the bare minimum. Hence, the strategy you've learned so far cashes in on the research completed by Wilbur: use the cases found in Steps One and Two, figure that all those cases from all those sources constitute a complete list of on-point cases, figure out where the collective Wilbur *stopped* running Key Numbers, and then *start* running Key Numbers where Wilbur *stopped* running Key Numbers. Make sense? If not now, it will.

Let's approach this monolith methodically. First, you'll learn the bibliographic features of the American Digest System. Second, you'll learn how to find the right Key Number or Key Numbers classifying your legal issue. Third, you'll learn where to start running those Key Numbers. And fourth, you'll learn where and when to stop running the Key Numbers. In other words, I'll follow the same four-part approach I've used in discussing the sources you learned about in Steps One and Two: (1) bibliography, (2) the Finding Phase (find the right Key Number), (3) the Use Phase (where to start running), and (4) the Updating Phase (where to stop running).

§ 8.2 The American Digest System: Bibliographic Information

Picture the problem. The West Company publishes nearly 10,000 volumes of court reports. Fourteen different sets of court reports: the seven regional reports, the two special state reports, and five different federal reports. These sets of books, which you learned all about in Chapter 4, contain all American cases worth worrying about.[2]

So there sits this huge pile of chronologically published cases. Somewhere in that pile sits the handful of cases on *your* legal research project. Your job is to find *all* cases on point and then choose the ones your reader needs to understand the legal problem and its resolution.

The West Company realized early in the game that it could not just publish cases chronologically. After all, they reasoned, few legal researchers are predisposed to wander over to the law library to browse around just to bone up on case law decided in January of 1945. No, chronological publication satisfied the need for speed but created huge problems when it came to "location."

The West Company also realized that it could not publish the cases in a chronological system and then turn around and publish the *cases themselves* in a subject matter arrangement. After all, each case might deal with as many as 10 different legal issues, requiring the republication of that one case in 10 different books dealing with 10 different subject matters. Such an approach would swell the West

[2]There are certain official reports in some states publishing the cases of lower courts. But the vast majority of legal researchers will find all the cases they need in West Company court reports.

Company's National Reporter System from 10,000 volumes to 100,000 volumes. Not a pretty sight.

§ 8.2(a) Headnotes

The West Company figured, therefore, that it needed to make the cases smaller, to smoosh them down to a smaller size so that it could publish the smaller-sized case in a set of books that wouldn't hog all the space in the law library. It thought and thought and concluded that "smoosh" was not exactly a good word to use to describe their new system and settled instead on another word meaning to "make smaller": digest.

The West Company decided that when it published the full text of a court opinion, it would instruct Wilbur[3] to write little paragraphs summarizing the points of law discussed in the court's opinion. These paragraphs would be called "headnotes." These headnotes would then become a little smooshed court opinion that could then be published in another set of books called *digests*. Legal researchers could then look stuff up in these *digests* and find all cases in the country dealing with the same point of law. What a stroke of genius!

So these days at the West Company an army of Wilburs reads all cases decided by all state and federal courts throughout the country. As Wilbur reads each case, he identifies the key points the court covers and writes a summary of what the court said. Those summaries become the headnotes appearing at the front of the court's opinion as published in the West report. And those headnotes are then assigned a Key Number and reprinted in the American Digest System so that you, the legal researcher, can "run" Key Numbers and locate all cases on the same point of law.

Your overall understanding of the American Digest System must begin with your understanding of headnotes. They are written by the West Company, not by the court. They are terribly written. They merely summarize a point of law. They should *never* be quoted or even paraphrased in legal writing.

To make certain you know what a headnote is and what a headnote looks like, I have reproduced the title pages of *Flowers v. District of Columbia* on the next two pages. Note that each headnote bears two numbers: (1) a Key Number and (2) a sequential number (1, 2, 3, 4). The Key Number corresponds to that point of law's classification in the American Digest System. The sequential number, as discussed earlier in Chapter 4, serves two functions.

First, the sequential number serves as a table of contents to the opinion itself. As you turn the pages of an opinion, you'll find bracketed numbers beginning some paragraphs of the opinion. A bracketed "3" would appear as "[3]," which would mark the point of the opinion prompting Wilbur to write the third sequential headnote. If you find brackets containing two numbers, that means that Wilbur went wild and wrote two headnotes to describe the same point of law. (Word has it that West editors are on the bonus system; the more headnotes they write, the higher their paychecks will be!)

[3]Yes, he works in the case-publishing division as well.

FLOWERS v. DISTRICT OF COLUMBIA D.C. 1073
Cite as 478 A.2d 1073 (D.C.App. 1984)

haustion of state entitlements and is tied to the state unemployment law. The nub of petitioner's claim is that after her initial disqualification by the District, denial of FSC benefits resulted in a double penalty. We affirm.

Petitioner voluntarily left her employment in the District to care for her infirm mother. Though understandable, she did not thereby have good cause for leaving her work, and she was appropriately assessed a seven week disqualification from benefits. D.C.Code § 46–111(a) (1981); *see Hockaday v. D.C. Department of Employment Services*, 443 A.2d 8 (1982). Petitioner did not challenge this determination, but instead claimed that she was entitled to reimbursement under the FSC program for those forfeited benefits. We disagree.

[1, 2] Under the FSC law, the terms and conditions of the state's law apply to claims for these supplemental benefits. *See* Note following 26 U.S.C. § 3304 at § 602(d)(2). Therefore, petitioner who was partially disqualified under District law is disqualified and statutorily ineligible to receive FSC benefits. *See* D.C.Code § 46–108(g)(8)(G) (Supp.1983); *cf. Steinberg v. Board of Review*, 34 Pa.Cmwlth. 294, 383 A.2d 1284 (1978). The FSC disqualification may only be purged by at least four consecutive weeks of employment subsequent to the filing of her initial District claim. D.C. Code § 46–108(g)(8)(G). Petitioner does not now claim that she has been reemployed. Accordingly, the order appealed from is

sequential headnote numbers

Geraldine FLOWERS, Appellant,

v.

DISTRICT OF COLUMBIA, Appellee.

No. 82–133.

District of Columbia Court of Appeals.

Argued July 5, 1983.

Decided July 12, 1984.

Mother brought action against District under principle of respondeat superior, alleging that tubal cauterization had been negligently performed and as proximate result she had become pregnant and given birth to healthy baby. The Superior Court, District of Columbia, John F. Doyle, J., ruled that mother could not pursue her claim that District must pay costs of rearing child, but permitted mother's other claims to be presented to jury, which returned verdict in mother's favor. The Court of Appeals, Kern, J., retired, held that mother was not entitled to recover costs of rearing her healthy but unplanned child.

Affirmed.

Ferren, J., filed dissenting opinion.

West Topic in Digest

West Key Number

1. Damages ⚷60

"Benefit rule" states that when defendant's tortious conduct has caused harm to plaintiff, and in so doing has conferred a special benefit to interest of plaintiff that was harmed, value of benefit conferred is considered in mitigation of damages, to the extent that such is equitable.

headnote

See publication Words and Phrases for other judicial constructions and definitions.

West Topic in Digest

West Key Number

2. Damages ⚷62(1)

"Avoidable consequences" doctrine is that one injured by tort of another is not entitled to recover damages for any harm

headnote

1074 D.C. 478 ATLANTIC REPORTER, 2d SERIES

that he could have avoided by use of reasonable effort.

See publication Words and Phrases for other judicial constructions and definitions.

3. Physicians and Surgeons ⚷18.12

Permitting parents to bring "wrongful birth" action alleging negligent performance of sterilization to force third person to rear financially their child would have potentially destabilizing effect on families, thereby implicating statutory public policy emphasizing importance of stable home environment and a secure family relationship for children. D.C.Code 1981, § 16–4501.

4. Physicians and Surgeons ⚷18.110

Mother who alleged that negligent performance of tubal cauterization proximately caused her to become pregnant and give birth to child was not entitled to recover cost of rearing her healthy but unplanned child.

Barry H. Gottfried, Washington, D.C., for appellant.

Leo N. Gorman, Asst. Corp. Counsel, Washington, D.C., with whom Judith W. Rogers, Corp. Counsel, Washington, D.C., at the time the brief was filed, and Charles L. Reischel, Deputy Corp. Counsel, Washington, D.C., were on the brief, for appellee.

John Lewis Smith III, Lee T. Ellis, Jr., Jeffrey S. Holik, and Andrew O. Eshelman, Washington, D.C., filed a brief for amicus curiae, The Medical Society of the District of Columbia.

Before FERREN, Associate Judge, and PAIR and KERN,* Associate Judges, Retired.

KERN, Associate Judge, Retired:

This appeal comes to the court upon an Agreed Statement in lieu of the Record on Appeal pursuant to DCCA Rule 10(k). According to the agreed statement of facts, after the birth of appellant's third child, appellant and the father of two of her children determined that they could not afford additional children. Therefore, on May 9, 1978, appellant underwent a laparoscopic cauterization to prevent her from becoming pregnant in the future. This surgery w[...]y Dr. Marsha Berkeley, as[...]chard Peters, both of whom [...] the District.

In October 1980, appellant filed suit against the District of Columbia under the principle of respondeat superior, alleging that the tubal cauterization had been negligently performed and as a proximate result she had become pregnant and given birth to a he[...]June 30, 1980.

App[...] the trial court compensation from the District of Columbia for: her medical expenses, her pain and suffering, and her lost wages, all incurred during her pregnancy;

—the wages she lost after the birth of her child until she could return to work;

—the cost of a properly performed tubal ligation she might undergo in the future; and,

—all costs of rearing her healthy baby until the child reached the age of 18.

The trial court ruled that appellant may not pursue her claim that the District, as a result of its doctors' negligence, must pay the costs of rearing her child. Otherwise, the court permitted appellant's other claims for relief to be presented to the jury and the jury returned a verdict in appellant's favor in the amount of $11,000.

Appellant only challenges the trial court's ruling *in limine* that her claim for child-rearing costs from the doctors might not be pursued. Appellant contends on appeal (Brief at 4), that

> when she negligently failed to perform an effective tubal cauterization, Dr. Mar-

* Judge Kern was an Associate Judge of the court at the time of argument. His status changed to Associate Judge, Retired, on May 25, 1984.

Second, the sequential number serves a vital role in Shepardizing cases, a role you'll learn all about in Chapter 9.

§ 8.2(b) Key Numbers: The Classification System

Once the West Company concluded that it needed to reprint headnotes in some other set of books so that researchers could look up case law, it then had to decide how to *arrange* those headnotes in that collateral set of books. Knowing of the limited number of ways to arrange information in the universe, West immediately sought counsel and referred to:

> **GOOD'S RULE OF RESEARCH #4:**
>
> **There are only three things you can do to a lawbook other than cuss at it:**
> **(1) the Analytical Approach,**
> **(2) the Index Approach, and**
> **(3) the Tabular Approach.**

West knew that it could use the Index Approach and develop a giant index cross-referencing you from index word to headnote (and then to case citation). Or it could use the Tabular Approach and create a giant table of cases (alphabetical listing of case names) but realized that it was the case you're looking for in the first place and that you wouldn't likely know the name of the case you were searching for. These two arrangements, it immediately saw, would not provide workable ways to *find* case law on a given point of law. (As we'll see below, the West Company does indeed have an index and a table as parts of the American Digest System, but these features do not form the major *finding device.*)

West was therefore left with the Analytical Approach and decided to create a huge analytical arrangement of all of American case law. Or, more precisely, it decided to create an analytical arrangement of all *headnotes* from the title pages of all cases so that the researcher could *find headnote* and then be referred to case citation in order to *find case.*

To build this gigantic analytical arrangement of American case law, West divided all of American law into approximately 435 topics. These topics might be quite broad, such as Constitutional Law, or quite narrow, such as Dead Bodies. West then analytically divided each topic into broad Roman Numerals, the Roman Numerals into letters—kind of like an outline for a high school English theme. It then analytically sub-sub-subdivided the topic into minute, analytical sub-sub-subdivisions, each bearing an analytical name. Once it named and listed these hundreds (and sometimes thousands) of analytical sub-sub-subdivisions of a given topic of law, the

West Company numbered them in order: the first was #1, the second #2, the third #3, and so on. Brilliant! Instead of giving these subdivisions just an unadorned, boring number, the West Company jazzed it up and came up with "Key Numbers." The key that unlocks the law, I guess.

So that you can see what a major West topic looks like, I've reproduced the "Physicians & Surgeons" topic on the following pages. Notice how the topic begins with regulatory matters, moves to substantive matters, and ends with procedural matters. You'll find that all West topics treat substance first in the lower and middle Key Numbers and procedure in the higher Key Numbers.

From here on, I'll refer to this topical breakdown—the actual listing of the Key Numbers and their corresponding names—as the "Menu." I'll even capitalize the word. It's *that* important. Note that it requires several pages to print the actual Menu in the digest. Repeat: note that it requires several pages to print the actual Menu in the digest.[4] Yes, use your highlighter pen for that one.[5]

[4] If I were teaching a course in legal research, one of the final exam questions would be: "How many pages are required to print the Menu of a West topic in the American Digest System?" The answer would be: "Repeat: note that it requires several pages to print the actual Menu in the digest."

[5] As a matter of fact, make certain you use lots of highlighter when reading this opus. Slash it with yellow marks on each page. Helps destroy the used book market!

The Menu

33

West Topic

PHYSICIANS AND SURGEONS

SUBJECTS INCLUDED

Practice of medicine, surgery, dentistry, or other healing art
Admission to practice
Registration, certification, and license of practitioners
Regulation of professional conduct
Mutual rights, duties, and liabilities of physician and patient

SUBJECTS EXCLUDED AND COVERED BY OTHER TOPICS

Privilege of professional communications, see WITNESSES
Public offices or employments, physicians in, see HEALTH AND ENVIRONMENT, OFFICERS AND PUBLIC EMPLOYEES
Testimony of physicians as experts, see EVIDENCE

For detailed references to other topics, see Descriptive-Word Index

Analysis

I. IN GENERAL, ⚿1–40.

II. NONCONSENSUAL CARE OR TREATMENT, ⚿41–47.

broad analytical breakdown of West Topic

I. IN GENERAL.

detailed breakdown with names of Key Numbers

⚿1. Power to regulate practice.
2. Constitutional and statutory provisions.
3. Authority to admit to practice.
4. Capacity and qualifications.
5. Registration, certificate, or license.
 (1). In general.
 (2). Application for registration, certificate, or license, and proceedings thereon.
 (3). Review of decisions of boards.
 (4). Operation and effect of registration, certificate, or license.
6. Practicing without authority.
 (1). Acts constituting unlawful practice or offense in general.
 (2). Dentists.
 (3). Osteopaths.
 (4). Obstetricians.
 (5). Opticians.
 (6). Christian Scientists.
 (7). Sale of drugs or appliances.
 (8). Defenses to prosecutions for practicing without authority.
 (9). Indictment, information, or complaint in prosecutions for practicing without authority.
 (10). Evidence in prosecutions for practicing without authority.
 (11). Trial of prosecutions for practicing without authority.
 (11½). Sentence and punishment.
 (12). Penalties and actions therefor.
7. Injuries to persons not patients in exercise of professional functions.
8. Privilege or occupation taxes.
9. Medical societies.
10. Regulation of professional conduct.
11. Revocation or suspension of certificate or license.
11.1. —— Authority to revoke or suspend.
11.2. —— Grounds for revocation or suspension.
11.3. —— Proceedings.
 (1). In general.
 (2). Complaint or accusation.
 (3). Evidence.
 (4). Hearing, findings and determination.
 (5). Review and reinstatement.
12. Relation to patient in general.
13. Contract of employment.
14. Degree of skill and care required.
 (1). In general.
 (2). Following professed or recognized school, system, or treatment.
 (3). Insurance of cure or benefit.
 (4). Depending on state of profession.
15. Acts or omissions constituting negligence or malpractice.
 (1). Errors of judgment and bad results.
 (2). Exercising as well as possessing skill, and diligence.
 (3). Persons required to exercise care.
 (4). Proximate cause of injury.
 (5). Particular acts or omissions of regular physicians and surgeons.
 (6). —— Abandonment of case.
 (7). —— Diagnosis.
 (8). —— Disclosure to patient.

33 9th D Pt 2—775 **PHYSICIANS & SURGEONS**

I. IN GENERAL.—Cont'd

⚷15. Acts or omissions constituting negligence or malpractice.—Cont'd
(9). —— Divulging communications and other breach of confidence.
(10). —— Eyes.
(11). —— Infection.
(12). —— Surgical operations in general.
(13). —— Anaesthesia.
(14). —— Sponges and other objects left in body.
(15). —— Unauthorized or unnecessary operation.
(16). —— X-rays.
(17). Practitioners other
(18). —— Chiropractors.
(19). —— Dentists in general.
(20). —— Anaesthesia by dentists.
(21). —— Nurses, attendants and therapists.
(22). —— Osteopaths.
(23). —— Psychiatrists, psychoanalysts and religious healers.
(24). —— Veterinarians.
16. Liability for negligence or malpractice.
17. Contributory negligence or fault on part of patient.
17.5. Medical malpractice panel.
18. Actions for negligence or malpractice.
18.1. —— Nature and form of action.
18.12. —— Rights of action and defenses.
18.15. —— Limitations.
18.20. —— Conditions precedent.
18.40. —— Pleading.
18.50. —— Issues, proof, and variance.
18.60. —— Presumptions and burden of proof.
18.70. —— Admissibility of evidence.
18.80. —— Weight and sufficiency of evidence.
(1). In general.
(2). Particular cases.
(3). —— Surgical procedures.
(4). —— Fractures and dislocations.
(5). Cause of injury; persons liable.
(6). Expert testimony requirement.
(7). —— Particular matters.
(8). —— Standard of practice and departure therefrom.
(9). —— Gross or obvious negligence and matters of common knowledge.
18.90. —— Questions for jury.
18.100. —— Instructions.
18.110. —— Damages.
18.120. —— Verdict and findings.
18.130. —— Review.
19. Duties and liabilities in examinations for insanity or inebriety.
20. Right to compensation.
21. —— In general.
22. —— Unauthorized practitioners.

(1½). Nature and form of remedy.
(1¾). Parties.
(2). Pleading.
(3). Evidence.
(4). Questions for jury.
(5). Instructions.

II. NONCONSENSUAL CARE OR TREATMENT.

⚷41. In general.
42. Substituted judgment; role of guardian or others.
43. Terminal illness; use or removal of life-support systems.
44. —— Substituted judgment; role of courts, physicians, guardians, family, or others.
45. —— Competent patients; living wills and other prior indications.
46. —— Dialysis.
47. —— Evidence and fact questions.

For detailed references to other topics, see Descriptive-Word Index

on-point Key Number

Note: The blank line after "18.110" and before "Damages" means that this Key Number is a subtopic of the preceding Key Number that has no blank line—here, Key Number 18, entitled "Actions for negligence or malpractice."

§ 8.2(c) Arrangement of Headnotes within Key Numbers

Once West has devised the Menu of a given topic by analytically subdividing it into Key Numbers, it then prints—immediately after the Menu—the actual headnotes in the digest sequentially by Key Number (I'll discuss the structure of the actual digests below). The headnotes under one Key Number might occupy just a few pages, or, in particularly "hot" areas, they might consume several hundred pages in a digest. It is vital, therefore, that you commit to memory the method West uses to *arrange headnotes within Key Numbers.*

West follows the same system of case arrangement in the digest that it uses in the footnotes of C.J.S.:

1. Supreme Court cases.
2. Federal circuit court cases.
3. Federal district court cases.
4. State court cases.

Some comments are in order. Federal cases are listed first, by hierarchy of court. Thus, if a Key Number has any Supreme Court cases classified to it, the headnotes from those cases appear first, each preceded by the designation "U.S." Then the headnotes from the federal circuit courts are listed *alphabetically by state* and given the designation, for example, "C.A. Pa.," which means the United States Court of Appeals that handles cases from Pennsylvania, which is another but extremely awkward way of saying the Third Circuit. As I mentioned in Chapter 6 above, this system of arranging federal circuit court cases alphabetically by state should earn the West Company the Boo of the Century Award. As you make your way toward that coveted status of Ace Legal Researcher, you must memorize which states are in which circuits so that "C.A. Cal." registers as "Ninth Circuit" in your mind and "C.A. Fla." registers as "Eleventh Circuit."

News Flash: as I was completing this book in the middle of 1992, the West Company—no doubt sensing their impending receipt of the Boo of the Century Award—actually changed the method of designating federal circuit court cases in the *Tenth Decennial, Part One* and in the current *General Digest.* Now, you'll be pleased to learn, the West Company designates these cases by circuit number! So in current digests, you'll see "C.A. 11 (Ga.)," meaning that it's an 11th Circuit case arising in Georgia. Unfortunately, the West Company continues to *sequence* the headnotes *alphabetically by state,* not *numerically by circuit.* Hiss. Boo.

But in all earlier digests, you'll have to know what state is in which circuit. I realize that you thought you could leave geography behind in junior high school, but you can't. To help you in this new geography course, I've provided below the following listing of states showing which states constitute which circuits. As an added bonus, the table shows the official Harvard *Bluebook* abbreviation of that state (which the West Company notoriously does *not* follow in its citations):

The States and the Federal Circuits

State	*Bluebook* Abbreviation	Circuit
Alabama	Ala.	5th Cir.
Alaska	Alaska	9th Cir.
Arizona	Ariz.	9th Cir.
Arkansas	Ark.	8th Cir.
California	Cal.	9th Cir.
Colorado	Colo.	10th Cir.
Connecticut	Conn.	2d Cir.
Delaware	Del.	3d Cir.
District of Columbia	D.C.	D.C. Cir.
Florida	Fla.	11th Cir.
Georgia	Ga.	11th Cir.
Hawaii	Haw.	9th Cir.
Idaho	Idaho	9th Cir.
Illinois	Ill.	7th Cir.
Indiana	Ind.	7th Cir.
Iowa	Iowa	8th Cir.
Kansas	Kan.	10th Cir.
Kentucky	Ky.	6th Cir.
Louisiana	La.	5th Cir.
Maine	Me.	1st Cir.
Maryland	Md.	4th Cir.
Massachusetts	Mass.	1st Cir.
Michigan	Mich.	6th Cir.
Minnesota	Minn.	8th Cir.
Mississippi	Miss.	5th Cir.
Missouri	Mo.	8th Cir.
Montana	Mont.	9th Cir.
Nebraska	Neb.	8th Cir.
Nevada	Nev.	9th Cir.
New Hampshire	N.H.	1st Cir.
New Jersey	N.J.	3d Cir.
New Mexico	N.M.	10th Cir.
New York	N.Y.	2d Cir.
North Carolina	N.C.	4th Cir.
North Dakota	N.D.	8th Cir.
Ohio	Ohio	6th Cir.
Oklahoma	Okla.	10th Cir.
Oregon	Or.	9th Cir.
Pennsylvania	Penn.	3d Cir.
Rhode Island	R.I.	1st Cir.
South Carolina	S.C.	4th Cir.
South Dakota	S.D.	8th Cir.
Tennessee	Tenn.	6th Cir.
Texas	Tex.	5th Cir.
Utah	Utah	10th Cir.
Vermont	Vt.	2d Cir.
Virginia	Va.	4th Cir.
Washington	Wash.	9th Cir.
West Virginia	W. Va.	4th Cir.
Wisconsin	Wis.	7th Cir.
Wyoming	Wyo	10th Cir.

Following the headnotes from federal circuit court cases, the West Company then lists the headnotes from federal district court cases alphabetically by state. In earlier digests, such headnotes are preceded by a designation such as "D.C.N.C.," which means one of the three federal district courts in North Carolina. Now, in the *Tenth Decennial, Part One* and the current *General Digest*, the West Company properly designates these cases as, for example, "M.D.N.C." (for Middle District of North Carolina).

Within one Key Number, when all the headnotes from federal cases have been listed, West then lists the headnotes from state cases alphabetically by state. Within any given state, the headnotes from the highest court will be listed first, followed by the headnotes from any intermediate courts of appeal. You'll see designations such as "Pa." used to designate the highest court in Pennsylvania, the Pennsylvania Supreme Court, and "Pa. Super." to designate the Pennsylvania Superior Court.

At this stage of your career, you should learn that West has its own system of abbreviating these courts and that the West abbreviations are *not necessarily* proper Harvard *Bluebook* abbreviations that should appear in your case citations. For a complete discussion of the proper abbreviation of courts in case citations, see C. Edward Good, *Citing & Typing the Law* 113-23 (LEL Enterprises 1992).

By knowing this order of headnotes appearing within any given Key Number, you can quickly turn to federal cases from a particular circuit (if you've got your Ph.D. in American geography) or to cases from a particular state.

You now know what headnotes are, what Key Numbers are, and how headnotes are arranged in digests. The final piece of the bibliographic puzzle is the digest itself. Once you become familiar with the structure of the American Digest System, you'll then be ready to run Key Numbers to find all cases on any given point of law from 1658 to the present day.

§ 8.2(d) The Structure of the American Digest System

Again, picture the problem. There sits a pile of 10,000 volumes of chronologically reported cases in 14 different sets of court reports (nine regional, two special state, five federal). You, the legal researcher, want to find just those cases dealing with your point of law. You do *not* want to check each of these volumes, volume by volume, for 10,000 volumes. No, you'd refuse and find something else to do for a living.

The West Company realized the dilemma and decided on *digesting* the cases by writing headnotes, which it would then print in big books called *Digests*. Its first problem concerned the *scope* of these big digests: would the books contain headnotes from the entire country? from just parts of the country? from state courts? from federal courts? Its second problem concerned *timing*: what time period would the books cover? How could they be supplemented to keep track of cases as they hit the shelves of the law libraries of the world?

Let's tackle the *scope* problem first, and then the all-important *timing* problem.

§ 8.2(d)(i) The Varying *Scopes* of West Digests

West decided to create a variety of digests, each with varying *scopes*:

Entire Nation

To cover the entire country, West created the American Digest System—a collection of digests containing the headnotes of *all* cases in the country, from state and federal courts, from the earliest days of American case law to the present day. These digests are called the *Decennial Digests* and the *General Digest*, both described in detail below.

Federal Cases

To provide access just to federal cases (Supreme, Circuit, District, and all other federal courts), West created a series of *Federal Digests*, collecting the headnotes from all federal cases from the earliest days of federal case law to the present day.

State Cases: Regions

Since the West Company had already structured its court reports by geographic region, it made good sense to create a digest for each regional report. At one time, such digests existed for all seven regions. But the regional digests for the *Southern*, *South Western*, and *North Eastern Reporters* have been discontinued.

State Cases: States

West also realized the provincial nature of American law practice. The vast majority of attorneys practice local, state law and could give less of a hoot about cases from neighboring states. State trial judges give even smaller hoots about out-of-state cases. To respond to these market desires, West created a separate digest for each of 47 of the 50 states.[6] One of these digests is called, for example, the *Georgia Digest*.

In sum, West has one gigantic digest system for the entire country (the Decennials and the Generals) and then smaller digests to respond to various submarkets: Federal Digests, Regional Digests, and State Digests. In your research career, you will likely use all these digests, changing from one to the other as the scope and nature of your research assignments change, or consulting the American Digest System to retrieve cases from the entire country *and* in the same research project checking a State Digest for a quicker look at the status of a given state's case law.

§ 8.2(d)(ii) Coping with the *Timing* Problem

Once the West Company had staked out the territorial *scope* of each digest, it then faced the age-old quandary in legal publishing: instantaneous obsolescence. West had to figure out how to stay up to date with its own shelf. In other words, each week West was adding case law to 14 different shelves in 14 different court reports. As time passed, somehow West had to grab all the headnotes from the shelf and print them in some ongoing digest system.

[6]The West Publishing Company does not publish digests for Delaware, Nevada, and Utah.

West didn't make all these momentous decisions all at once. Its system evolved over time and is still evolving. At the close of the 19th Century, West decided to collect the headnotes from all cases decided since the beginning of time to 1896. It gathered together all the headnotes from all the cases for the previous 250 years or so, alphabetized them by Main Topic name, and sequenced them by number ("section numbers," not Key Numbers, were used at that time), and printed them in a giant digest called the *Century Digest.* Thus, for all you history nuts, here's your source, here's where you can find all the early cases in American case law. For everybody else, the chances of your using this source are virtually nil. You will, after all, rely on the research of Wilbur, which has gone well beyond the old *Century Digest.*

Then the West Company had to decide how often it would gather together all the headnotes of the world, alphabetize them by Main Topic, and sequence them by Key Number. The "decade" seemed like a good time period, so the West Company created the *First Decennial Digest,* which covered the period between 1897 and 1906. In this *First Decennial,* the West Company gathered together all the headnotes from all the cases decided *after* the *Century Digest,* alphabetized them by Main Topic, sequenced them by Key Number, and printed them in a set of big, huge digests. If you look this set in the face, which totals 25 volumes, you'll find the "A" topics in the beginning volumes and the "Z" topics in the ending volumes. Sometimes, a topic will begin in one volume (through a certain Key Number) and then end in the next volume. You'll find the Menu at the front of the topic in the beginning volume.

And so in 1916, West gathered together all the headnotes from all the cases decided *after* the *First Decennial,* alphabetized them by Main Topic, sequenced them by Key Number, and printed them in the *Second Decennial Digest,* covering the period 1907 through 1916. The process then continued with the *Third Decennial* appearing in 1926, the *Fourth Decennial* in 1936, and so on to the *Eighth Decennial* in 1976.

A chart showing these digests, their respective coverages, and the number of digest volumes in each set appears as follows:

Digest	Dates	# Volumes
First Decennial	1897-1906	25
Second Decennial	1907-1916	24
Third Decennial	1917-1926	28
Fourth Decennial	1927-1936	34
Fifth Decennial	1937-1946	49
Sixth Decennial	1947-1956	36
Seventh Decennial	1957-1966	38
Eighth Decennial	1967-1976	50

Now get out your "honer" so that you can "finely hone" a skill that must be finely honed for you to become an Ace Legal Researcher: the skill of mathematical subtraction. Can you handle it? Can you "subtract one"? Take the *"Third Decennial"* as an example. See the "3" in "third"? Now "subtract one." Good, got the resulting "2"?

Great. Now change that "2" to a "20" and put a "6" on it. Get it? The *Third Decennial* ended in "1926," the *Fifth Decennial* in 1946, the *Eighth Decennial* in 1976. All these decennials end in the year ending in "6" in the decade "one less" than their name. Of course, you can work it the other way as well. Take the year, add one, and you get the name of the decennial. You'll find that this astute mathematical insight pays some dividends in your life as a legal researcher.

In 1981, the West Company pulled a fast one on us. We were all expecting to have to wait another five years, until 1986, to receive the *Ninth Decennial Digest.* But all of a sudden, right there on the shelves, a new digest materialized, the *Ninth Decennial, Part One*. The *Ninth Decennial, Part One* covered the years 1977 through 1981. Naturally, in early 1987 we began to receive the *Ninth Decennial, Part Two.* And now as I write this in the fall of 1992, the shelf is beginning to receive the *Tenth Decennial, Part One.*[7]

The entire system, covering all state and federal cases from 1658 to 1992, appears as follows:

Coverage of the American Digest System

Digest	Dates	# Volumes
Century	1658-1896	50
First Decennial	1897-1906	25
Second Decennial	1907-1916	24
Third Decennial	1917-1926	29
Fourth Decennial	1927-1936	34
Fifth Decennial	1937-1946	49
Sixth Decennial	1947-1956	36
Seventh Decennial	1957-1966	38
Eighth Decennial	1967-1976	50
Ninth Decennial, Part One	1977-1981	38 (5 years)
Ninth Decennial, Part Two	1982-1986	48 (5 years)
Tenth Decennial, Part One	1987-1991	Just beginning to emerge in the summer of 1992.

You should be starting to shudder. For you can see what *running Key Numbers* might entail: using a Key Number or several Key Numbers and tracing them throughout a digest system stretching back to the beginning of time. And what do you find when you *run Key Numbers*? Headnotes. Miles and miles of headnotes. And what do you do with those headnotes? You read the suckers, all of them classified to your Key Number, searching for those revealing cases on point. And what do you do when you

[7]As of July 1992, the *Tenth Decennial, Part One* appeared in 11 volumes, the 11th volume covering through part of the "Criminal Law" topic.

"hit" a headnote revealing a case on point? You write down its citation. And then what do you do? You go to the shelf, get that case, and read the damned thing. And it's just one out of hundreds. Any takers?

Why do all that? Why do that if that's exactly what Wilbur had to do to write all that background authority in C.J.S., Am. Jur. 2d, A.L.R., treatises, legal periodical articles, and Restatements of the Law? No reason at all. No reason why you should re-do what Wilbur has already done. What you'll do, as described in detail below, is to pick up running Key Numbers where Wilbur stopped running Key Numbers, thereby cutting down the basic chronological case research to a bare minimum.

But first, the structure of the American Digest System remains incomplete. After the West Company puts together a decennial digest, cases continue to hit the shelves, every week, like clockwork, for 10 years until the next decennial gathers together all the headnotes, alphabetizes them by Main Topic, sequences them by Key Number, and prints them in the next decennial. *Actually, the time period is not 10 years since the West Company puts out the decennials in installments—Part One and Part Two. Effectively, the West Company has turned the decennial digest system into a quintennial digest system.*

§ 8.2(d)(iii) Solving the *Supplementation* Problem

West thus faced another dilemma: cases were hitting the shelves each week but the digest system was gathering together their headnotes and printing them in big digest books only every 10 years (now every five years). It had to develop some method of collecting headnotes, alphabetizing them by Main Topic, sequencing them by Key Number, and printing them in a regular and much more frequent way. To solve this problem, it developed the ever-popular, if sometimes mind-numbing . . . *General Digest.*

To fill in the time gap between the publication of the latest decennial digest and the present day, the West Company publishes an ongoing series of *General Digests.* In the first month after the end of a decennial period, West publishes "Volume 1" of the next series of *General Digests.* This "Volume 1" contains *all 435* Main Topics in the West Digest System. It collects all headnotes from all court reports, alphabetizes them by Main Topic, sequences them by Key Number, and prints them in a single volume. This "Volume 1" will cover approximately *one month* of time on the 14 court report shelves. Then, not surprisingly, along comes "Volume 2" of the *General Digest.* It picks up where Volume 1 left off, collects all headnotes from all court reports, alphabetizes them by Main Topic, sequences them by Key Number, and prints them in a single volume. Then comes "Volume 3," which does the same thing, picking up where Volume 2 left off. And then comes "Volume 4," and "5," and "6," hitting the shelves at the rate of one per month. *Each volume contains the entire West System, all 435 Main Topics from "A" to "Z."*

To become a true Ace Legal Researcher, you must understand several important differences between a *General Digest* volume and a *Decennial Digest* volume. First, as mentioned above, a *General Digest* volume contains *all* Main Topics in the digest system, whereas a *Decennial Digest* volume contains just a few topics. Because the *General Digest* volume contains *all* topics, it does not have enough space to print the Menu of each topic. In other words, you cannot find the complete analytical breakdown of a Main Topic, with all the Key Numbers named and listed, in a *General Digest* volume. If the *General Digest* did print the Menus *each month*, it would require nearly 1,000 pages just to print those Menus. The *absence* of the Menus in the *General Digest* volumes has major implications for your research technique. Repeat: the *absence* of the Menus in the *General Digest* volumes has major implications for your research technique. Another one of those final exam questions.

Second, because a *Decennial Digest* volume covers more time (10 years, or now five years), it likely has quite a few headnotes classified to each Key Number. A *General Digest* volume, on the other hand, covers only a few weeks of time and consequently can have a Key Number with *no headnotes* classified to it during that small amount of time. These "headnote-less" Key Numbers occur quite frequently and West treats them the way all law publishers treat information that doesn't exist: they leave it out! This phenomenon, known in scientific circles as *antimatter*, gives rise to:

GOOD'S RULE OF RESEARCH #19:

A great deal of legal research involves looking for what's *not* there.

Thus, if you were to use the *General Digest* for the period covering 1987 to 1991 (which is currently being superseded by the *Tenth Decennial, Part One*), you'd be confronted with 59 volumes worth of digest. Keep in mind that *each volume* contains *all West Topics*. Thus, a complete search for your research project would require looking in *all 59 volumes*. Fun—especially when, after looking through all 59 volumes, you find that only volumes 17, 27, and 31 contained headnotes classified to your Key Number. To ascertain this fact, you had to pick up Volume 1, look up your Key Number, give it a great big "nope, nothing there," close the book, pick up the next volume, look up your Key Number, give it a great big "nope, nothing there," close the book, pick up the next . . . and run screaming from the main library reading room. A great deal of legal research indeed does involve looking for what's not there. (You'll discover below, much to your relief, the shortcut enabling you to avoid engaging in the rather stupid task of opening books and looking for what's not there.)

Using the *General Digest*, you will soon learn, will become part and parcel of your skills as an Ace Legal Researcher. In any research projects involving case law research, you will use the *General Digest* as one of the means of updating your basic chronological research to the present day. The trick, of course, lies in realizing that a good friend of yours—Wilbur—also used the same *General Digest*. If you could just figure out where Wilbur *stopped*, then you would know precisely where to *start* running Key Numbers to the present day.

§ 8.2(d)(iv) Understanding the *Digest Overlap* Phenomenon

What happens when two universes occupy the same space simultaneously?

Various physicists, cultists, and others who voted on the Elvis Commemorative Stamp Design Contest[8] have been struggling with this dilemma in physics since the dawn of time. The phenomenon crops up, of course, in the nether world of legal research, where, you are no doubt learning, time does tend to bend.

Picture the problem facing the West Company at the end of 1991. In 1987, the West Company published the *Ninth Decennial, Part Two*, covering the years 1982 through 1986. Then, beginning in the month of January 1987, it began publishing the *General Digest, Seventh Series.* (Note: Please don't ask what the "Seventh Series" means. I honestly don't know. Presumably, it's the seventh *General Digest* published by the West Company. How the West Company updated the decennials before that time is a mystery to me.)

That *General Digest* then continued for 59 volumes, coming out at the rate of almost exactly one per month for five years. This five-year period ended in December 1991. Then, the West Company began to change these 59 volumes of *General Digest* into the new *Tenth Decennial, Part One.*

Here's what it had to do. The West Company had to assemble a team of the unemployed—probably a team of unemployed physicists—to act as its Super Key Number/Headnote Recollation Team. This team of crack collators, or should I say, this crack team of collators, started at the first West Topic: Abandoned Property, Key Number 1. It collected all those headnotes from the General Digest, Volume 1. Then it went to Volume 2, and 3, and 4, and 5, and on up to 59, grabbing all headnotes classified to Abandoned Property Key Number 1. When it got all of them, it then arranged them by court, federal headnotes first, then state. Mopping its collective brow, the team then turned its attention to Abandoned Property Key Number 2, grabbing all the headnotes from all 59 volumes and arranging them by court. On to Abandoned Property Key Number 3, the crack team marched. And on and on through all Key Numbers in the first West Topic, Abandoned Property. Finished with that daunting task, the crack team then tackled the next West Topic, and the next, and the next . . . .

As the West Company completed the various topics, it would begin to publish the *Tenth Decennial, Part One.* The first volume, for example, which hit the shelf in the spring of 1992, contains the topics "Abandoned and Lost Property" through "Appeal and Error (Key 122)." And, in the next year or two, volumes in the *Tenth Decennial, Part One* will continue to hit the shelves.

During this period, legal researchers experience a condition known as *Digest Overlap.* On the shelf, there sits the *General Digest, Seventh Series*; it covers the years 1987 through 1991. On the shelf, there sits part of the *Tenth Decennial, Part One*; it too covers the years 1987 through 1991. See? *Digest Overlap.*

[8] I personally endorsed the Fat Elvis version, which lost by a landslide.

During this period of time, you will notice legal researchers in various parts of the law library sitting in the Lotus Position chanting in strange-sounding voices. They are trying to invoke the grace of the Legal Research Gods to bestow upon them *legal research topics beginning with the letter "A."* Or maybe even "B."

How come? Because during this period of *Digest Overlap*, it's a great deal easier to use the *Tenth Decennial, Part One* (which might be complete only through the letter "B") than the *General Digest*. After all, in the *Tenth Decennial, Part One* a legal researcher has to open only *one* book, for *one* look, to find case law decided in the five-year period from 1987 through 1991. The researcher relegated to the *General Digest*, the poor slob over there assigned the project on Zoning Law, must check all 59 volumes of the *General Digest Seventh Series* to find all case law over the five-year period from 1987 through 1991.

All together now . . . ommmmmm, ommmmmm, ommmmmm. Pray to the Legal Research Gods for an assignment beginning with the letter "A."

§ 8.2(d)(v) A Graphic Depiction

The following figure shows the structure of the American Digest System.

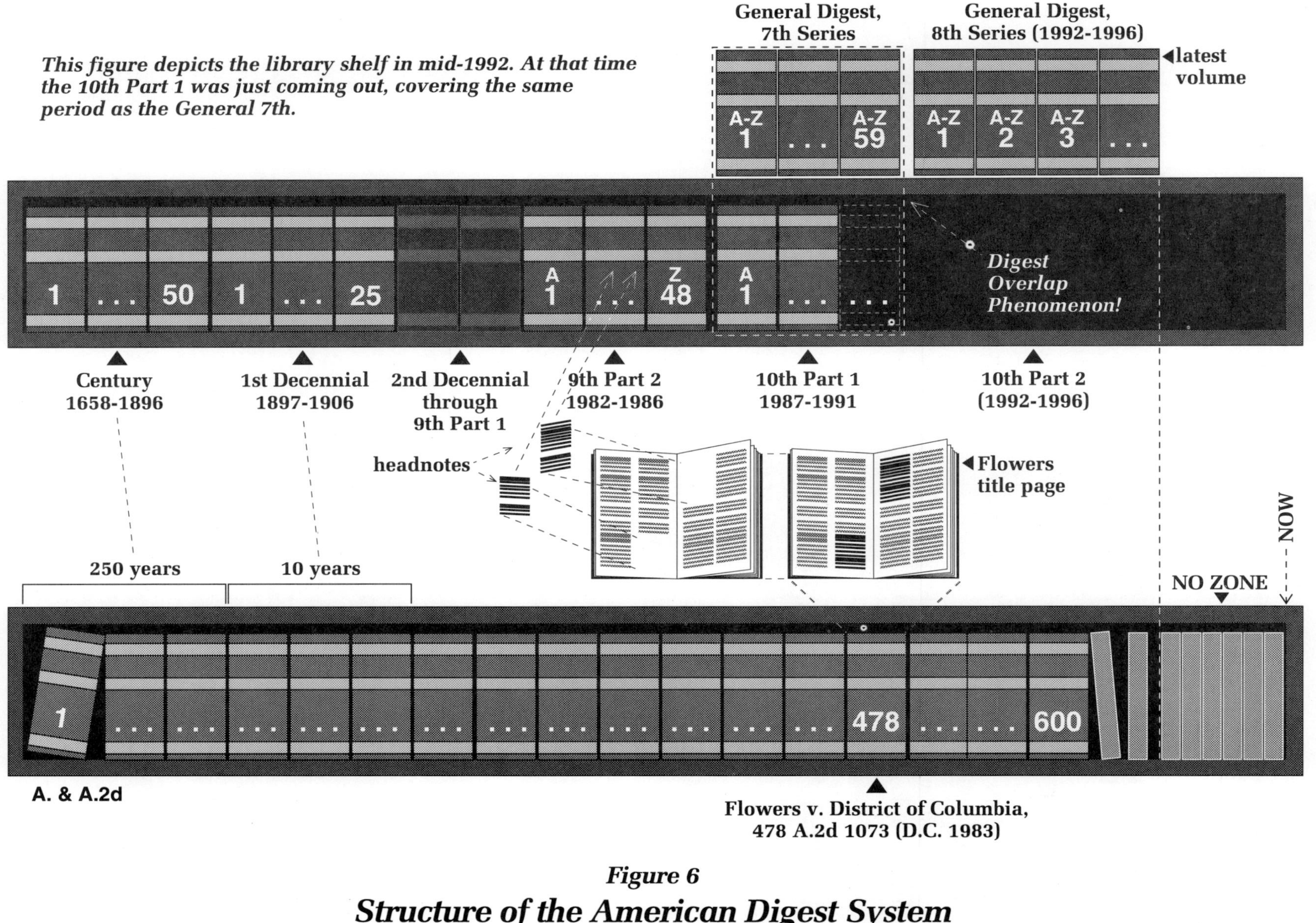

Figure 6

Structure of the American Digest System

§ 8.2(e) Additional Bibliographic Features

Before going further, let me pause for a moment and summarize. The West Company collects Key Numbers from the entire country in its American Digest System, which is divided into *Decennial Digests* and, to keep the system current, *General Digests.* These two digests contain all state and federal cases decided since the dawn of time to the present day. To become an Ace Legal Researcher, you must commit to memory both the scope and the time coverage of these digests.

For those not interested in researching the case law of the entire country, West provides *Federal Digests, Regional Digests,* and *State Digests.* These, as their names suggest, collect the headnotes from cases from the federal court reports, the regional reports, and a single state.

In most of these digests, you can find the West Topic broken down analytically at the front of the Topic in the digest. Remember, however, that in the *General Digest* the Topics are *not* broken down, named, and numbered at the front of each topic, for the simple reason that each volume of the *General Digest* contains *all* West Topics. If the West Company reprinted each Menu of all 435 topics in each volume of the General Digest, it would consume over 1,000 pages just to print these Menus.

Thus, you can use the Analytical Approach to find the right Key Number by consulting likely West Topics in the latest Decennial Digest. Then, by deductive reasoning, you can figure out the exact Key Number that likely covers your particular research problem.

You might remember, however . . .

GOOD'S RULE OF RESEARCH #4:

There are only three things you can do to a lawbook other than cuss at it:
(1) the Analytical Approach,
(2) the Index Approach, and
(3) the Tabular Approach.

Remembering this vital rule, you might think that the American Digest System has other "finding aids" to help you locate the right Key Number. And you'd be dead right.

In fact, you'd be right if you concluded that the digest itself also provides an Index Approach and a Tabular Approach. *Approach* to what? To *finding* the right Key Number. We'll get to a more thorough discussion of Key Number Location Skills in the "finding" section below, but at this point you do need to know the bibliographic features of the *Descriptive Word Index* and the *Table of Cases.*

§ 8.2(e)(i) The *Descriptive Word Index*

You will find a *Descriptive Word Index* with *each component* of the American Digest System. Thus, the *Sixth Decennial Digest* has its own *Descriptive Word Index*, as does the *Fifth*, the *Fourth*, and the *Ninth Decennial, Part Two.* And you'll find a separate *Descriptive Word Index* at the back of each volume of the *General Digest.*

This Index is perhaps unique in all of legal literature. Most indexes refer you directly to the information being indexed. For example, the *Index to Annotations* indexes A.L.R. annotations, the *Index to Legal Periodicals* indexes legal periodical literature, and the *General Index* in C.J.S. indexes the text of the C.J.S. legal encyclopedia. You might think, therefore, that the *Descriptive Word Index* indexes CASES. But this time you'd be dead wrong.

The *Descriptive Word Index* indexes not CASES, but KEY NUMBERS. Since the Key Number System is an analytical breakdown of all American case law, then the *Descriptive Word Index* is . . . hold on . . . an Index to an Analysis. Told you this is a weird world.

In the *Descriptive Word Index* you can play the word games of the TARP Rule and discover references to Key Numbers that classify cases concerned with those index words. The index entries, you must realize, refer you to Key Numbers, not to cases.

§ 8.2(e)(ii) The *Tables of Cases*

Each component of the American Digest System also has a *Table of Cases.* For example, at the *end* of the *Seventh Decennial Digest* you will find several volumes containing an alphabetical listing of all cases decided in the "seventh decennial" time period, that is, between 1957 and 1966. You'll find an identical *Table of Cases* for each of the *Decennial Digests*, for each component of the *Federal Digests*, for each *Regional Digest*, for each *State Digest*, and for each individual volume of *General Digest.*

In these *Tables of Cases* you will find some very useful and some quite useless information. The useful information consists of the citation to the case and any case history higher up in the court system. Thus, if you know the *name* of a case and roughly when it was decided, you can find the *citation* to the case by using the *Table of Cases* in the appropriate *Decennial Digest.* As a bonus, you'll get the citations to any case history decided by higher courts. That's good information, but you can readily see that it has little to do with Key Number research.

That's where the useless information comes in. In addition to the citation and case history, the *Table of Cases* also lists the Main Topics and Key Numbers used to classify all the legal issues in that case. "Why is that useless?" you might legitimately ask. Because even if you get that information from the *Table of Cases*, you're still going to go *read* the case in the West Company court report. And what will you find on the title page of the case itself? You got it. The Key Numbers. I can imagine only one situation where the Key Number cross-references might be useful: if a researcher has a case name and citation but for some reason does not have access to the actual case as reported in a West Company court report.

So mark it down in your notes that there is indeed a Tabular Approach to *finding* Key Numbers but that no one in his right mind is likely to use that approach in the real world of legal research.

You will find that the *Table of Cases* comes in very handy when you have to find what I call the Cocktail Party Cases. You see, every Saturday night lawyers go to cocktail parties. And what do lawyers talk about when they gather socially? Right. Case law. So one lawyer says, "Did you hear about the *Jackson v. Fulbright* case just handed down by the Ninth Circuit?" "No, what's its cite?" "Don't recall, but you ought to try to find it. Sounds like it's right on point to your case."

So what do you do when the lawyer you're working for comes in Monday morning all lathered up about the *Fulbright* case? After determining that it's a recent case decided by the Ninth Circuit, you hightail it to the most recent volumes of the *General Digest* and work backwards in the *Tables of Cases*. Sooner or later you'll find a reference to the case the attorney seeks. And your picture goes on the attorney's piano!

§ 8.2(e)(iii) The Author's Subterfuge

Time for me to fess up and admit that I've been holding something back from you. I did so intentionally because I didn't want to complicate an otherwise crystal clear discussion of this murky area of legal research: Key Numbers and the American Digest System.

The *General Digest* has a rather nice feature that will save you an enormous amount of time. In the back of each volume, you'll find the *Descriptive Word Index*, the *Table of Cases*, and another feature we'll discuss a bit later. Well, guess what. These indexes and tables *cumulate* within each 10 volumes of *General Digest*. Here's how it works. In Volume 2 of the *General Digest*, the *Descriptive Word Index* and the *Table of Cases* will add the index words from Volume 2 and the cases from Volume 2 to the *Descriptive Word Index* and *Table of Cases* that were in Volume 1. In a word, Volume 2 cumulates Volume 1. Then, in Volume 3, the *Descriptive Word Index* and the *Table of Cases* will cumulate those in Volumes 1 and 2. Volume 4 does the same to Volumes 1, 2, and 3. And so on up to Volume 10. In that volume, the *Descriptive Word Index* and the *Table of Cases* cumulate all those from Volumes 1 through 10.

Then Volume 11 starts all over again with a *Descriptive Word Index* and a *Table of Cases* for just that volume. Then the index and table in Volume 12 will cumulate those in Volume 11. And on up to Volume 20, which cumulates 11 through 20. Then the process starts all over again.

Thus, when the attorney comes in on Monday morning swooning over the *Fulbright* case, off you go to the latest volume of the *General Digest* to look up the case in the *Table of Cases*. And then you work your way backwards in each *tenth* volume.

Now please do not be confused. The only features of the *General Digest* that cumulate are the *Descriptive Word Index* and the *Table of Cases* (and one other I'll explain below). The headnotes arranged by Key Number obviously do not cumulate. If they did, then how big would Volume 10 be? As big as all 10 volumes combined. A book four feet thick!

§ 8.3 The Finding Phase: How to Find the Right Key Number

Actually, you've already found a Key Number or several Key Numbers that classify the legal issues in your fact situation. As you researched in C.J.S., Am. Jur. 2d, A.L.R., legal periodicals, treatises, and Restatements, you undoubtedly began your "research notes." On legal pads, laundry receipts, matchbook covers, and other available scraps, you began to write down the citations to on-point cases. When curiosity got the best of you, you hauled off and retrieved those cases from the shelves. The books you used for your case reading were the notorious West Company reports. And on the title pages
{28,29} of those cases {28,29} you found . . .

KEY NUMBERS.

This approach, which I call the "Back Door Approach," is the most efficient way to determine *initially* the identity of your Key Number or Key Numbers. By finding cases on point and then seeing what Key Numbers the West Company's editors used to classify the issues involved in those cases, and consequently in your case, you can conclude that West would use the same Key Numbers to classify the identical legal issues in all future cases. Hence, you figure, all you need to do is run those same Key Numbers and you'll find all other cases on point. Right?

Well, maybe. A few dangers lurk in this mysterious world of legal research, dangers that can destroy your efforts and demolish your growing reputation as an Ace Legal Researcher.

You do indeed *initially* use the Key Numbers found on the title pages of on-point cases. But you do *not* run off stark raving mad, foaming at the mouth and run these Key Numbers without first following:

GOOD'S RULE OF RESEARCH #20:

Woe be unto the legal researcher who runs a Key Number without first *verifying* that Key Number.

Here's the danger. The West Company often must *revise* an existing Main Topic in the American Digest System. Or it might have to create an entirely *new* Main Topic, which might derive from some existing Main Topics such that legal issues that *used to appear* in a Main Topic might now appear in some brand-new Main Topic. So what inevitably happens to those legal researchers who fail to follow Good's Rule of

Research #20? You got it. They run Key Numbers that are no longer valid, fail to find cases, and incorrectly conclude that there are no new cases.

And how do I know? Simple. It's happened to me. Several times. You'd think I'd learn, huh.

So before you rush off to run the Key Numbers you found on the title pages of on-point cases, please pause to engage in these three steps of *verifying a Key Number*: (1) the Analytical Approach, (2) the Index Approach, and (3) the Peel-the-Label Approach. Let's look at each in turn.

§ 8.3(a) Verifying Your Key Number: The Analytical Approach

The Analytical Approach simply entails your going to the latest *Decennial Digest*,
looking up your Main Topic {30,31}, seeing that your Key Number is indeed there, and **{30,31}**
looking around for other potentially relevant Key Numbers. Why the latest *Decennial Digest*? Because you remember from the discussion earlier in this chapter that the "Menus" of each Main Topic are printed only in the *Decennial Digests* and could not possibly be reprinted in each volume of the *General Digest* because they would eat up too many pages. If you're using a *Federal Digest*, then go to the latest hardbound edition of the *Federal Digest*, find your Main Topic, and verify that the Key Numbers are still used and that others, more on point, don't exist.

Let me pause here, before discussing the Index Approach and the Peel-the-Label Approach, to relate a real-world anecdote showing how vital the Analytical Approach can be.

I used to use a jurisdictional topic involving federal diversity of citizenship in some of my legal research courses. Once I wanted to update my materials, which were in dire need of more recent cases. So, in clear violation of Good's Rule of Research #20, I ran off stark raving mad, foaming at the mouth and ran the Key Number classifying the leading cases in this particular field of law. If memory serves, the Key Number was "Courts" Key Number 311. I ran and ran and ran and found no new cases. "This can't be," I whined. Then, after thumping my forehead with the heel of my hand, I went to the latest *Decennial Digest* and *verified* my Key Number using the Analytical Approach. Right there before my eyes in the Main Topic "Courts" was a statement: "The *Courts* Main Topic has been revised such that federal issues are now found in the new Main Topic *Federal Civil Procedure*."

§ 8.3(b) Verifying Your Key Number: The Index Approach

The Index Approach involves using the latest *Descriptive Word Index* {32} in the latest **{32}**
Decennial Digest. Alternatively, if you're working with a "hot" legal topic that is rapidly evolving, then you might check the *Descriptive Word Indexes* at the backs of the "10" volumes in the *General Digest* (remember, they cumulate in each 10th volume). This Index Approach will give you a "fact word" approach to finding other

Key Numbers that the West Company might have used to classify similar cases.

You might strike paydirt with the Index Approach if your research problem is what I call "fact specific" rather than "law specific." Let me explain. A "law specific" problem is one clearly involving a known and identifiable area of law. A federal diversity of citizenship case would be such a problem. In other words, one cannot imagine a judge writing an opinion of law in such an area and using any legal theories that might prompt an editor at the West Company to grab some extraneous Key Number to classify the issues in that case. Thus, when you find such a case, you can pretty well rest assured that the Key Numbers appearing on the title page are the ones used to classify those issues and that there are not other, equally pertinent Key Numbers out there lurking and laughing at you. Thus, in a "law specific" problem, you simply verify your Key Number with the Analytical Approach to make certain that the Main Topic hasn't been revised or that some new Main Topic isn't now used to classify current cases involving the same legal issues.

Not so with "fact specific" research problems. In such a problem, you've got a statement of facts that could give rise to several legal theories being used by judges to resolve the issues. Perhaps another anecdote would best demonstrate the dangers in a "fact specific" research problem.

Back in the early 1970s, right after my graduation from law school, I served as an editor at the National Legal Research Group, a company performing legal research services for practicing attorneys throughout the country. We were researching a rather novel case for an attorney. It seems his client was sitting in a restaurant eating a hamburger. Meanwhile, another patron, in her car outside, was parking in a parking space perpendicular to the restaurant. When the patron went to hit her brakes, she hit the accelerator instead. The car plowed through the brick wall right into plaintiff's french fries. Needless to say, the plaintiff was miffed (and seriously injured) and brought suit against the deeper of the two pockets, the restaurant.

Our legal researcher found a case pretty much on point.[9] It involved the liability of a shopping center for injuries sustained by a plaintiff patron walking on a shopping center sidewalk. Another shopping center patron, parking a car, hit her accelerator instead of the brake. The car jumped the curb and smashed into the plaintiff. The court held that the shopping center was not responsible for erecting a barrier to guard against such a possibility. No liability.

The West Company classified that case to Negligence Key Number 51, entitled "Precautions against injury; Barriers, or covering or guarding dangerous places." Our researcher took that Key Number, ran off stark raving mad, foaming at the mouth, ran the Key Number throughout the American Digest System, and found no other cases on point.

Bad news for the attorney representing the plaintiff in the restaurant case. So we wrote up the Memorandum of Law as best we could, making a stab at a few supportive "policy" arguments.

[9] *Mack v. McGrath*, 150 N.W.2d 681 (Minn. 1967).

About two weeks later, I was editing some other memo for some other attorney. That problem also involved the negligent design of parking lots, though the facts differed substantially from the restaurant case. In any event, there I was editing that other memo when I came across a discussion of a case involving the liability of a restaurant for injuries sustained by a patron clobbered by a car jumping the curb of a perpendicular parking space and smashing into the restaurant's brick wall.[10] Yes, indeed. The case was dead on point to the attorney's case analyzed in the *first* memo. It even involved the *same kind of defendant*!

So I picked up the phone, called the first attorney, and said, "Well, we've done some more research . . . ." That was true! "And guess what we found?" I gave him the facts of the restaurant case and its citation, and promised to mail him a copy right away. Naturally, he used the case to extract a huge settlement from the restaurant's insurer.

We escaped with our reputation as Ace Legal Researcher still intact. But I knew we had blown it. What went wrong?

I went to the law library and looked up the second case. Whereas the first case was classified to Negligence Key Number 51, the second case—involving a restaurant, which was an "inn" under the common law—was classified to Main Topic "Innkeepers" Key Number 10.3, which was entitled "Injury to person of guest; Defects in premises or appliances in general." Two identical cases classified not only under different Key Numbers but under different Main Topics! Why? Because the judges used two different legal theories to dispose of these "fact specific" situations.

I then went to the *Descriptive Word Index* and found under the fact words "Parking Lots" a cross-reference to the Innkeepers Key Number 10.3. If the researcher had verified his Key Number with an Index Approach, he would have discovered the identical fact situation classified under an entirely different Main Topic and entirely different Key Number.

If *you* have a "fact specific" problem, I urge you too to verify your Key Numbers by consulting the appropriate *Descriptive Word Indexes.*

§ 8.3(c) Verifying Your Key Number: The Peel-the-Label Approach

If you think my tongue is firmly in my cheek, you're right. It is. But the Peel-the-Label Approach is indeed a very valid approach to Key Number verification. Let me explain.

When the West Company revises a Main Topic or adds a new Main Topic, it announces this publishing event on the spine of the *General Digest* containing the new Menu of the new or revised Main Topic. Now in librarian lingo, the *General Digest* is clearly a set of "reference" books. A "reference" book means if you try to sneak it out of the law library, the Automatic Book Detector that sends radioactive rays through your body each time you enter and exit the law library sets off the most horrifying alarms and flashing red lights, prompting the entire law library to look at you with

[10]*Denisewich v. Pappas*, 198 A.2d 144 (R.I. 1964).

total disgust and armed guards to surround you as you sheepishly hand over the offending title squirreled away in your bookbag. Anyway, to discourage such embarrassments, and to maintain their "reference" collections, the Reference Librarians come equipped with little labels that say "REF" and that they prominently display on the spines of "reference books" and that then hide the crucial "New Topic" or "Revised Topic" information on the spines of the *General Digest* volume containing just the New Topic or Revised Topic you need to complete your research. To guard against *missing* this vital information, you then sneak a peek, make sure no one's looking, and "peel the label" to see if that particular volume has a "New Topic" or "Revised Topic" notice on the spine.

I'm only kidding. Please believe me. The Reference Librarians wouldn't dare cover up such information. So please do *not* peel any labels. You'll be sorry if you do, for they too are wired to those same alarms and flashing lights . . . .

Quite seriously, you do have to scout out the spines of the latest *General Digest* series. Failure to do so will cause extreme pain and embarrassment. Let me prove my point.

In the mid-1980s, I taught a two-week paralegal training course at the United States Department of Justice for paralegals serving the U.S. Attorneys' Offices and other branches of Justice. In one course, I was using a research topic involving the Freedom of Information Act (FOIA). The class, using Step One and Step Two sources, had found quite a few on-point cases, all classified to Main Topic "Records," Key Number 14 (entitled "Access to Records or Files"). Many class members ran off stark raving mad, foaming at the mouth and ran Records Key Number 14 in the American Digest System covering the time period not covered by their background research. And they found *no new cases*. No new cases on the Freedom of Information Act? Impossible.

One class member, however, did it the right way and *verified* the Key Number first. By looking at the spines of the *General Digest*, she saw part of a notation peeking out from beneath the "Reference" label. Carefully looking both ways to make certain no one was watching, she "peeled the label" and found a notation saying "Including Revised Topic Records." By using the Peel-the-Label Approach, she discovered that Records Key Number 14 *did not even exist*! The numbers in the new revised Main Topic went like this: 10, 11, 12, 13, 15 . . . . Then she looked at the end of the Main Topic and found that 24 new, additional Key Numbers had been created to accommodate the myriad issues facing the courts in FOIA litigation.

Here's what had happened: in the old days, way back in the 1960s when FOIA was passed, the West Company simply classified the smattering of cases under the broad Key Number 14, "Access to Records or Files." But then the cases began to roll out of the courts, so the West Company had to change the Key Numbering system to accommodate the issues confronting the courts. Needless to say, the West Company cannot very well go back to older volumes of court reports and put little Post-it Notes on the title pages saying, "Hey, fool, use this Key Number at your peril. It no longer exists! Ha, ha, ha, ha, ha, ha . . . ." Instead, the West Company changes the Main Topic and announces the change on the spine of the *General Digest* where the change first appears. And, of course, along comes the Reference Librarian with his reference labels saying "REF," which he promptly puts on the spine to make sure no one takes the book out of the law library. In doing so, he hides this vital information from soon-to-be-hoodwinked legal researchers.[11]

§ 8.3(d) The Finding Phase: Summary

So there you have it. You find the right Key Number or Key Numbers from the title pages of on-point cases found in Steps One and Two. You then verify those Key Numbers by checking out the Menu of the Main Topic in the latest *Decennial Digest* (the Analytical Approach). If the research problem is "fact specific," you verify the Key Number by playing word games in the appropriate *Descriptive Word Index*. And finally you remain ever vigilant, carefully watching the spines of the latest *General Digest* volumes for New Main Topics or Revised Main Topics.

Then, and only then, do you begin basic chronological case research: running Key Numbers in the American Digest system.

§ 8.4 The Use Phase: Where to Start Running Key Numbers

Now for the fun part.

You've found and verified a Key Number or several Key Numbers to run in the American Digest System to find on-point case law. Many legal researchers will simply mosey over to the American Digest System and run their Key Numbers {33} *without* **{33}**
any thought about overlapping the research already completed by the background sources they've read.

You, on the other hand, having read this riveting bestseller, know better. You know that it makes no sense to duplicate the research of Wilbur. He's already researched your issue and written about it in C.J.S., Am. Jur. 2d, A.L.R., legal periodicals, and Restatements of the Law. In those sources and in any available supplements, he has cited cases on point. And how did he find these cases on point? Did they fall off the shelves into his waiting arms? Did he trip over them in the aisles? Did his boss provide a list?

No. Wilbur ran Key Numbers in the American Digest System to find those cases. Do you, armed with your Key Numbers (the same ones Wilbur used) want to re-do what Wilbur has already done?

Of course not.

So here's the trick: your strategy is (1) to figure out where Wilbur stopped researching in the West court reports (the Stop Cite), (2) to find out where that point in the court reports is digested in the American Digest System, and (3) to run Key

[11]I'm only kidding!

Numbers in the digest system from that point to the present day. By using this strategy, you will reduce Key Number research to the bare minimum.

Let's see how it works.

§ 8.4(a) Where Wilbur Stopped: the Stop Cite

Please recall the *second most important page in all of legal research*, originally discussed in Chapter 6 in § 6.5(d). You'll find this page at the *front* of any West Company supplementation feature. For example, at the front of the C.J.S. pocket part, you'll find a table, which tells you the precise volume and page number in each West court report where Wilbur stopped his research. The volume number and page number, from any *one* given court report, constitute the Stop Cite.

Below I've typed part of the Second Most Important Page in All of Legal Research so that you can see, as examples, the actual Stop Cites for F.2d and A.2d. The
{9} entire page appears as Page 9 in the Visual Aids.

The Second Most Important Page in All of Legal Research

This Cumulative Annual Pocket Part contains selective supplementary material derived from decisions closing with cases reported in:

. . .

Federal Reporter, Second Series............................943 F.2d 1319

. . .

Atlantic Reporter, Second Series...........................596 A.2d 373

. . .

Suppose you don't use C.J.S. or any other West Company publication. In that event, you won't find the *second most important page in all of legal research*, for most other publishing companies unfortunately do not provide that information in their supplements. Well, all is not lost. You can figure out a perfectly workable Stop Cite yourself: just spot the most recent case cited in a supplement and use its citation as the Stop Cite. It won't precisely mark where Wilbur stopped, but you'll know he at least got that far in a particular court report.

The important point is this. In the system of court reports publishing American case law, a volume and a page number is not only a citation showing "location information." That citation also shows a precise week in time. Thus, if a researcher found a case at 596 A.2d 373 and that researcher was thorough in citing all cases up until that time, then it makes little sense to research the law *before* that time, that is, to the left of 596 A.2d 373 on the shelf. No, you want only to research to the *right* of 596 A.2d 373 on the shelf, from the point where your background source *stopped*.

To grasp this notion, you must also realize that the point in time represented by

596 A.2d 373 is the identical point in time represented by 943 F.2d 1319. Take a careful look at the Visual Aids for Chapter 6 above. Also study Figure 5 on page 79. You absolutely must understand this concept before we can proceed.

Conceptually, think of the Stop Cite as the end of the shelf as it existed when the background source author completed his research. The very next week, advance sheets began to hit the shelves and continued, one each week, to the present day. Those volumes of court reports no doubt contain on-point cases. You, therefore, must *begin* your research where the background sources *stopped*. In the case of C.J.S., the source tells you where it stopped by listing all Stop Cites on the *second most important page in all of legal research.*

Please make a mental note: when you learn how to do federal legislative research in Chapter 12, the *second most important page in all of legal research* will become vitally important. So expend the mental energy now to learn the significance of the information appearing on this page.

§ 8.4(b) Where You Start

Naturally enough, you *start* where Wilbur *stopped*. There's one slight problem, however. Wilbur tells you where he stopped by giving you a Stop Cite on the *second most important page in all of legal research.* He does not tell you where in the American Digest System he stopped running Key Numbers.

So wouldn't it be great if you could take a Stop Cite and find out exactly where in the digest system that particular point in time is digested? If you could find out where your Stop Cite is digested, then you'd know where Wilbur *stopped* running Key Numbers. And if you know where Wilbur *stopped* running Key Numbers, you then know where to *start* running Key Numbers. Well, if you have the volume and page number of *any* West Company court report, you can find out exactly where in the digest system that case is digested by referring to . . . ta-dah . . .

THE SINGLE MOST IMPORTANT PAGE IN ALL OF LEGAL RESEARCH! {34} **{34}**

At the front of each volume of the *General Digest* (always pick the latest one), you will find a table showing where each volume and page of each court report in the entire National Reporter System is digested. You'll find a separate table for each West court report so that if you have a Stop Cite from A.2d, you can determine exactly where that citation in A.2d is digested in the digest system. And if you know where that citation exists in the digest system, *you then know where Wilbur stopped running Key Numbers.* After all, it would be that digest that Wilbur used to find that case in the first place.

Let's see what the table might look like, using A.2d as an example. Although the Visual Aids for this chapter will show the process unfold and samples of the pertinent pages, I thought I'd type part of the table for illustration purposes. As I write this book in the summer of 1992, the *SINGLE most important page in all of legal research* from Volume 8 of the *General Digest* looks like this:

The Single Most Important Page in All of Legal Research

ATLANTIC 2d—Cont'd

Vol.	**Page**		**Vol.**	**Page**	**Digest**
. . . .					
511	310	to	513	42	1 General 7th
513	43	to	514	723	2 General 7th
514	724	to	515	1078	3 General 7th
. . . (similar entries for 53 more *General Digest* volumes)					
588	1066	to	590	105	57 General 7th
590	106	to	591	796	58 General 7th
591	797	to	592	148	59 General 7th
592	149	to	593	477	1 General 8th
593	478	to	594	905	2 General 8th
594	906	to	596	373	3 General 8th
596	374	to	597	806	4 General 8th
597	807	to	598	1098	5 General 8th
598	1099	to	599	1052	6 General 8th
599	1053	to	600	1003	7 General 8th
600	1004	to	601	1387	8 General 8th

From the above, you can readily see that if your Stop Cite is 596 A.2d 373, then that particular citation is digested in Volume 3 of the *General Digest.* That volume, therefore, is the last volume of the *General Digest* that Wilbur used when he ran Key Numbers to find all those cases he cited in the background sources.

And if Wilbur *stopped* running Key Numbers at the end of Volume 3, then you *start* running Key Numbers in Volume 4.

Before we see some tricks of the trade in actually running Key Numbers, let's pause and look at the *Digest Overlap* Phenomenon. As you can see from the above table, the *General Digest, 7th Series* ended in Volume 59. This was the final volume published in December of 1991. Those 59 volumes will be collated and magically transformed into the *Tenth Decennial, Part One.* But that decennial won't be complete for 18 months or so. During the interim, this table will show both the *General Digest 7th Series* (covering 1987-1991) and the current *General Digest 8th Series* (covering 1992-present). When the *Tenth Decennial, Part One* is complete, the *General Digest 7th Series* will disappear from the tables on the *single most important page in all of legal research* and will be replaced by a single entry for the *Tenth Decennial, Part One.*

Let's also pause to summarize what you've learned. We keep track of time in the judicial system by volume and page numbers in any given court report. If you have a citation showing where someone stopped researching in a court report, you can then consult the *SINGLE most important page in all of legal research* to determine where that court report is digested in the digest system. Where that citation is digested is where you *start* running Key Numbers.

In a nutshell, so to speak, you merely have to compare the information on the
SECOND most important page in all of legal research {9} with the information on the **{9}**
SINGLE most important page in all of legal research {34}. That comparison will always **{34}**
tell you exactly where to *start* running Key Numbers.

Finally, if you understand the concepts behind those two pages, you're well on your way to becoming an Ace Legal Researcher.

§ 8.4(c) Where You Stop

Typically, when you begin to run Key Numbers, you'll begin in some volume of the current *General Digest*, at the point where Wilbur stopped running Key Numbers. There might be times when you fail to find good background authority or cannot trust the background authority you've found (some obscure treatise or some flimsy law review article). In that case, you have to trace Key Numbers throughout the American Digest System, back through the *Decennial Digests* until you've reached what you consider to be the Dark Ages.

Even when you run Key Numbers through previous *Decennial Digests*, at some point you reach the dreaded *General Digest* volumes. Recall why they are "dreaded." In one volume of a *Decennial Digest* you find 10 years' worth (or five years' worth) of headnotes. In one volume of a *General Digest*, however, you find one month's worth of case law. Thus, running Key Numbers through the *General Digest* can be a painful experience. You open the first volume, consult your Key Number, find out that it's not there because no cases were classified to that Key Number during that one-month time period, go to the next volume, find no cases there either, and the next, and the next . . . no wonder you're losing your mind.

§ 8.4(c)(i) Table of Key Numbers

Well, there is a better way. A shortcut will enable you to determine which volumes in the *General Digest* have *no headnotes classified to your particular Key Number* before you even pick up the volume. Now don't worry, I haven't flipped into ESP or tea leaves or other weird devices for predicting the future. Instead, I'm simply a heavy user of . . .

THE TABLE OF KEY NUMBERS {35}. **{35}**

In the back of *each volume* of *General Digest* you'll find a "Table of Key Numbers." This table lists all Main Topics in the American Digest System along with all Key Numbers under each topic. The table then shows which volumes of the *General Digest* contain headnotes classified to that particular Key Number.

Now, stay with me for a minute.

The Table of Key Numbers is that other feature in the *General Digest* that cumulates within each 10 volumes. Thus, in Volume 1, you'll find a Table of Key Numbers just for Volume 1. But in Volume 2, you'll find a Table of Key Numbers for Volumes 1 and 2. In Volume 3, you'll find a Table of Key Numbers for Volumes 1, 2, and 3. And so on up to Volume 10, which has a Table of Key Numbers for Volumes 1-10. Then, in Volume 11, the process starts all over again. In Volume 11, you find a Table of Key Numbers just for Volume 11. Then, in Volume 12, you'll find one for Volumes 11 and 12. And so on up to Volume 20, which has a Table of Key Numbers for Volumes 11-20. Volume 21 then starts the process all over again. And on and on throughout the next five-year period.

Thus, when you begin to run Key Numbers in the *General Digest*, the *first* thing
{36} you do is to check the Tables of Key Numbers {36} in the back of each 10th volume and in the latest volume. Then, making sure that no one comes along to mess up your system, pull out each volume of *General Digest* having cases classified to your Key Numbers, just about an inch or two right there on the shelf. Then pull each volume off and run Key Numbers in those volumes having headnotes classified to your Key Number. Ignore all the others; you won't find headnotes there.

§ 8.4(c)(ii) Running Key Numbers

Running Key Numbers, of course, is not exactly the most thrilling of experiences, for it entails reading headnotes quickly to ascertain that the cases they summarize either
{37} are or are not on point {37}. You hope to have a research problem with a "thin" headnote, not a problem with a "fat" headnote. Unfortunately, as you'll discover when you see the Visual Aids for this chapter, you'll find out that Wally and Mipsie's and Dr. Schwartz' case is classified under a very fat headnote entitled "Damages." That is, *all* medical malpractice cases involving the issue of recoverable damages are classified under just *one* Key Number. Rats. That means that you have to read each headnote until you reach the damaged body part clearly eliminating it from consideration. You'd prefer, of course, to have a "thin" headnote such as "Damages for Wrongful Conception." But who said life was fair or legal research was fun?

So off you go, running Key Numbers in the *Decennials* if necessary and through the pertinent volumes of the *General Digest* (after having checked the Table of Key Numbers). And then you run your Key Numbers to the *end* of the *General Digest*. And then you've finished?

§ 8.4(c)(iii) The NO ZONE

No. You haven't finished. There remains the evil "NO ZONE," not to be confused with "OZONE" or lack thereof.

You must realize that each West court report is growing at the rate of *one advance sheet per week*, while the *General Digest* is growing at the rate of *one volume per month*. Thus, the shelf itself is always ahead of the digest. Put another way, there exists, beyond the digest, another realm, another dimension in time, perhaps a whole new and bizarre universe where light bends and researchers make mistakes. That, friends, is the NO ZONE.

The following schematic shows this newly discovered, scientifically documented sphere of confusion.

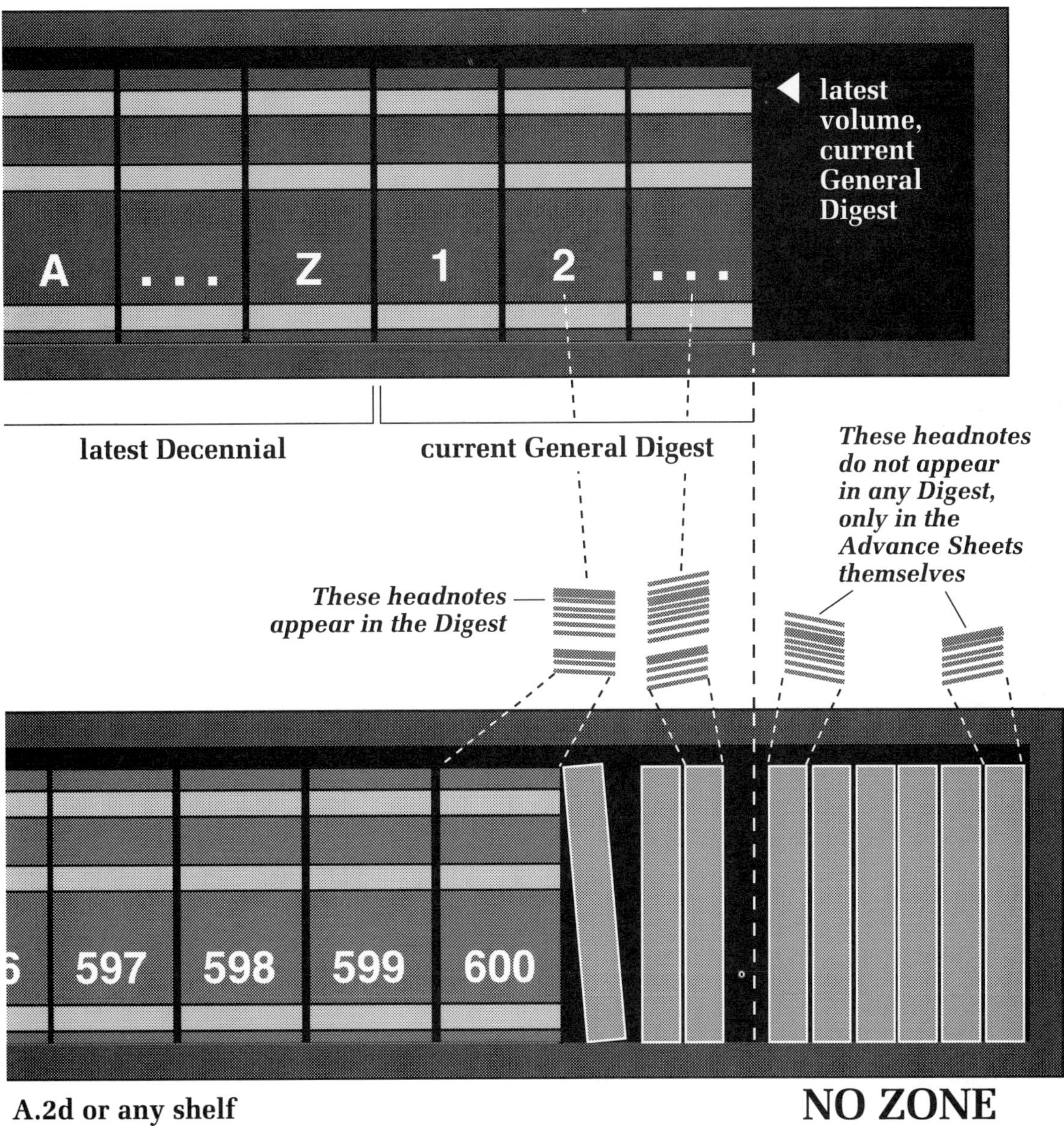

Figure 7

The NO ZONE

As you can see from the above figure, every time the *General Digest* tries to catch up with the advance sheets, along comes another advance sheet stretching out the NO ZONE farther and farther until another *General Digest* volume comes along to shorten it. But the *General Digest* never catches up, and the NO ZONE is always there. For example, the *average size* of the NO ZONE in F.2d is *12 volumes*. That's 18,000 pages of federal circuit court case law that is *unretrievable* in the American Digest System. The *only* way you can retrieve those cases is to follow:

GOOD'S RULE OF RESEARCH #21:

You must always run Key Numbers through the NO ZONES of each court report having relevant cases.

"And how do I find out where the NO ZONE begins in any given court report?" you ask.

"Simple," I respond. "On the **SINGLE most important page in all of legal**
{34} **research** {34}." Notice on the table in Section 8.5(b), the one showing the *single most important page in all of legal research*, that the NO ZONE for A.2d would begin at 601 A.2d 1387. The page number of that citation leads me to believe that page 1387 *ends* volume 601. If so, then your NO ZONE *begins* at 602 A.2d page 1. If that volume is an advance sheet, you run Key Numbers in the *front* of that advance sheet. If that volume is a bound volume, you run Key Numbers in the *back* of that bound volume.

"How many NO ZONES do I have to worry about?" you ask fearfully.

"All containing potentially relevant cases," I respond fearsomely.

If you're conducting a *national* legal research problem, then you'd have to run Key Numbers through:

1. All 7 *Regional Reporters*.
2. The 2 West state reporters (N.Y.S.2d, and Cal. Rptr. 2d).
3. Pertinent federal reporters (probably F. Supp. and F.2d, and maybe S. Ct., depending on the legal issue).

Believe me, this task—running Key Numbers through the NO ZONES of pertinent court reports—is the most burdensome task of all *and* the most important task of all. If you fail to make it a habit *always* to run Key Numbers through *all* pertinent NO ZONES, then the odds are *100%* that you will miss a crucial on-point case at some point in your career. Every case ever decided, every case ever published, every case you care about makes it grand debut on the shelf in the NO ZONE. There it sits all by itself for several weeks, if not several months, before its headnote is grabbed by the latest *General Digest* volume. The *only* way to retrieve this case is by running Key Numbers through the NO ZONE.

I can make NO ZONE research a bit less burdensome by urging you to use the "Week Numbers" on the spines of advance sheets {38}. In many law school libraries {38}
and large law firm or federal agency libraries, you'll find "dual subscriptions" to the advance sheets. If you try to keep track of volumes and pages as you make your way through the dual subscriptions, you'll go blind and bats. But if you focus on the sequential "Week Number" marking the beginning of your NO ZONE, then you can readily determine which advance sheet pamphlet awaits your next move.

Running Key Numbers through the NO ZONES is a burden, at best. Usually, the NO ZONE will begin in an advance sheet, but sometimes it might begin in a bound volume. To run Key Numbers in a bound volume, look in the *back* of the book and you'll find the Key Number Digest. In an advance sheet, you'll find the Key Number Digest in the *front* {39}. In either place, look up your Main Topic. If no cases in that {39}
volume are classified to your Main Topic, the Main Topic's name will simply be omitted. Under a Main Topic having cases in that volume classified to the topic, you'll find the Key Numbers and headnotes arranged just as they are in the digests themselves: sequentially by Key Number, by type and hierarchy of court within Key Number. If no cases in that volume are classified to a particular Key Number, the Key Number is simply omitted. Therein lies the burden of running Key Numbers through the NO ZONE. When doing it, you'll no doubt recall:

GOOD'S RULE OF RESEARCH #19:

A great deal of legal research involves looking for what's *not* there.

And therein lies the trap. Running Key Numbers through the NO ZONE usually does not bear fruit. It's common to make it all the way through a NO ZONE and find zilch, zero, zip. But you must remember that in the NO ZONE sinister forces and weird time dimensions can wreak havoc on your research technique and ruin your growing reputation as an Ace Legal Researcher. These sinister forces combine to conspire to bring you to your knees. They begin by planting this tempting thought in your overworked head:

"Why bother?" these forces whisper.

"You didn't find cases the last time you ran Key Numbers through the NO ZONE," they egg you on.

"You'll save time if you skip it this time," they tantalize.

Sometime the forces resort to out and out bribery:

"Forget it this time, and we'll buy you a beer," they coo.

These forces, don't you see, are well aware of:

GOOD'S RULE OF RESEARCH #22

When you run Key Numbers through the NO ZONE, you'll find no cases there. When you *fail* to run Key Numbers through the NO ZONE, your opponent will find the cases there.

§ 8.5 The West Key System: A Quick Review

The American Digest System is the *only* subject matter rearrangement of *all* of American case law. Using it, without doubt, is the most difficult and confusing part of legal research. To master the intricacies of the system will require patience, time, and practice on your part. But make no mistake: mastering the West Key System is part and parcel of becoming an Ace Legal Researcher. Failing to master its intricacies will only delight one person: your opponent (and, perhaps, the sinister forces awaiting you in the dreaded NO ZONE).

So here's a quick review. West divided all of American law into 435 subject matter
{30} categories called Main Topics {30}. It divided each Main Topic into subtopics and
{31} subsubtopics and subsubsubtopics {31}. When its analytical arrangement of a Main
Topic was complete, it numbered each analytical subpart and gave that subpart a
sequential Key Number. Editors at the West Company could then write headnotes for
the zillion cases it publishes, classifying each headnote to the appropriate Key
Number. It could then print these headnotes (1) on the title page of the case itself
{28,29} {28,29}, (2) in the back of the bound volume where the case is published or in the front
{39} of the advance sheet where the case is published {39}, and (3) in the appropriate digests
so that legal researchers could find any case on any point of law in America from the
{33,37} 1600s to the present day {33,37}.

These digests make up a national series of digests called the *Decennial Digests*, published every ten years since 1906 and every five years since 1981, and the *General Digest*, published every month to fill in the time gap between the latest *Decennial Digest* and the present day. Other digests include the four *Federal Digests*, the four *Regional Digests*, and the 47 *State Digests*.

You, the legal researcher, faced with the task of retrieving all cases on a given
point of law, can identify the correct Key Numbers and trace them through the digests,
a task known in the trade as "Running Key Numbers." To identify the correct Key
Number, you will find on-point cases in background sources and see which Key
Numbers the West Company uses, by studying the title pages of those on-point cases
{28,29} as reported in the West Company court reports {28,29}. But before rushing off stark
raving mad, foaming at the mouth to run those Key Numbers, you will *verify* those Key
Numbers by checking the Main Topic in the latest *Decennial Digest* (Analytical
{30,31} Approach) {30,31}, by consulting the *Descriptive Word Index* in the latest *General* or
{32} *Decennial Digest* (Index Approach) {32}, and by perusing the spines of the current

General Digest volumes to make certain that no new Main Topics have been created or that your Main Topic has not been recently revised (Peel-the-Label Approach).

Then, armed with the correct Key Numbers, you will *begin* running Key Numbers where your background sources *stopped* running Key Numbers. You can figure out the exact spot by comparing any Stop Cite found on the *second most important page*
in all of legal research (the table at the front of the C.J.S. pocket part) {9} with the **{9}**
appropriate table found on the *single most important page in all of legal research* (the
tables appearing at the front of the latest *General Digest*) {34}. **{34}**

When you find out where Wilbur *stopped* in the American Digest System, you then *start* running Key Numbers at that same point all the way to the end of the current *General Digest*. To make this onerous task more palatable, you check the *Table of Key*
Numbers {35, 36} in the back of each 10th volume in the *General Digest* and in the back **{35,36}**
of the latest volume of the *General Digest*. These tables reveal which volumes of the preceding 10 volumes actually contain cases classified to your Key Numbers.

Then, finally, you bail out of the *General Digest* and return to the actual shelves
of the court reports themselves {38}. You check the *single most important page in all* **{38}**
of legal research {34}, for it tells you exactly where the digest system *stopped* **{34}**
collecting headnotes in *each* set of West court reports. Having established the exact beginning of each NO ZONE in each pertinent court report, you then run Key Numbers through the NO ZONES to the last advance sheet on the shelves for each pertinent court report.

You then sigh with relief, "Finished. Finally I've finished." You walk away from the shelf, back to your study alcove or back to your apartment, ready to write your Memorandum of Law.

As soon as you round the corner of the shelves and head back to your study alcove, the librarian, who's been lying in wait watching your every move, sneaks to the shelf you just left and places the next advance sheet at the end of the shelf.

In it, naturally enough, is . . . a case on point.

A strange world, indeed. Legal research. A task without end.

§ 8.6 Running Key Numbers: A Roadmap for Research

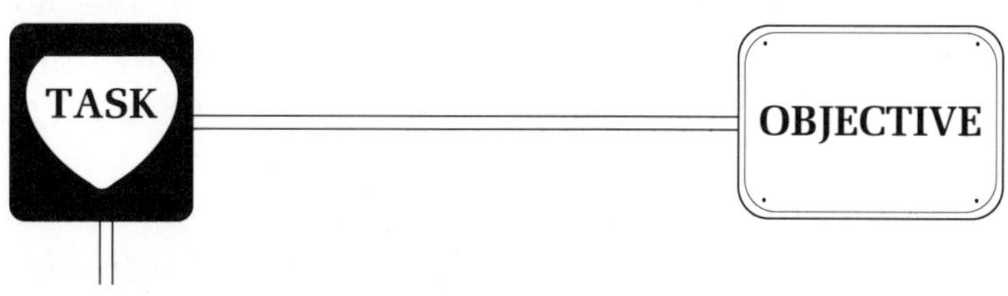

Task	Objective
Find the Correct Key Numbers:	
Check title page of case.	Find correct Key Numbers.
Verify Key Numbers:	
1. Check Main Topic in latest *Decennial Digest*.	Look for other potential Key Numbers.
2. Check *Descriptive Word Index* in latest *Decennial* or *General Digest*.	Look for other potential Key Numbers.
3. Check spines of latest *General Digest* volumes.	Look for new Main Topics or revised Main Topics.
Run Key Numbers:	
1. Check *second most important page in all of legal research* at front of C.J.S. pocket part.	Jot down Stop Cite for any given report (use A.2d as an example).
2. Check *single most important page in all of legal research* at front of latest volume of *General Digest*.	Establish the volume in the *General Digest* where the Stop Cite is digested.
3. Go to the *Table of Key Numbers* in the back of each 10th volume of *General Digest after* the volume established in step 2 above and look up your Key Numbers.	Jot down the volumes of *General Digest* containing cases classified to your Key Numbers. Ignore all others.
4. Run Key Numbers in those volumes of *General Digest*.	Jot down cites to on-point cases.

5. Return to the *single most important page in all of legal research* at the front of the latest volume of the *General Digest.* For each court report containing cases you should find, jot down the beginning of the NO ZONE (look at the end of the table for each court report).	Establish beginning points of each pertinent NO ZONE.
6. Run Key Numbers in *all* pertinent NO ZONES.	Jot down cites to any on-point cases.

§ 8.7 Key Numbers: Visual Aids {28-39}

In the Visual Aids booklet, I have reproduced selected pages from the variety of sources and features you would use in running Key Numbers to find all on-point cases. These are pages you would encounter in researching Wally and Mipsie's case. On each page, in the box, you'll find my commentary showing exactly what the researcher is doing to find Key Numbers, verify Key Numbers, and run Key Numbers in digests and NO ZONES.

Please note that these pages are selective. In the real world of legal research, you would consult many more pages, especially those you'll undoubtedly stumble over in your very first efforts. You will, most likely, go down lots of dead ends, locating irrelevant information, getting frustrated, and, yes, perhaps even *losing your mind.*

But if you'll follow the above instructions, step by step, and study the Visual Aids, page by page, you'll begin to learn how to do legal research *without losing your mind.*

CHAPTER 9

STEP FOUR: SHEPARDIZING CASES

§ 9.1 Strange Little Men Shooting Arrows

As you read cases, you undoubtedly will notice that one case cites other cases. Indeed, one case might cite scores or hundreds of other cases. One case gets its law from these previous cases—the doctrine of stare decisis in action. And, no doubt, in your research, you often *find* other on-point cases simply by reading on-point cases and then looking up the other cases they cite.

Perhaps you didn't know it, but each case in American jurisprudence has inside the opinion itself a strange little man with a bow and arrow. This little man is a shooter of "citation arrows." As the court that wrote the opinion cites each case in the opinion, the little man gets out another arrow and "shoots" that previous case with a "citation arrow." Necessarily, the shooter of citation arrows can only aim in one direction on the shelf—to the left, back in time, to previous cases the court is citing to support its analysis of the law.

Of course, when you pick a case off the shelf and read it, you can instantaneously see all the previous cases shot by the little man with citation arrows. Right there in the opinion are citations to those previous cases, and, if you're so inclined, you can then retrieve those cases from the shelf and read them. As you do, of course, you'll find that each of them has a strange little man, who, in turn, is shooting previous cases, which, if you're so inclined, you can retrieve and read and find other strange little men who're shooting previous cases, which have strange little men shooting previous cases, which have . . . . A strange world indeed.

I realize you might be doubting my sanity right now. So to prove that cases really do have little men shooting citation arrows at previous cases, I uncovered a rare depiction of this phenomenon as it actually unfolds in the law library. An enterprising photographer, in the stealth of night, actually captured this shooting war by taking the following picture:

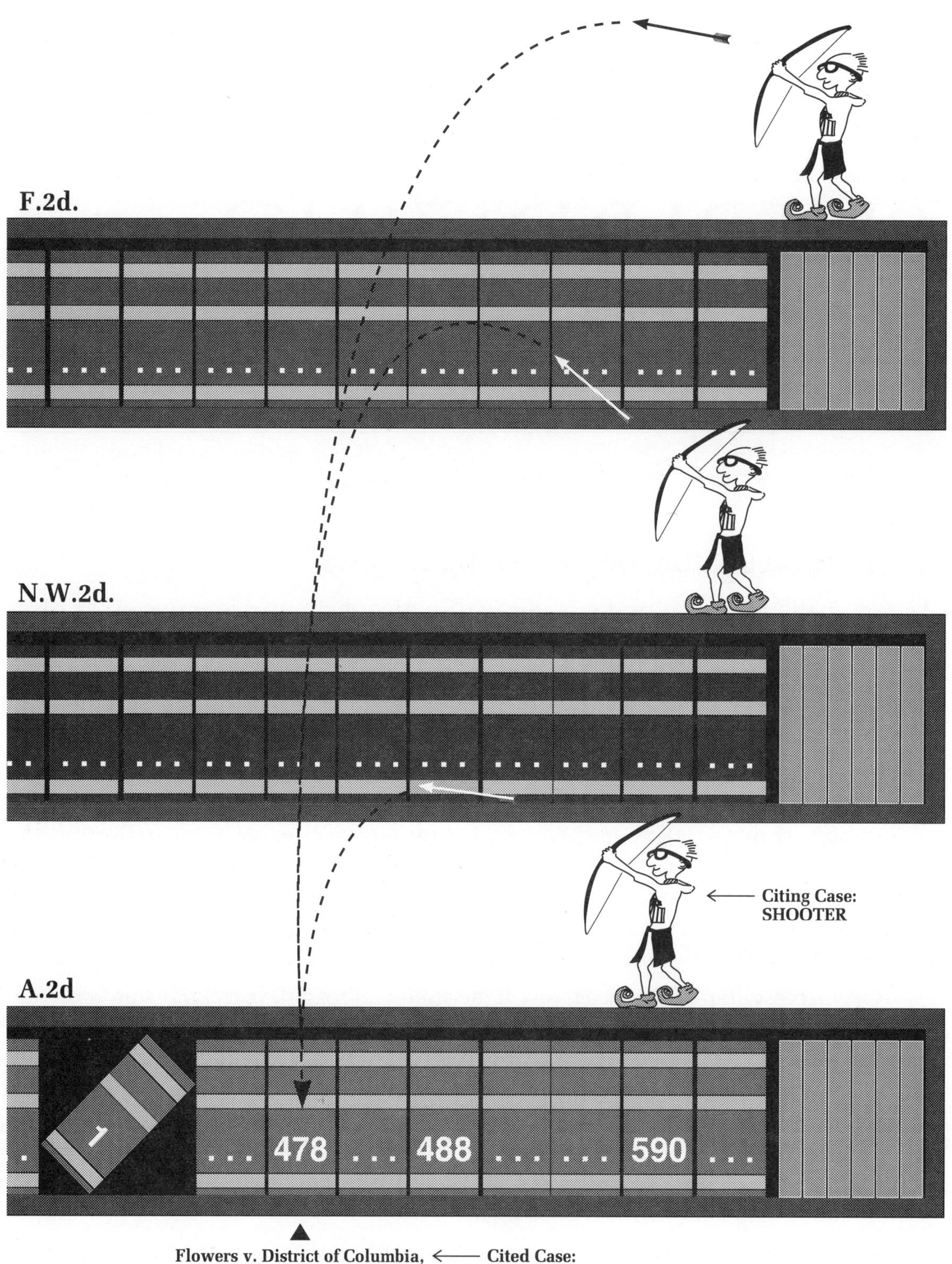

Figure 8
Strange Little Men Shooting Arrows

§ 9.1(a) Your Case Becomes a Target

So you've found a case on point. Perhaps it's *Flowers v. District of Columbia*, a case involving the recoverability of damages for the costs of rearing an unwanted child born as the result of a negligent sterilization operation. You can pick up *Flowers*, read it, and actually see all the other cases shot by the little man in *Flowers* as he shot previous cases throughout the law library. In fact, *Flowers* might be the case depicted in the figure above.

Now *Flowers* was decided in 1983. Sometime during that year the law librarians of the universe put the advance sheet containing *Flowers* on the shelf. At that magic moment in time, *Flowers* became not only a "Shooter of Citation Arrows" but also a "Target." When *Flowers* made its grand debut on the shelf, guess what happened? Suddenly, all over the universe, legal researchers began to *find Flowers* as they were researching cases involving doctors who had botched sterilization operations and greedy parents who had seen the opportunity to fleece a rich doctor and plaintiffs' lawyers who had seen big bucks in their futures. Lots of researchers all over the world began to pick *Flowers* from the shelf. These researchers began to *cite Flowers* in their trial briefs to judges. These judges then began to *cite Flowers* in their opinions. Those opinions were then appealed by the losers, the appellants, who also *cited Flowers* in their briefs to appellate courts. Finally those appellate courts wrote opinions and sent them to the West Publishing Company. The West Publishing Company then published those opinions, first in advance sheets and later in bound volumes, and sent them to the law librarians of the universe.

And the law librarians of the universe put advance sheets and later bound volumes on the library shelves. Suddenly sitting on those shelves, leering at *you*, the legal researcher who has just pulled *Flowers* from the shelf, are cases with strange little men inside the opinions *shooting citation arrows at* Flowers!

And you can't see them. But they're there.

Thus, *Flowers*, indeed *every case* in American case law, is both a shooter of citation arrows (which you *can* see, just read the opinion) and a target of citation arrows (which you *can't* see because they happened *after* the case was published in the court report).

You can readily see that your task as a legal researcher is to uncover those cases taking potshots at your case, for those cases might very well do some very nasty things to your case. Before moving on to a study of the methods you'll use to uncover these cases shooting at your case, let's define some terms.

§ 9.1(b) "Citing Cases" and the "Cited Case"

The *cited case* is the one you've found in the research process. It's the one you intend to use in your memo or brief. It's the one you're worried about, as you look paranoically around the library knowing that those other cases—the *citing cases* that lurk there—are shooting your case with citation arrows (because they involve the same point of law) or perhaps with Scud missiles (because they're reversing or overruling your case).

§ 9.1(b)(i) Two Kinds of Citing Cases

These citing cases can be one of two kinds (and it is vital that you learn these two distinctions right now). One citing case that cites your case might be . . . are you ready? . . . *your case*. That's right. Your case might have cited your case. (I know, this really gets weird.) But think about it. What might have happened in your case? Mightn't the loser have gotten mad enough to appeal the case higher up in the court system? And if the loser appealed, when did that appeal take place? *After* your case was already printed and sent to the shelf. So perhaps in *Flowers* the loser appealed the case to a higher court and that higher court then wrote an opinion affirming (or worse, *reversing*) the case you're about to rely upon in your memo or brief. So one citing case is: the same case higher up on appeal in the appellate process. A later *Flowers* might cite the *Flowers* you're about to stake your reputation on. The opinion or opinions arising in the appellate process are called *case history*.

As you strive toward the status of Ace Legal Researcher, you'll begin to pay attention to the status of the court deciding the cited case. You'll see that the cited case was decided by an intermediate appellate court and immediately begin to worry that the case might have been appealed to the highest state court. Or you'll notice that the cited case was decided by the highest state court, recognize that the issue involved is a pure state law issue, realize that no *federal* appeal could possibly take place, and then calm down and realize that the chances are slim indeed that your cited case has any subsequent case history whatsoever. In sum, you simply begin to hearken back and remember:

GOOD'S RULE OF RESEARCH #1:
Woe be unto the legal researcher who fails to notice the status of the court deciding the case.

The other citing cases are just that: *other* cases. That is, *Jones v. Smith* or *Green v. Hale* or any other case from anywhere in the country might cite your case. These other cases (citing cases) might stand up and applaud the reasoning in your case (the cited case) or they might hold their bellies and laugh at the stupidity of the reasoning in your case. Or, and here's the real danger, if your case is kind of old, perhaps the court that decided your case no longer likes its doctrine or its reasoning. Suppose the court decides in a later case that your case has got to go. That later court, the same one that decided your case in the first place or a higher court with the power to do so, might very well *overrule* your case, yes that one, yes the one you're about to cite in your memo or brief, the same one that your opponent will astutely point out to the judge was overruled in the recent case of *Jones v. Smith*.

As I write this chapter, attorneys in Washington are arguing the case of *Pennsylvania Planned Parenthood*. Now I do not know what the outcome of that case will be. Perhaps *Roe v. Wade* will stand, perhaps it will be overruled, perhaps it will be changed in some way. Whatever the result, *Roe v. Wade* is a court opinion sitting on the shelf in your law library. If you want to find it, I can tell you it was decided in 1973. So choose the correct *Table of Cases* in the correct *Decennial Digest* and you can find its citation in a flash! In any event, there it sits. It's a *cited case*. Soon the Supreme Court opinion in *Pennsylvania Planned Parenthood* will hit the shelf, 19 years down the shelf to the right of *Roe*. What do you think, will *Pennsylvania Planned Parenthood* cite *Roe*? Of course. It might even *overrule Roe*, which will mean that *Roe v. Wade* is no longer the law of the land. Or it might change *Roe* in some way. Or it might let *Roe* stand as solid precedent. The point is this: if you found *Roe* in the research process, you would certainly have to worry about little men with citation arrows taking a potshot at your case. And to discover the identity of those strange little men shooting arrows at your case, you will "Shepardize" your case.

To summarize, your case is the *cited case*. The *citing cases* are of two kinds: (1) the same case (involving the same parties) higher up in the court system citing your case and (2) other cases (involving entirely different parties) from all over the country citing your case.

These citing cases can do various things to the cited case:

Type of Case	Effect on Your Case
1. Same Case	affirm, reverse, modify, vacate, deny certiorari, etc.
2. Other Case	overrule, follow, distinguish, criticize, question, etc.

The problem for you, the legal researcher, is to *find* the citing cases. If you fail to look, I can make you one absolute promise: the day will come when you cite to a court a case that has been reversed on appeal by a higher court or overruled by some later court. The court receiving your brief will not be amused. Your opponent will.

To wrap up your case law research skills, you must learn how to find these *citing cases*, these shooters of citation arrows. You must learn how to "Shepardize."

§ 9.2 *Shepard's Citators*

Early in the development of the American legal publishing industry, people realized they needed a way to discover what had "happened" to a given case. They could look up a *Flowers*, for example, read it, and see what cases it had cited. But they couldn't see those citation arrows raining in from other cases all over the library. A man named Mr. Shepard provided the solution: a series of books enabling the legal researcher to look up the citation to the cited case and find citations to all the citing cases.

§ 9.2(a) The Need for Shepard's

Citing earlier cases in a court opinion is the doctrine of stare decisis in action. Because court opinions cite other court opinions, it became necessary in American law to develop a system enabling legal researchers to look up the cite to one case and find references to all later cases that have cited that case. The researchers would have several motives for wanting to find all these "citing cases," the ones citing the case the researchers are about to rely upon. First, the researchers would want to find out if the case was appealed to a higher court and, if so, what that higher court "did" to the case. Did it affirm? Reverse? Modify? Second, they would want to learn if some entirely different and later case cited the opinion they are about to rely upon. Did a later court "overrule" the doctrine of the case they've found? Did a later court "follow" their case, "distinguish" it, "criticize" it, or otherwise cite it? If so, the chances are that those later cases are similar to the case they've found and to the legal problem they're researching. Finally, if the researchers located a state case in a West regional reporter, they would also like to obtain the "parallel" cite to the same case in the official state report.

A company called Shepard's developed such a system, which allows researchers to look up the cite to their case, the *cited case*, and obtain citations to other cases that have cited their case, the *citing cases*. The system is a giant series of books known as *Shepard's Citators*.

§ 9.2(b) The Structure of Shepard's

Shepard's is a huge system of tables delighting those who get a kick out of reading bus schedules. The tables, published in large bound volumes supplemented with interim supplements and cumulative monthly red-colored supplements, allow you to look up the *citation* to virtually any case decided in the United States. Listed below that citation will be a list of citations to all other cases that have cited your case.

Since Shepard's is a system based on case citations, the Shepard's Company naturally based its series of tables on official and unofficial court reports. Shepard's has a separate set of volumes for each of the seven regional reporters, for each state, for the Supreme Court of the United States, for the United States courts of appeals (F. and F.2d), and for the United States district courts (F. Supp. and F.R.D.).

§ 9.2(c) *Cited Case* and *Citing Cases*

As discussed above, the *cited case* is the one you Shepardize. Let's assume you want to Shepardize *Flowers v. District of Columbia*, a negligent sterilization case you have already found in the law library. When you Shepardize *Flowers* in *Shepard's Atlantic Citations*, you'll find a list of case citations that have cited *Flowers*. *Flowers* is the *cited case*. Those listed are the *citing cases*.

To review, *citing cases* can be one of two types: the *same case* or *other cases*. The *same case* would be a later disposition of the same lawsuit, usually by a higher court. A higher court could *affirm, reverse, modify, vacate, deny certiorari,* etc. These references would constitute the *subsequent case history* the Harvard *Bluebook* requires you to include in each case citation.

Other cases are those that have cited *Flowers* because they involve the same or similar legal issues found in the cited case. You should be aware that *other cases* can "do" something to the *cited case.* Of most importance, a later, *other case* could *overrule* the *cited case. Other cases* might also *criticize* the *cited case, explain, follow,* or *harmonize* it, etc.

§ 9.3 How to Shepardize a Case

Read this section in the law library with a recent bound edition of a regional Shepard's in front of you. As I discuss the various features of Shepard's, consult that feature in the bound volume you have in front of you.

Following is a step-by-step method for Shepardizing a case to obtain both subsequent case history and citations to other on-point cases citing your case. The discussion will follow the technique of Shepardizing *Flowers*. But if you do not have *Shepard's Atlantic Citations*, you may choose any other Shepard's for any other regional reporter. The features will be the same, and you'll be able to follow the discussion.

§ 9.3(a) Step One: Select the Correct *Set* of Shepard's

I kid you not. Many first-time legal researchers will pick the wrong *set* of Shepard's to Shepardize a case. I've taught thousands of law students and paralegals, and invariably, in every class, some students will come to me moaning and groaning that they can't Shepardize. They'll be trying to Shepardize an A.2d case in the P.2d Shepard's. Or they'll be trying to Shepardize an F. Supp. case in the F.2d Shepard's. I've even watched one poor soul trying to Shepardize a *case* in the federal regulations Shepard's! So please be careful: the first step is finding the correct *set* of Shepard's. (Most libraries shelve the Shepard's at the end of the respective court report, but some have what's called a "Shepard's Alcove" where *all* Shepard's are shelved.)

§ 9.3(b) Step Two: Select the Correct *Volume*

When you've found the correct *set* of Shepard's in the law library, look at the spines of the bound, burgundy-colored volumes. The spines will list their coverage by volume numbers. For example, if you wanted to Shepardize *Flowers v. District of Columbia*, 478 A.2d 1073, you'd select the volume that states: Vol. 2, Part 4 1986, 356 A.2d - 498 A.2d[1] {40}. The point is that you want to select the *first* bound volume **{40}**

[1]The actual volume in the summer of 1992 one would use to Shepardize *Flowers*. One day in the future, this volume might be recompiled to cover a broader time period.

coverage of the particular case. (Subsequent bound supplements or paperback supplements will cover the case, but they will not list the parallel citation, which might be needed for correct case citation.)

When you select the correct volume for your first look, be sure to identify the *supplements* within that set of Shepard's you'll need to update your research. Typically, each set of Shepard's has (1) at least one bound volume, (2) perhaps one or more interim bound supplements, (3) an annual paperback supplement (usually tan or a pale yellow), and (4) a cumulative monthly paperback supplement (red).

Once you've identified the correct books within the correct set, you should then complete the following substeps during your early experience as a legal researcher. As you gain experience and advance toward your goal of becoming an Ace Legal Researcher, you'll be able to skip these substeps and proceed directly to Step Three.

§ 9.3(b)(i) Substep Two-A: Turn to the Preface in That Volume

Read the Preface to familiarize yourself with the overall system of Shepard's. Within
{41} the Preface, find the section entitled: "Analysis of Case Citations" {41}. Notice it states that the *citing in-region cases* and *federal cases* have been "analyzed" to determine what the *citing cases* did to the *cited case.* While it was developing its system, the Shepard's Company realized it could not just *list* the cases citing your case. That list might extend to several hundred cases citing your case. Suppose *one* of those cases *reverses* your case. What are you supposed to do? Look up hundreds of cases in search of just *one* that reversed your case? Nope. You'd find something else to do for a living.

Shepard's anticipated this problem and solved it by including this "Analysis" feature. Thus, in addition to *listing* the citations of cases citing your case, the editors at Shepard's "analyze" these *citing cases*, determine what effect they had on your case, and reveal this effect by sticking little abbreviations before the citations to the *citing cases.* (As you'll learn below, the Shepard's company shows you not only the effect the *citing case* had on the *cited case.* It shows the exact point of law in the *cited case* that prompted the *citing case* to cite the *cited case.*)

Return your attention to the "Analysis of Case Citations" part of the Preface. Notice that it then states that the resulting "history" (same case higher up citing your case) or "treatment" (other case citing your case) is shown by a little letter abbreviation preceding the citing case reference. These letter abbreviations showing "history" will reveal necessary subsequent case history for the correct citation of the case you are Shepardizing. The abbreviations showing "treatment" will reveal other on-point cases around the country citing your case.

Looking further in the "Analysis of Case Citations" section of the Preface, notice what cases are *not* analyzed. The Preface states, in *Shepard's Atlantic Reporter Citations*, that each "Atlantic Reporter case and federal court case" has been analyzed. Well, if those are the ones that *are* analyzed, then what cases are *not* analyzed? Nonregional and nonfederal court cases. Thus, in a regional Shepard's, you'll find that the cases listed from the same regional reporter and from the federal court reporters will have the little letter abbreviations showing what those cases did to your case. Other cases, those from out of the region, will not be analyzed. Their citations will just be listed. No little letter abbreviations will appear. To find out what they did to your case, you'll have to look them up.

§ 9.3(b)(ii) Substep Two-B: Turn to the "Abbreviations—Analysis"

Now, in the Preface, turn over several pages and find the section entitled: "Abbreviations—Analysis" {42}. Notice there are two groups of letter abbreviations. The first group, called "History of Case," shows case history abbreviations. These will precede the *same cases* that cite your case, i.e., the same case higher up in the court system. The second group, called "Treatment of Case," will precede *other* cases that have cited your case. The "History" abbreviations reveal the subsequent case history that the Harvard *Bluebook* requires you to include in your case citations. The "Treatment" abbreviations reveal other on-point cases you might want to consult in your research. **{42}**

Focus on both groups of abbreviations and familiarize yourself with them. A true Ace Legal Researcher has pretty much committed them to memory so that a "j" automatically tells the researcher that the *citing case's* dissenting opinion cited the *cited case.*

§ 9.3(b)(iii) Substep Two-C: Turn to the "Abbreviations—Reports"

Now find the section entitled: "Abbreviations—Reports." Note the unique citation abbreviations Shepard's uses to list the *citing cases*. Shepard's isn't trying to be difficult by not complying with ordinary rules of citation. Rather, it had to develop its own, compact abbreviation system to list tens of millions of *citing cases* throughout the Shepard's system.

§ 9.3(b)(iv) Substep Two-D: Study the "Illustrative Case"

Now find the section entitled: "Illustrative Case" {43}. This section shows you a sample column from a page of Shepard's. In large brackets stretching down the right of the column, it shows the order in which *citing cases* are listed. For those of you who aspire to the status of Ace Legal Researcher, recall the words of that great sage: **{43}**

> GOOD'S RULE OF RESEARCH #23:
>
> **Woe be unto the legal researcher who fails to learn the *order* Shepard's uses to list cases citing your case.**

By knowing the order Shepard's uses to list cases, you'll increase your efficiency as a Shepardizer and won't waste precious time as I used to do in my law student days when I was fumbling around in the law library.

For state cases, Shepardized in the Regional Shepard's (A., P., So., N.W., N.E., S.W., S.E.), here's the order:

In parentheses immediately below the bold-faced page number of the case you Shepardize, you'll find the "parallel citation" if any exists. Then you'll find eight groups, each of which is explained by the corresponding number on the "Illustrative Case" page.

1. **Case History.** The first cases listed will be case history. If the case has been affirmed, reversed, denied certiorari, or has received any other case history event, those citations will be listed at the top of the column. In this first group of listings, you might see some preceded with the little letter "s," which means "same case." If the volume number of such a listing is lower than the one you are Shepardizing, then that reference probably is to prior case history. If the volume number is higher, then that listing is some subsequent proceeding in the same case, and probably is not the kind of subsequent case history that must be included in the correct citation. The really important subsequent case history will be tagged with the little letter abbreviations you saw in the "Abbreviations–Analysis" section. So watch for "r," "a," "m," "v," "U S cert den," and so on. These are the ones that must appear in the subsequent case history part of your case citations.[2]

2. **In-state Cases.** Then you'll find *other cases* from the same state citing your case. The list will simply move from case history to in-state cases without any special announcement, but you can tell where in-state cases begin by the abbreviations: they'll change from "history" abbreviations to "treatment" abbreviations. (See how important it is to memorize the list of abbreviations?)

3. **Federal Cases.** Then you'll find any *other* (not same) federal cases citing your case. (If federal cases appear as part of case history, they, of course, will be cited at the top of the column, not at position #3. The most likely event of this kind is the denial of certiorari by the Supreme Court of the United States.)

4. **In-region Cases.** Then you'll find out-of-state but in-region cases citing your case. These cases will be listed alphabetically by state, their states' abbreviations centered in the column itself.

5. **Out-of-region Cases.** After the out-of-state, in-region cases, you'll find the out-of-state, out-of-region cases listed alphabetically by state. At this point you'll notice that the "analysis" features disappear, for out-of-state

[2]Please see Chapter 6 of *Citing & Typing the Law* (LEL Enterprises 1992).

and out-of-region cases are not analyzed, just listed.

6. **A.B.A. Journal.** If your case has been cited in an *American Bar Association Journal* article, the citation to that article will appear next.

7. **A.L.R.** If your case has been cited by an A.L.R. Annotation or if an A.L.R. Annotation has dealt with the subject matter of the case, cites to A.L.R. Annotations will appear next. Please note that if your case has been *reported*—that is, the full text of its opinion has been published in A.L.R.—such A.L.R. citation will appear as a "parallel citation" in parentheses at the top of the list. When you find such a citation in parentheses, you then know that an on-point A.L.R. Annotation will follow the report of that case in A.L.R.

8. **Treatises.** Finally, Shepard's will include citations to "selected" legal texts, i.e., treatises, that cite your case. With all due respect, these citations are really disguised advertisements, for the "selected" legal texts, naturally enough, are those published by Shepard's or its parent company, McGraw-Hill. The abbreviations of these citations will be meaningless and will prompt you to turn to the "Abbreviations—Reports" section each time to discover the name of the treatise and its author or authors.

§ 9.3(b)(v) Substep Two-E: Get Out Your Magnifying Glass

Before you actually Shepardize the *Flowers* case, there's one more thing you need to know. Look at the listings of citations on the "Illustrative Case" page {43}. If you're **{43}** under 30 you'll probably be able to see some tiny superscript numbers appearing before some of the page numbers in the *citing case* references. If, like me, you're approaching **old-fogey-hood** and need bifocals or other visual assistance, then get out your magnifying glass and scout out these microscopic numbers.

Now recall earlier in this book when I was explaining the headnotes on the title pages of cases. There I pointed out that headnotes have sequential numbers (1, 2, 3, and so on). I also pointed out that these sequential numbers serve two purposes. The first purpose was a "table of contents" function for the opinion itself. The second function, I said back there, had to do with Shepardizing cases. Well, here we are.

When you see a tiny superscript "2" or "3" or whatever, that means that the case citing your case cited it for the proposition of law represented by *that sequential headnote* on the title page of your case. Thus, if you're only interested in the fourth headnote on the title page of your case, you only have to pay attention to those analyzed cases bearing a superscript "4" before their page references.

Please note, however, that this superscript number feature is part of the "analysis" feature of Shepard's. Recall that in the regional Shepard's only in-region and federal cases citing your case are analyzed. Out-of-region cases are not analyzed and consequently don't have any little letter abbreviations or any superscript numbers.

Those cases might be right on point, but you have no way of knowing until you look them up and quickly read their prefatory statements and their headnotes.

§ 9.3(c) Step Three: Find the Correct Volume and Page Numbers

If you're Shepardizing 478 A.2d 1073, turn in the correct volume of Shepard's until
{44} you find the page that begins the listings for "Volume 478" {44}. Look at the top of the pages for the "**VOL.**" references. Keep looking until you find the page that contains the "**VOL. 478**" references. Coverage for your particular volume might stretch on for several pages, so begin to focus on the page references, which will be indicated as "**-1073-**." When you find the correct page, the listings that follow are those cases citing
{44} your case. If your page number is omitted {44}, that means your case has not been cited during the coverage of that volume of Shepard's.

§ 9.3(d) Step Four: Supplement in All Supplements

Once you've Shepardized in the first bound volume covering your case, you must then
{45} repeat the process in all subsequent supplements {45}. Usually that will entail consulting a paperback annual supplement (yellow or tan) and a monthly paperback supplement (red). For many sets of Shepard's, however, you'll also find one or more interim bound supplements.

To make certain you've consulted all supplements, you can check the front cover of the red-colored monthly supplement. There you will find a box entitled "What Your Library Should Contain." The volumes listed there show the complete set of Shepard's for that particular court report.

§ 9.3(e) Step Five: Beware the NO ZONE

In an overall legal research project you will have already run Key Numbers in the appropriate NO ZONES to make certain you've found all cases on point up to the present day. So there's certainly no reason why you'd have to run Key Numbers again in the NO ZONES created by Shepard's Citators. But some legal research projects involve *only* Shepardizing cases. Paralegals, for example, might "cite check" the citations found in a brief about to be submitted to a court. One of their tasks would be to Shepardize all cases cited in that brief to make certain all case history was included in each citation and to make certain that the cases had not been reversed or overruled.

If your research assignment, therefore, involves only Shepardizing cases, you must beware of the inevitable NO ZONES created by the *monthly* schedule of supplementing the shelves that are growing *weekly*.

At the front of the latest Shepard's supplement (the red-colored paperback), guess
{46} what you'll find? *The second most important page in all of legal research!* {46} There you'll find the same table you found at the front of the C.J.S. pocket part. On this table,

Shepard's tells you exactly where it stopped grabbing the citations of *citing cases.* But if you'll compare the actual shelves in your law library, you'll find that the volume number of the latest advance sheet on any of these shelves is *always* greater than the end of Shepard's coverage. Hence, you've got another NO ZONE.

And the *only* way to find cases in this NO ZONE? You got it: you must run Key Numbers through all issues of a court report beyond the point where Shepard's stopped.

So if your attorneys ask you to Shepardize some cases, be sure to ask the attorneys which Key Numbers they're interested in. They're likely to say: "We don't want you to run Key Numbers. We want you to Shepardize."

To which you smugly reply: "It's impossible to Shepardize without also running Key Numbers. Otherwise, I'll miss cases in the NO ZONE."

When they ask what the NO ZONE is, just tell them to buy their own copy of *Legal Research . . . Without Losing Your Mind.*

§ 9.4 Shepard's: A Roadmap for Research

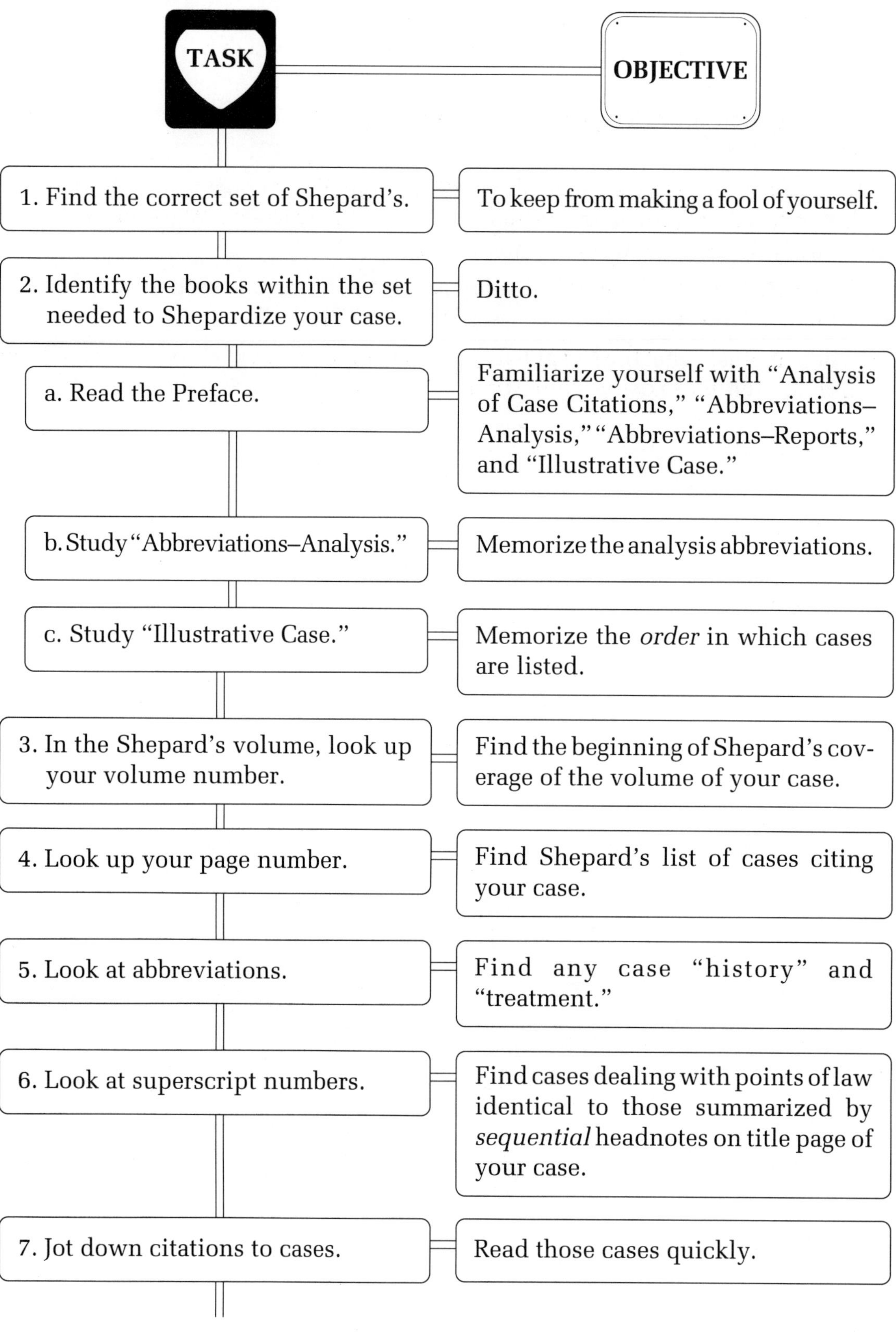

TASK	OBJECTIVE
1. Find the correct set of Shepard's.	To keep from making a fool of yourself.
2. Identify the books within the set needed to Shepardize your case.	Ditto.
a. Read the Preface.	Familiarize yourself with "Analysis of Case Citations," "Abbreviations–Analysis," "Abbreviations–Reports," and "Illustrative Case."
b. Study "Abbreviations–Analysis."	Memorize the analysis abbreviations.
c. Study "Illustrative Case."	Memorize the *order* in which cases are listed.
3. In the Shepard's volume, look up your volume number.	Find the beginning of Shepard's coverage of the volume of your case.
4. Look up your page number.	Find Shepard's list of cases citing your case.
5. Look at abbreviations.	Find any case "history" and "treatment."
6. Look at superscript numbers.	Find cases dealing with points of law identical to those summarized by *sequential* headnotes on title page of your case.
7. Jot down citations to cases.	Read those cases quickly.

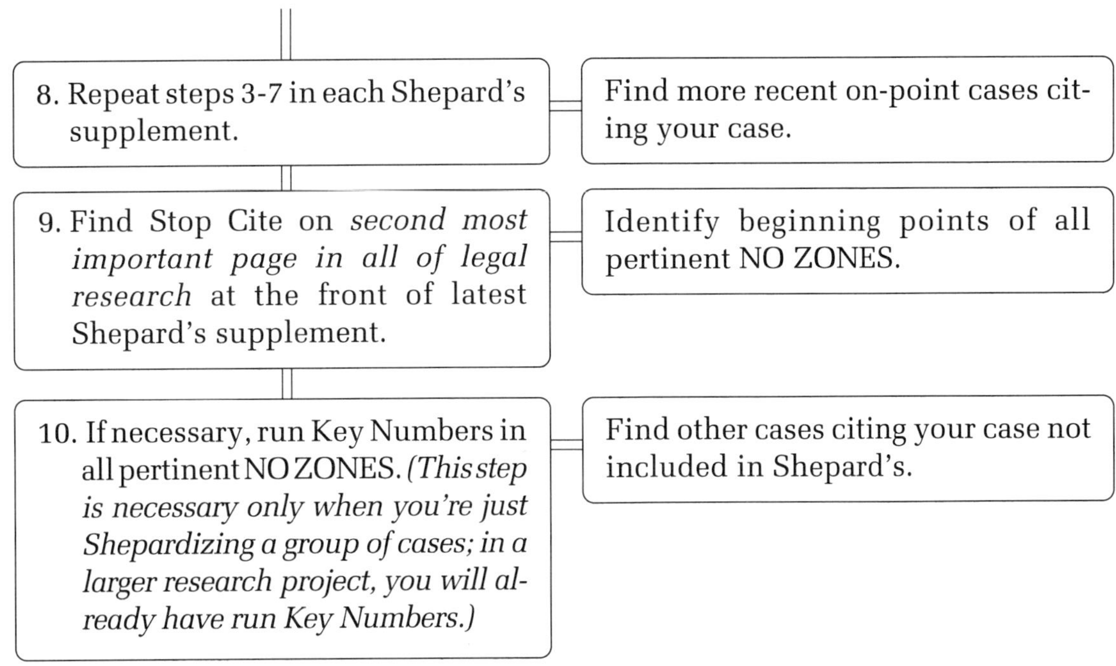

§ 9.5 Shepard's: Visual Aids {40-46}

In the Visual Aids booklet, I have reproduced selected pages from the Shepard's volumes used to Shepardize *Flowers v. District of Columbia.* In the box on each page, you'll find my commentary showing exactly what the researcher is doing to Shepardize a given case.

Please note that these pages are selective. In the real world of legal research, you would consult many more pages, especially during your first experience with Shepard's. You would, most likely, go down lots of dead ends, locating irrelevant information, getting frustrated, and, yes, perhaps even *losing your mind.*

But if you'll follow the above instructions, step by step, and study the Visual Aids, page by page, you'll begin to learn how to do legal research *without losing your mind.*

CHAPTER 10

CASE LAW CONCLUDED

§ 10.1 Time Out

When you've made it this far, you clearly deserve a break. You'll be glad to know that the worst is over, that case law research is the hardest, and that when you've descended this far down, there's only one way to go. By the same token, you'll be sad to learn that our next topic—legislative research—necessarily will return you to case law, Key Numbers, and NO ZONES.

But before we tackle the remaining types of legal research—legislative and administrative law—let's pause a moment and rehash what you've learned (or should have learned). Following then are, for lack of a better term, some Cliffs Notes on the first nine chapters of the book. Don't tell your friends about these Cliffs Notes, or they'll be tempted to skip the first nine chapters and just read Chapter 10.

§ 10.2 The Litigation Explosion

A brief tour around the National Reporter System vividly demonstrates the litigation explosion. In the ten-year period from 1957 to 1966, the West Company published 127 volumes of F.2d, the book publishing federal circuit court law. During the same period it published 112 volumes of F. Supp., the book publishing federal trial court decisions. In the state case law arena, during that same period the West Company published 82 volumes of N.E.2d, the book publishing the decisions of New York, Ohio, Illinois, Indiana, and Massachusetts.

During the ten years from 1982 to 1991, F.2d consumed 285 volumes, F. Supp. required 249 volumes, and N.E.2d totaled 179 volumes. The following table shows this growth in total volumes and in percentage increases:

Report	1957-1966	1982-1991	Increase	Percentage
F.2d	127	285	158	124%
F. Supp.	112	249	137	122%
N.E.2d	82	179	97	118%

For legal researchers, these data bring good news and bad news. First, the good news: business is very good out there; there's lots of litigation going on; lots of briefs to be written; lots of research to be done. And the bad news: as more and more cases are decided and published, research becomes more and more difficult, and the chances of making a mistake by missing an on-point case become ever greater.

Consequently, here at the beginning of your legal career, you must develop legal research skills that will enable you to locate on-point cases quickly and efficiently. Naturally, you are well on your way to achieving this goal by having shelled out your hard-earned money for this tome on *how to do legal research without losing your mind.*

§ 10.3 The Quarry

So the quarry is quite large and quite foreboding: over 10,000 volumes of court reports published by the West Company alone. Its National Reporter System includes seven regional reporters (A., P., So., N.E., S.E., N.W., S.W.), all of which are in their second series (A.2d, P.2d, So.2d, N.E.2d, S.E.2d, N.W.2d, S.W.2d). The National Reporter System includes two special state reporters (N.Y.S., Cal. Rptr.), both of which are in their second series (N.Y.S.2d and Cal. Rptr. 2d). The National Reporter System includes five federal reporters (F., F. Supp., F.R.D., B.R., S. Ct.), one of which is in its second series (F.2d).[1]

As you tour the stacks in search of on-point cases, your quarry peers down at you from ominous-looking shelves. It seems to be taunting you, saying "Watch out, be careful, don't miss a case, you just walked right past one . . . ." The laughter and cackles from the lawbooks make you want to enter med school and become a psychiatrist.

Somewhere, you know, somewhere in those 10,000 volumes are cases on your point of law. Your job is to find them. Your job is to find *all* of them. Your job is to not *miss* a key case, one right on point, one found by the judge, one found by your opponent, one found by everybody but you. Terrifying.

§ 10.4 The Initial Quest

As you tour the stacks of the National Reporter System, you get the eerie feeling that someone has been here before, someone researching the precise issue you are researching, someone who has suffered the pains and, yes, citation arrows shot by strange little men in the books themselves. "Surely someone has researched my topic before," you lament.

Indeed "someone" has. And that someone is our good friend Wilbur. Wilbur. The drone who works for every legal publishing company. The tireless researcher who has

[1]As this book goes to press in late 1992, F.2d is approaching its 1000th volume. The entire legal profession is betting in office pools around the country on the way the West Company will go. Will it be 1001 F.2d? Or 1 F.3d? This writer predicts 1 F.3d. You heard it here first, folks.

written C.J.S., Am. Jur. 2d, A.L.R. Annotations, treatises, legal periodicals, and even Restatements of the Law. Wilbur has done it all on virtually every conceivable topic of law.

And what has Wilbur done? He has found cases on point. And how did he find cases on point? He engaged in *basic chronological case research*. And what is that?

Running Key Numbers in the American Digest System!

So if Wilbur's done it all, why redo what Wilbur has already done? No reason at all.

Your strategy, your quest, thus becomes:

> ***Step One:*** Use general background sources to find general discussions of your legal topics. These sources include C.J.S., Am. Jur. 2d, and A.L.R.
>
> ***Step Two:*** Use specific background sources to gain critical analysis of your legal topics, some ideas for arguments, and some passages you can quote in your brief or memo to impress your judge, law professor, or boss.

Once you locate these background materials, you then figure out that it would be stupid to retrace Wilbur's steps in the law library. Instead of redoing what Wilbur did to find all those cases he cited in the footnotes of those sources, why not pick up his research where he stopped? Brilliant.

§ 10.5 The Quest Continues: Where Wilbur Put His Pencil Down

Most background sources give little clue about where they stopped researching the topics they discuss. Most only give a copyright date, information that is way too general to form the basis of a research strategy. One source, C.J.S., does tell you where it stopped researching, where Wilbur put his research pencil down. On *the second most important page in all of legal research* {9}, which you can find at the front of any **{9}**
C.J.S. pocket part, you can determine exactly where C.J.S. stopped collecting cases in *each component of the National Reporter System*. Of course, you need not know where Wilbur stopped in *all* court reports. You only need to know where he stopped in *one* court report. For if you have a volume number and a page number of *any* court report, that citation marks a precise moment in time, a precise week of the year (since all court reports grow weekly with the addition of yet another advance sheet).

So if you've got lots of background research, an on-point A.L.R. Annotation, some good law review articles, perhaps some treatise discussion, then your research is probably complete *as of the time that Wilbur put his pencil down in the C.J.S. pocket part*. In other words, if all these little Wilburs are rushing around at the same time of year putting together pocket parts in C.J.S., Am. Jur. 2d, A.L.R., and supplemented treatises, why not use the C.J.S. pocket part as an overall calendar?

The C.J.S. pocket part, then, with its *second most important page in all of legal research*, can serve as an overall guide to let you know exactly where Wilbur put his pencil down, exactly where Wilbur *stopped* researching case law. This precise point, you know by now, is the Stop Cite.

§ 10.6 The Quest Continues: Where You Pick Your Pencil Up

When time is short, it's probably a safe bet to rely on the C.J.S. pocket part as an overall guide to where Wilbur put his pencil down. You might try to "psych out" other supplemented sources simply by jotting down the citation to the *latest* case they cite and using that citation as your Stop Cite. "If they found that case," you reason intelligently, "they must have gotten that far."

Whatever the source—the C.J.S. pocket part, U.S. Code supplementations, which we'll learn about next, or a "psyched out" background source—the clever legal researcher, indeed the Ace Legal Researcher, tries to establish a Stop Cite marking the exact point where a background authority stopped researching.

Once you've established a Stop Cite, you then go to the *SINGLE MOST IMPOR-*
{34} *TANT PAGE IN ALL OF LEGAL RESEARCH* {34}, the tables in the front of the latest volume of the *General Digest.* These tables show where every volume and every page of every West report is digested in the American Digest System. Then, quite simply, you pick a Stop Cite from the C.J.S. pocket part (any report will do since they are all marking the same moment in time). You then look up your Stop Cite in these tables. You will then find exactly where Wilbur stopped running Key Numbers—exactly where Wilbur put his pencil down.

At that point, you pick your pencil up and begin to run Key Numbers from that point on.

§ 10.7 The Quest Continues: Some Warnings

You've found on-point cases in your background research, and you've read these cases in West reports. You've seen on their title pages the Key Numbers the West Company uses to classify your legal issues. But in your Key Number work, you recall the admonition not to run off stark raving mad, foaming at the mouth, and use a Key Number without first *verifying* that Key Number. After all, Key Numbers change. New Main Topics are created. Main Topics are revised.

So you use the Analytical Approach to check out your Key Number. You simply
{30,31} look up your Main Topic in the latest *Decennial Digest* {30,31} and see that, yes indeed, your Key Numbers are still there and, yes indeed, their names do analytically describe the issues you are interested in, and, yes indeed, there are no other Key Numbers you should consult.

Or you use the Index Approach to check out your Key Number. You simply look up some factual or legal words in the *Descriptive Word Index* of the latest *Decennial*
{32} *Digest* {32} or the *Descriptive Word Index* in each 10th volume of *General Digest.* These words might cross-reference you to some other equally on-point Key Numbers.

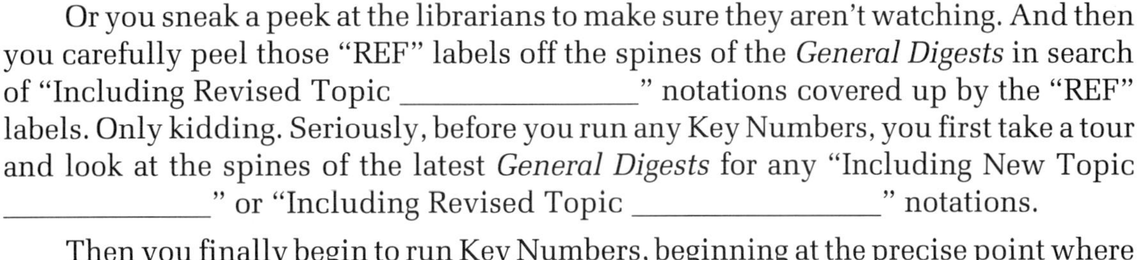

Or you sneak a peek at the librarians to make sure they aren't watching. And then you carefully peel those "REF" labels off the spines of the *General Digests* in search of "Including Revised Topic _______________" notations covered up by the "REF" labels. Only kidding. Seriously, before you run any Key Numbers, you first take a tour and look at the spines of the latest *General Digests* for any "Including New Topic _____________" or "Including Revised Topic ________________" notations.

Then you finally begin to run Key Numbers, beginning at the precise point where Wilbur stopped, picking up your research pencil where he put his down.

§ 10.8 The Quest Continues: Some Shortcuts

Toward the end of decennial periods, which are really quintennial periods these days, the *General Digests* loom large. In a five-year period, which will turn into the next "____ Decennial, Part One" or "_____ Decennial, Part Two," more than 60 to 70 volumes of the *General Digest* will appear on the shelf. Perhaps the *SINGLE MOST IMPORTANT PAGE IN ALL OF LEGAL RESEARCH* has told you to start running Key Numbers in volume 23 of the *General Digest*.

Instead of running your Key Numbers in all volumes from volume 23 to the present, you first take a shortcut to see *which* volumes of the *General Digest* actually
have headnotes classified to your Key Numbers {35,36}. In the back of, say, volume 30, **{35,36}**
you find the Table of Key Numbers, look up your Key Numbers, and find that only volume 25 has a headnote classified to your Key Numbers. Then you check the same Table of Key Numbers in the back of volume 40 and find that volumes 31, 33, and 39 have headnotes classified to your Key Numbers. Then you do the same in volumes 50, 60, and so on. Each time, when you discover which volumes in the *General Digest* have headnotes classified to your issues, you pull those volumes out an inch on the shelves. Then making absolutely certain that no one comes along and pushes them back in until you are finished with them, you run your Key Numbers in those marked volumes, jotting down the citations to on-point cases, and threatening to flatten anyone who dares to come along and mess up your system.

§ 10.9 The Quest Continues: Putting Your Pencil Down

Just as Wilbur had to put his pencil down when he concluded his research, so too must you put your pencil down. Many researchers put theirs down at the end of the *General Digest*. And they make a drastic mistake. They lose their reputations as researchers in the dreaded NO ZONE.

The *General Digests* are never up to date. The librarian puts a new volume of the *General Digest* on the shelf each *month*. The same librarian puts an advance sheet for each West report on the shelves each *week*. There are *always* cases on the shelves that are *not* digested in the *General Digests*. The *only* way to retrieve these cases is to . . .

RUN KEY NUMBERS THROUGH THE PERTINENT NO ZONES.

To do so, you face two questions: (1) which NO ZONES? and (2) where do the NO ZONES begin?

The "which NO ZONE" question is answered by the scope and type of your legal research topic. If you're researching a federal legal issue, then your NO ZONES are those in F. Supp., F.2d, and S. Ct. If this federal legal issue is a civil procedure problem, then add the F.R.D. NO ZONE. If it's a bankruptcy problem, then add B.R. If, on the other hand, you're researching a state law issue and the attorney wants only in-state cases, then your NO ZONE lies in the Regional Reporter publishing the decisions of that state. If your attorney wants case law from the entire country, then your NO ZONES lie in *all Regional Reporters* and the *two State Reporters.* If some federal diversity of citizenship cases could affect your issue, then add the NO ZONES in F. Supp. and F.2d.

Fun, huh?

The "where does the NO ZONE begin" question is answered by the *SINGLE*
{34} *MOST IMPORTANT PAGE IN ALL OF LEGAL RESEARCH* {34}. Go to the tables appearing at the front of the latest *General Digest* volume. Look at the *bottom* of the table for each pertinent court report. There you'll find the volume and page number where the latest *General Digest* volume *stopped* collecting headnotes from the reports themselves.

That's where your NO ZONE begins.

You must run your Key Numbers through those advance sheets *beyond* the point
{38} where the *General Digest* stopped collecting cases, that is, through the NO ZONE {38}. As you engage in this delightful task, you'll find out that many law libraries subscribe to *two* copies of each advance sheet. So be careful and make certain you don't duplicate your work and run Key Numbers in each advance sheet volume *twice.* To guard against this wasted effort, pay attention to the "Week Number" on the spine of the advance sheet. That's the sequential number (from 1 to 52) at the bottom of the spines. Identify the Week Number beginning your NO ZONE and then make sure you cover all advance sheets beyond that number, skipping over duplicate copies. If you try to keep track by volume and page number, you'll go blind, or perhaps even lose your mind.

You can finally put your pencil down after you've run your Key Numbers through *all* advance sheets in *all* pertinent NO ZONES.

§ 10.10 The Quest Ends: Strange Little Men Shooting Arrows

The only remaining task involves Shepardizing cases to find out if your cases have been shot with citation arrows by those strange little men. Actually, as you move ever closer to your ultimate status of Ace Legal Researcher, you'll find out that Shepardizing occurs throughout the legal research process. You might, for example, begin your research in A.L.R., find a crucial on-point case, and *immediately* Shepardize it to see if it's been reversed or overruled and to find a list of all other cases citing it.

But at some point in your research, you must Shepardize *all* cases you intend to use in your memo or brief. Failure to do so can result in all sorts of horrible things, ranging from flunking your legal research course to being sued for legal malpractice.

I remember well my third year of law school. I was working part time for an attorney who was representing a construction company sued by a worker injured on a job site. The job site was located on federal property, so the attorney faced a "choice of law" problem in the case. He had already won at trial and needed some research for his appellee's brief. When he received the appellant's brief, he sent me a copy with instructions to "try to tear it apart."

It didn't take long.

The appellant based his entire argument on a federal district court case decided by the United States District Court for the District of Maryland. Naturally, I got the case and read it. And then, naturally enough, I Shepardized it. Bingo!

I called the attorney with some amazing news: the appellant had relied upon a federal district court case that had been *reversed* on appeal by the Fourth Circuit. The case was totally worthless.

Needless to say, we won. The poor client who had staked his claim with the opposing counsel was out of luck. I'm sure he never learned the true reason for the defeat. If he had, he could have sued his attorneys for breaking one of the most basic rules of lawyering:

GOOD'S RULE OF RESEARCH #24:

You must Shepardize *every* case you use in your memo or brief.

And that's it. That's case law legal research: find the drudge work somebody else has already done, cash in on it, and bring it up to date.

Let's move on to statutes and the battle of the titans:

The Case of Anita and Clarence.

CHAPTER 11

THE AMERICAN LEGISLATIVE SYSTEM

§ 11.1 Federal vs. State

Since the ratification of the United States Constitution in 1789, the United States Congress has had certain powers to use in governing the country. Among others, the Congress has the power to regulate commerce among the several states, to promote the general welfare, to pass all laws necessary and proper . . . and on and on. The Tenth Amendment to the Constitution, rarely used in constitutional jurisprudence, essentially says that all the power the Congress does *not* have is reserved for the states. And the Supremacy Clause of the Constitution has been interpreted to mean that if Congress passes a law and a state passes a conflicting law, the federal law takes priority and "preempts" the state statute.

I pretend no special knowledge of Constitutional Law and do not intend to write any treatise on legislative powers (I couldn't even if I wanted to). I start this chapter with these Constitutional allusions merely to make a single point: in the law library you'll find one great big "code" of *federal statutes* and you'll find 50 separate "codes" of *state statutes*. I am going to concentrate my teaching in this book on federal statutes, showing you how to find federal statutes, how to find cases interpreting those statutes, and how to update those statutes and cases to the present day. When you learn the necessary research methods, you'll be able to transfer them quite easily to the realm of state statutory research; the publication techniques, after all, are virtually the same.

§ 11.2 The Federal Legislative Process

Since 1789 Congress has been meeting to enact laws governing a vast range of human behavior. Every two years, the entire 435-member House of Representatives is up for re-election. Because the Senatorial terms are six years, only one-third of the Senate is up for re-election every two years. The significant number for Congress is "two" because "a Congress" is a two-year affair. Each Congress since the First Congress has been numbered sequentially.

Each Congress lasts two years and has two sessions. Each two-year Congress is sequentially numbered. For example, the 100th Congress began in January of 1987 and ended the last day of December 1988. The first year of a two-year Congress is called the First Session, the second year the Second Session.

During any given Congress, only 400 to 600 federal statutes will be passed. A great deal of "legislative history" material, however, is produced. When faced with a problem involving the interpretation of a federal statute, attorneys routinely try to find these materials in order to ascertain the "legislative intent" of a particular statute.

Basically, there are four types of legislative history materials: (1) House and Senate Bills, (2) Committee Hearings, (3) Committee Reports, and (4) Floor Debate.

§ 11.2(a) Bills

During each Congress as bills are introduced in the House or Senate, they are assigned sequential numbers. The first bill introduced in the House is designated H.R. 1, the first in the Senate S. 1. Thus, H.R. 12,453 is the 12,453rd bill introduced in the House in a particular Congress.

Each Bill retains its number throughout the legislative process even though it probably will undergo significant changes. Thus, H.R. 12,453 will read one way "as introduced," but will probably read differently "as reported out by committee," or "as amended on the floor of the House," or "as amended on the floor of the Senate," or "as reported out by a conference committee," or "as passed by the House and the Senate." The bill's content and wording change; its number remains the same during a particular Congress. If the bill fails to pass, however, it must be reintroduced in the next Congress, at which time it will receive a new bill number.

Bills are published in a variety of places. Each bill is first separately published. Upon introduction, many bills will be published in the *Congressional Record.* When reported out by committee, the bill will appear with the committee report. When passed by the House, the bill will probably appear in the *Congressional Record.* When passed by the Senate, the bill will likely appear in the *Congressional Record.* So even though bills are separately published, the *Congressional Record* represents the most likely place the ordinary legal researcher could retrieve a House or Senate Bill.

§ 11.2(b) Committee Hearings

After its introduction in the House or Senate, each bill will be referred to the appropriate House or Senate committee. The committee might decide to hold "hearings," a proceeding designed to find facts necessary to informed legislative action. The committee might invite, or force through its subpoena power, interested or expert witnesses to testify at the hearing. Witnesses might accompany their oral testimony with a prepared written statement. All questions, answers, and written reports will be transcribed and published separately as a paperback "committee hearing."

Each reader of this book, of course, has witnessed at least part of a committee hearing. The older, more seasoned readers, remember the Senate Watergate Hearings or the House Impeachment Hearings during Nixon's twilight years. And everyone on the face of the globe witnessed the Senate Judiciary Committee Hearings featuring Judge Clarence Thomas and Professor Anita Hill.

A committee hearing does not receive any special number. It is separately published and is referred to by the title that appears on the front cover of the published hearing. Hearings are retrievable alphabetically by title in most law library card catalog or electronic database systems.

§ 11.2(c) Committee Reports

When a majority of committee members agrees on a version of the bill, the committee will write and publish a "committee report." The committee report will reprint the changed bill and then proceed to explain why each change was made. Most authorities agree that the committee report represents the most telling evidence of "legislative intent." Consequently, a court will often cite the committee report when interpreting a particular federal statute. Legal researchers, therefore, should try to get their hands on the committee reports on a federal statute when the meaning of that statute is at issue.

During each Congress as committee reports are issued in the House or Senate, they receive a sequential number. Since 1969, these numbers have incorporated the Congress number so that current committee reports appear as H.R. Rep. No. 97-12, the 12th committee report issued by a House committee during the 97th Congress, or S. Rep. No. 97-26, the 26th committee report issued by a Senate committee during the 97th Congress. Before 1969, the committee report numbers did not reveal the Congress number. They appeared as H.R. Rep. No. 12 or S. Rep. No. 26 without identifying the Congress.

Committee reports are separately published in paperback editions. A private source, however, does publish the committee reports of significant pieces of legislation. *United States Code Congressional and Administrative News*, published by the West Publishing Company, prints the full text of all public laws chronologically. In addition, for important statutes, USCCAN (pronounced "yoos-can" in Jersey and "use-can" everywhere else) also publishes the committee report on the bill that was ultimately passed. Because USCCAN is widely available to attorneys and judges, and because of various tables it features in the back, you will become intimately familiar with this source as you continue your quest to become an Ace Legal Researcher.

§ 11.2(d) Floor Debate

When a bill is "reported out" by a committee, it returns to the floor of the House or Senate for the vote. At that time, floor debate is likely to take place. Although courts do not pay a great deal of attention to the substance of floor debate in their attempts to ascertain legislative intent, it is frequently necessary to find and cite passages from floor debate.

All floor debate is transcribed in the *Congressional Record*, which is published daily in a source appropriately known as the *Daily Edition*. The *Daily Edition* has two sections, one for the House and one for the Senate. Each section is separately paginated. At the end of each year, however, the entire mass of *Daily Editions* is bound into the *Congressional Record*, which is published in sets of sequentially numbered volumes with each volume set containing sequentially numbered pages. Many separate books are needed to house one year's output. Thus, volume 123 might have ten separate books as parts of volume 123. Separate pagination for House and Senate activities disappears in bound editions of the *Congressional Record*.

§ 11.3 Why Attorneys Seek Legislative History Materials

When Congress enacts a federal statute, it cannot foresee all circumstances in which the statute might apply. Congress essentially leaves it up to the federal courts to work out in individual cases the exact application of the statute. When a court must apply a federal statute to a given set of facts in a given case, it wants to apply the statute in such a way that the purpose of Congress is carried out. Courts must thus ascertain the purpose of Congress or its "legislative intent." To do so, courts will turn to these legislative history materials, a judicial technique of "statutory construction."

Referring to the "notes" of a legislative body in order to get inside "the minds of the legislators" has been going on for more than 400 years in the common law system. The earliest English treatise on statutory interpretation, written sometime before 1572, had this to say about the process we follow today:

> The statute shall be taken . . . *ex mente legislatorum* [in the minds of the legislators], for that is chiefe to be considered, which, althoughe it varie in so muche that in maner so manie heades as there were, so many wittes; so manie statute makers, so many myndes; yet, notwithstandinge, certen notes there are by which a man maie knowe what it was . . . . And so, in our dayes, have those that were the penners & devisors of statutes bene the grettest lighte for exposicion of statutes.[1]

§ 11.4 A Note on Legislative History Research

Researching legislative history materials is an art form in itself and usually beyond the curriculum of most courses on legal research. I believe, however, that people

[1]Anonymous, *A Discourse upon the Exposicion & Understandinge of Statutes* 151-52 (Thorne ed. 1942).

graduating from law school or paralegal school should at least know how to compile a legislative history on an enacted piece of federal legislation. Consequently, at the end of Chapter 12, I'll offer a step-by-step method you may use to locate bills, hearings, committee reports, and floor debate on any given federal statute. Before you can understand either the importance of legislative history or the means of retrieving it, however, you must first focus your attention on federal statutes themselves, the means of their publication, and the methods used for their retrieval and supplementation. Then, at the end of the next chapter, I'll share with you a method you can use to compile legislative histories.

§ 11.5 Federal Statutes

When Congress enacts a bill and the President signs it, the statute becomes effective immediately unless it specifically states otherwise. A law, therefore, could affect the lives of 250 million Americans immediately. The governed, of course, want to know about such a law immediately. At least theoretically they want to know about it right away. Certainly lawyers in Washington and even a few "outside the Beltway" want to learn of these statutes right away, for they affect the commercial and personal lives of their clients.

To satisfy this need for speed, Congress publishes all legislative laws the same way all case law is published—"chronologically." Congress does not wait around to publish laws by subject matter, even though it would be a great deal easier to locate federal statutes published in a subject matter arrangement.

§ 11.6 Chronological Publication of Statutes

Since 1957, Congress has classified and numbered each law it passes as a "public law" (Pub. L. No.) or a "private law" (Priv. L. No.). A public law applies to the general public or a sector of the public. A private law, on the other hand, applies only to a named individual or a named group of individuals. For example, some years ago, Congress enacted a private law giving Mamie Eisenhower the right to send her mail without postage charge. Similarly, after the American hostages were released by Iran in 1981, a bill was introduced to exempt these Americans from federal income taxation during their captivity. Unfortunately for the hostages, the bill did not pass. If it had passed, it would have been a private law, applying only to the named individuals, and not to you and me.

Each public law enacted is given a sequential number, which incorporates the Congress number. Thus, *Pub. L. No. 97-443* is the 443rd public law passed by the 97th Congress. Private laws are given similar but separate sequential numbers.

Before 1957, however, each law enacted was given a sequential "chapter number" without regard to the law's public or private classification or to the precise Congress in which it was passed. Thus, chapter 231 might be the 231st law enacted by the 81st Congress, or it might be the 231st law enacted by the 82d Congress.

Each law is first published in "slip law" form, that is, individually. Instead of waiting around for enough law to accumulate to warrant publication of a hardbound volume, Congress publishes each law separately and chronologically to satisfy the need for speed.

§ 11.6(a) Marking Legislative Time

These slip laws are comparable to the "advance sheets" you learned about in the case law portion of this book. Slip laws do differ from advance sheets, however. Whereas an advance sheet publishes quite a few cases, each slip law publishes just one federal statute. And whereas advance sheets hit the shelves regularly—once each week for each court report—slip laws arrive in a haphazard way, tending to bunch up at the end of two-year Congresses. Finally, in the study of case law, you learned that a volume number and a page number of any given court report marks a precise moment in time, a precise week when that particular case hit the shelves of the nation's law libraries. In the legislative process, on the other hand, we mark time, not by volume and page number of advance sheet, but by public law number. Thus, *Pub. L. No. 101-302* is a more recent event in time than *Pub. L. No. 101-301*, just as *932 F.2d 414* is a more recent event than *931 F.2d 1201*.

§ 11.6(b) The *Statutes at Large*

At the end of each year, all laws, public and private, are bound into hardbound volumes of the *Statutes at Large*. Each volume is sequentially numbered as are the pages within each volume. The *Statutes at Large*, currently numbering over 100 volumes, has been published since 1789 when Congress first began to legislate. Every law ever passed by Congress can be found in the *Statutes at Large*. Thus, for citation purposes, every federal statute could be cited to a particular volume and a particular page in the *Statutes at Large*. We could, for example, cite every federal law to its *Statutes at Large* location, e.g., 93 Stat. 123, volume 93 of the *Statutes at Large* at page 123. And for research purposes, we could locate and read federal statutes in the chronological publication, the *Statutes at Large*. But we would not be very smart researchers if we did.

§ 11.7 Topical Publication: *Revised Statutes* & *United States Code*

Publishing federal statutes as slip laws and then in the hardbound *Statutes at Large* certainly satisfies the need for speed. But chronological publication by itself creates huge problems of location and revision. Legal researchers do not search for statutes on the basis of time; can you imagine an attorney saying "I guess I'll run over to the law library to bone up on the statutes enacted by Congress in late June of 1949." No, instead, they seek federal laws governing a particular subject matter.

Also, laws as passed and published in the *Statutes at Large* are frequently amended or repealed at a later date. Yet no one instructs the subscribers to the *Statutes at Large* to tear out the pages of a repealed statute or to rewrite the pages of an amended statute. Indeed, an amendment does not totally revise and rewrite the older statute it is changing. Instead, the amendment merely states that certain words are to be added or certain words are to be deleted. To get an up-to-date picture of the current wording of the amended statute, one would have to consult the original wording in the *Statutes at Large* and the amending legislation in a later volume of the *Statutes at Large* and then "cut and paste" together the current correct wording. Not a whole lot of fun. Certainly not one of those Kodak Moments.

It thus became clear that only one publication of federal statutes was not enough. Those statutes should be revised to throw out repealed laws and change amended laws. Some system aiding "location" and "revision" had to be devised.

In the late 1800s Congress responded to these twin needs of "location" and "ongoing revision" by ordering the revision and republication of all laws passed.

§ 11.7(a) *Revised Statutes of 1875*

In the 1860s Congress ordered the revision of all federal statutes. All statutes were divided into 74 classifications called "titles." Within each title, all laws relating to that classification were logically arranged and assigned sequential section numbers. The section numbers ran sequentially throughout the 74 titles, totalling nearly 6,000 sections. Amended laws were rewritten to reflect the changes. Repealed laws were discarded. Also, only those laws of a "general and permanent" nature were included in the revision. Others were omitted from the new, up-to-date publication. Thus, a legal researcher could locate in one place all federal statutes concerning a particular subject matter. The researcher also could obtain the text of a statute as amended instead of having to retrieve the original statute from the *Statutes at Large* and the amendment from the *Statutes at Large* and then "cut and paste" the statute together to obtain its current wording.

When the revision was complete, Congress enacted the *Revised Statutes* into positive law, many of which remain in force to this very day. The enactment of the *Revised Statutes* automatically repealed the identical laws published in the *Statutes at Large*. Oddly (but perhaps predictably) enough, after the enactment of the *Revised Statutes*, numerous editorial mistakes were discovered. Congress had to order another revision in 1878 but the "revision of the revision" was never enacted into positive law.

Unfortunately, in 1875 Congress did not provide for a rapid system of ongoing revision. Thus, researchers would have to locate a statute in the *Revised Statutes* and then locate and "cut and paste" any subsequent amendments found in the *Statutes at Large*.

§ 11.7(b) *United States Code*

In 1926, Congress finally resolved the twin problems of "location" and "ongoing revision." Congress authorized creation of the *United States Code* to publish all "general and permanent" laws of the United States in a subject matter arrangement.

The United States Code Commission and the House Committee on Revision of Laws devised 50 broad subject classifications called "titles." For example, title 26 would contain all Internal Revenue laws; title 29 would contain all laws dealing with Labor; title 42 would contain all laws dealing with the Public Health & Welfare. A table showing these titles and the subject matter of the statutes they contain appears below:

Titles of the *United States Code*

1 General Provisions
2 The Congress
3 The President
4 Flag, Seal, etc.
5 Government Employees
6 Official & Penal Bonds
7 Agriculture
8 Aliens & Nationality
9 Arbitration
10 Armed Forces
11 Bankruptcy
12 Banks & Banking
13 Census
14 Coast Guard
15 Commerce & Trade
16 Conservation
17 Copyrights
18 Crimes
19 Customs Duties
20 Education
21 Food & Drugs
22 Foreign Relations
23 Highways
24 Hospitals, Asylums
25 Indians
26 Internal Revenue Code
27 Intoxicating Liquors
28 Judiciary & Judicial Procedure
29 Labor
30 Mineral Lands & Mining
31 Money & Finance
32 National Guard
33 Navigation & Navigable Waters
34 Former Navy title now in title 10
35 Patents
36 Patriotic Societies & Observances
37 Pay of Uniformed Services
38 Veterans' Benefits
39 Postal Service
40 Public Buildings, Property & Works
41 Public Contracts
42 Public Health & Welfare
43 Public Lands
44 Public Printings & Documents
45 Railroads
46 Shipping
47 Telegraphs, Telephones, etc.
48 Territories & Insular Possessions
49 Transportation
50 War & National Defense

From the *Revised Statutes* and the *Statutes at Large*, the committee extracted all federal statutes of a "general and permanent" nature, rewrote amended laws, and discarded repealed laws. These rewritten laws were then classified to the appropriate subject matter title. Within each title the committee logically arranged the laws and then assigned each law a section number. To allow for future growth, the committee intentionally left gaps in the numbering system. The entire *United States Code*, thus, constitutes a huge *analytical arrangement* of all general, permanent, and current federal statutes.

To provide a continuing system, Congress decided to complete a new edition of the *United States Code* once every six years, although the next edition did not appear until 1934, eight years after the first codification in 1926. Now the *United States Code* is rewritten and reissued every six years. At the writing of this book in 1992, the current edition is the 1988 edition, which will be replaced by the 1994 edition. That edition, the 1994 edition, however, won't hit the shelves as a completed work until sometime in late 1995 or early 1996. As titles are completed, the volumes will be sent to the libraries of the world, slowly forming a completed version of the *United States Code*.

Attorneys and the general public, however, cannot wait around for six years to gain subject matter access to federal statutes. (And they certainly can't wait around an additional two years to get the six-year revision.) To fill in the six-year period, the *United States Code* provides five interim supplements. The first year after a new Code is published, "Supplement I" will appear, containing all new laws and the rewritten versions of amended laws. The second year, "Supplement II" will appear. Since it cumulates the material in Supplement I, the first supplement can be discarded. The process continues through "Supplement V." Then the next edition of the entire Code will be published.

As you can see, many federal laws—those that are general, permanent, and current—are republished in the *United States Code* even though they also appear in the *Statutes at Large*. Thus, for legal citation purposes, many federal statutes could be cited either to the *Statutes at Large* or the *United States Code*. And for research purposes, you could find and read a statute in the *Statutes at Large* or find its amended and up-to-date version in the *United States Code*. But as we'll see in the next section, your legal research will rarely occur in the official version of the *United States Code*, for it is just too doggone slow to attract discerning researchers who insist on being truly up to date. Fortunately for these discerning researchers, there are two other places where codified federal laws are published: in two private versions of the *United States Code*.

§ 11.7(c) The Private Codes: U.S.C.A. and U.S.C.S.

Researchers face two main problems with the official *United States Code*. First, it is slow. The entire Code is updated every six years (1988, 1994, 2000, 2006, and so on). (It's weird seeing those 2000 dates!) Even though interim supplements fill in this six-year time gap, these supplements are notoriously slow in making their grand debut on the nation's library shelves. They come out piecemeal, one volume containing the new stuff for titles 1-11, the next picking up with title 12 through 18 (as an example), the next (half a year later) fixing up the next several titles. Researchers, especially Ace Legal Researchers, won't stand for such dillydallying.

The second problem with the official *United States Code* vexes researchers even more. When a researcher must research a federal legislative problem, the researcher, naturally enough, goes to the *United States Code* and looks up the applicable statute.

The statute might say something like this:

> Copyright protection subsists, in accordance with this title, in original works of authorship fixed in any tangible medium of expression, now known or later developed, from which they can be perceived, reproduced, or otherwise communicated, either directly or with the aid of a machine or device.[2]

Terrific. Why not run off to your computer and whip up an instant analysis of the precise meaning of that linguistic disaster. Dean Richard Wydick, of the University of California at Davis Law School, calls such gibberish "cosmic detachment."[3]

To find out exactly what federal statutes mean, researchers must . . . *get control now, I know this is terrible news* . . . research case law. That's right. Case law. For in our system of law, the federal courts, and ultimately the Supreme Court of the United States, have the power to interpret the laws passed by the legislative branch. After all, the ultimate enforcement of law, whether civil or criminal, takes place in the federal courts. So federal judges must face the language of the legislative law, no matter how unartful, figure out what it means, apply it to the set of facts in a given case, and then write an opinion of law explaining what the statute means and how it will apply in the real world.

Legislative researchers, then, must be able to find case law. And in the *United States Code* they will find absolutely zero case law.

So not only is the *United States Code* notoriously slow, it does not provide (indeed it was not intended to provide) any references to the thousands of cases that have cited and interpreted federal legislative law.

Researchers cannot wait for 18 months while the interim supplements to the Code finally update the *preceding* calendar year. Also, researchers want to find not only the applicable federal statute but all cases interpreting that statute. Thus, the market was ripe for the major legal publishing companies to publish their own versions of the *United States Code.*

§ 11.7(c)(i) *United States Code Annotated*

The West Publishing Company responded with *United States Code Annotated* or U.S.C.A. *United States Code Annotated* publishes the full text of all titles and all sections of the *United States Code.* Anyone, of course, can publish the full text of all general and permanent federal legislation—not exactly copyrighted information. So the title numbers and the section numbers in U.S.C.A. are identical to those you'll find in U.S.C.

Also, West was sitting in the catbird's seat. When the U.S. Congress cranked up the project to codify all federal laws, guess who it turned to for help? You got it. The West Company. Indeed, Roy G. Fitzgerald, Chairman of the Committee on the

[2]17 U.S.C. § 102(a) (1988).

[3]Richard Wydick, *Plain English for Lawyers* at 63 (Carolina Academic Press 1990).

Revision of the Laws of the House of Representatives, back in 1926, paid homage to the West Company in the Preface to the first edition of the *United States Code*:

> Under the auspices of the committees of the House and the Senate the actual work of assembling and classifying the mass of material has been done by the West Publishing Co. and the Edward Thompson Co. These two houses have subordinated their private interests to the public good and have produced a result which would not have been possible without them.

So while the West Company was helping the Congress codify its laws, it was, most likely, simultaneously setting type so that it could publish the first private version of the Code.

West was sitting in the catbird's seat for another reason: the West Company was publishing all of American case law; it was writing headnotes summarizing points of law found in the nation's case law; much of that case law was interpreting provisions of the *United States Code*; so all West had to do was "lift" the headnotes from the cases it was already publishing and reprint those headnotes in its version of the *United States Code*. Voilà! Along came *United States Code Annotated*.

The "annotated" in *United States Code Annotated* simply means that the code includes cross-references to cases interpreting each section. This means that you, the legal researcher, can look up any given federal statute, read it in U.S.C.A., and then find at your fingertips the headnotes from *every case in the country that has interpreted your particular code provision*.

Providing access to case law, however, was not enough. The West Company realized that the official form of supplementing the Code—interim, annual, hardback, slow supplements—would not serve its market well. It needed to speed up this supplementation process. It did so by providing cumulative annual pocket parts, which really do come out shortly after the year is over. To provide even more rapid supplementation, U.S.C.A. provides four pamphlets,[4] each supplementing the entire Code and each adding to, i.e., not cumulating, the preceding pamphlet. Each year these pamphlets usually are dated June, September, November, and January. Then, in February or March of each year, the new legislation found in the four pamphlets is dispatched to the new pocket part of the appropriate volume containing the appropriate title and section affected by new legislation and by new cases interpreting each section. The quarterly pamphlets then disappear from the shelf until the process begins anew the following May or June.

§ 11.7(c)(ii) *United States Code Service*

In the mid-1970s, Lawyers Cooperative Publishing Company introduced its version of the Code to compete with U.S.C.A., calling it *United States Code Service* (U.S.C.S.).

[4]In some particularly prolific years, West must produce as many as six of these "quarterly" pamphlets.

Lawyers Co-op bought the older *Federal Code Annotated* and added some rather attractive research aids:

1. References to law review articles analyzing any given section of the Code.
2. Headnotes to administrative decisions interpreting any section of the Code.
3. Citations to A.L.R. annotations dealing with any section of the Code.

These additional research aids, *which justify your using U.S.C.S. in addition to U.S.C.A.*, frightened the West Company into action. In more recent volumes of U.S.C.A. and in current supplement features, you'll find cross-references to more West publications and to "Law Review Commentaries."

U.S.C.S., however, follows the ordinary practice of Lawyers Co-op, which is to include only "selective" references to case law. The broader, more comprehensive coverage of cases provided by U.S.C.A. should, therefore, attract you to U.S.C.A. as your primary research tool. The clever legal researcher, that is, truly Ace Legal Researchers, will use both: U.S.C.A. as a case finder, U.S.C.S. as a law review and A.L.R. finder.

§ 11.8 Names and Sections of Federal Statutes

When drafting a statute, the authors frequently give it an official name. For example, the statute says, "This act may be cited as the Economic Recovery Act of 1984." Even if a statute is not given an official name, it often assumes the name of its sponsor, e.g., the Hatch Act, the Gramm-Rudman Act. Other statutes might even obtain a "popular name" such as the "Lindbergh Act," which made kidnapping a federal crime after Charles Lindbergh's baby was kidnapped.

Each federal statute enacted and published chronologically in the *Statutes at Large* has its own sectioning scheme. It might have sections 1, 2, 3, 4, 5, and so on. Each section might have subsections such as (a), (b), (c), (d), and so on. If a statute is "general and permanent," however, it must be reprinted in the appropriate title of the *United States Code*. And if it is a new statute, it must be assigned sections in U.S.C. that totally differ from its original sectioning scheme. These different sections for the same piece of legislation often cause confusion and can best be demonstrated by example.

Suppose Congress is concerned about student living conditions in the nation's law schools. On December 1, 1981, we'll assume, it passed the Law Student Relief Act, which was public law number 97-106. The Act, of course, was chronologically published in the *Statutes at Large*, volume 94, page 123.

Suppose section 1 of this Act requires each law school to provide sleeping sofas in the student lounge for between-class naps. Section 2 makes it a federal crime for the law school dean not to provide such sofas. Section 3 gives the federal courts jurisdiction to hear any civil action for damages arising under the statute. The statute with its three sections permanently resides in the *Statutes at Large*.

Because our hypothetical statute was "general and permanent," it had to be reprinted in the *United States Code*. But since the three sections pertained to different subject matters, they parted ways and resided in the appropriate titles of the Code. Because section 1 concerned the "Public Health and Welfare," it was codified in title 42 and assigned, let's say, section 2015. Section 2 concerned "Crimes" and was codified in title 18 as section 3211. Section 3 pertained to the "Judiciary" and was codified in title 28 as section 3414. The following table shows this process of "codification":

Original Section	Code Title	Code Section
§ 1	42	§ 2015
§ 2	18	§ 3211
§ 3	28	§ 3414

The statute stays in the Code under its new section numbers until it is repealed, perhaps in response to a concerted lobbying effort by law school deans. It forever stays in the *Statutes at Large* regardless of any repeal or amendment. Quite possibly, section 2 gains notoriety as more and more law school deans are prosecuted and sent to prison and becomes widely known as the Law Student Relief Act § 2. Like the Clayton Act § 7, or the Sherman Act § 1, the Law Student Relief Act § 2 is known and partially cited by its original section number even though its codified citation is 18 U.S.C. § 3211 (1988). The correct citation of this famous statute is:

Law Student Relief Act § 2, 18 U.S.C. § 3211 (1988).

It is very important for you to understand that section 2 in the above citation is the original section number of the statute as passed and as published in the *Statutes at Large*. The same statutory provision is republished in the *United States Code* and assigned Code section 3211 in title 18, which contains all criminal laws. Often in legal research, you'll find cases referring to a statute as "§ 734(a)" in "Title VII." Yet the citation will be "42 U.S.C. § 2000(e)(2)(a) (1988)." Are these two different statutes? What does the court mean "Title VII"? Is that "Title 7" of the Code, which reprints all statutes dealing with "Agriculture"?

No. When a statute is passed and published in the *Statutes at Large*, it might be divided into various "Titles." These are *not* the same titles as the 50 titles of the *United States Code*. Also, each statute has its own sectioning scheme. So "Title VII, § 734(a)" in the *Statutes at Large* might end up as "§ 2000(e)(2)(a)" in "Title 42" of the *United States Code*.

Isn't this fun?

Well, maybe not, but it's the career you've chosen, so you might as well get used to a world where "title" sometimes does not mean "title."

Why is it so important that you understand these fine distinctions? Perhaps so you can avoid a mistake made by a law student of mine who looked for hours in "Title 7" of the *United States Code* (Agriculture) for the Civil Rights Act of 1964, which was called "Title VII, § 734."

§ 11.9 "Enacted" Titles of the *United States Code*

Originally the *United States Code* merely provided a convenient means to locate federal law by subject matter and to keep federal law up-to-date by adding new legislation, changing amended legislation, and weeding out repealed legislation. If, however, there was a difference in the way a statute was worded in the *Statutes at Large* and the *United States Code*, the *Statutes at Large* would govern. The *Statutes at Large* provided positive evidence of the wording of a statute, while the *United States Code* served only as "prima facie evidence."

This distinction is still valid today for most federal statutes. The wording in the *Statutes at Large* must govern any conflicts. Congress, however, has embarked upon a campaign to *enact* many of the *United States Code* titles themselves.

Many of the 50 titles in the Code concern subject matter that should be acted upon by Congress in a concerted way. Thus, as an example, instead of enacting criminal laws bit by bit, publishing each bit chronologically in the *Statutes ai Large*, and republishing all bits in title 18 of the Code, Congress decided to revise all criminal laws at one time and then to enact title 18 itself. Congress has acted similarly with 22 of the 50 titles in the Code. The titles themselves, with their codified sectioning schemes, are enacted. The *United States Code* thus becomes positive evidence of the wording of the law in any of these 22 titles. Oddly enough, the enacted title is published in the *Statutes at Large* and, of course, republished in the *United States Code*. Now the sections are the same in both places. And if a different wording appears, the *United States Code* governs.

Some legal organizations make a crucial distinction between the *Statutes at Large* and the *United States Code* in their citation and research systems. The Tax Division of the Department of Justice, for example, requires its attorneys to read and cite to the *Statutes at Large* for any federal law in an *un*enacted title. If the title is enacted, the attorney must use the *United States Code*.

Why make such a distinction? Well, sometimes there is a difference in the wording so that the *Statutes at Large* wording governs any of the unenacted titles. For example, in one case a judgment was reversed just because the attorney had cited the *United States Code*, and it turned out that the wording in the *Statutes at Large* differed. The difference altered the entire outcome of the case. Here's what the judge said:

> We do not know what source of United States law is used in the Commissioner's office but we would be surprised if they [sic] were not the same as that commonly used by a judge, namely, *United States Code* or *United States Code Annotated*. The mistake, therefore, is perfectly natural. But no one denies that the official source to find United States laws is the *Statutes at Large* and that the Code is only prima facie evidence for such law.[5]

For citation purposes, the *Bluebook* distinguishes between enacted titles and unenacted titles only if the wording does differ, in which case the writer should cite the *Statutes at Large*. As a basic rule, the *Bluebook* provides: if a federal statute is in

[5]*Royers, Inc. v. United States*, 265 F.2d 615, 618 (3d Cir. 1959).

the Code, cite to the Code; if not in the Code, cite to the *Statutes at Large*. For research purposes, you should probably become accustomed to using U.S.C.A., but you should be aware that the wording of the statute you're citing might very well be different in the *Statutes at Large*. If your statute comes from an *un*enacted title, that other wording will govern your case. A list of enacted titles appears in the Preface of the latest *United States Code* or Interim Supplement.

§ 11.10 Legislative Law: Conclusion

In your study of the federal legislative system, you undoubtedly saw numerous parallels with the judicial system. Both systems produce "law": statutes in the legislative branch, cases in the judicial branch. Both these documents vitally affect the lives of millions of people. For that reason, people, i.e., "clients," are willing to shell out big bucks to law firms to find these cases and statutes, read them, understand them, and advise the clients how to comply with the law (or legally avoid the heavy burdens imposed upon them by the law).

These documents—statutes and cases—are published chronologically, statutes in the *Statutes at Large*, cases in the National Reporter System (the seven regionals, the two state reporters, and the five federal reporters). This chronological system of publication satisfies the need for speed. It also provides a permanent resting place for all law to sit chronologically on the shelves of the nation's law libraries.

But this chronological system created havoc when it came to "location" and "revision." So some form of "topical publication" was needed in addition to "chronological publication."

"Let's publish it twice!" the legal publishers all yelled in unison, visions of multiple invoices dancing in their heads.

And so they did. The West Company realized that case law was too bulky to publish twice, so they smooshed it down to a manageable size by writing "headnotes" to points of law. Then they printed these headnotes in the American Digest System, *the only subject matter rearrangement of case law in existence*.

Statutes, everyone agreed, were not so bulky. So Congress, and then West, and then Lawyers Co-op, all decided to publish federal statutes twice, first chronologically in the *Statutes at Large* and again by subject matter in the *United States Code*.

And then someone pointed out that no one, not the brightest person on earth, could possibly understand what a federal statute means. That person, indeed all legal researchers, would have to figure out what statutes mean by locating federal cases that have interpreted these statutes. So the West Company, owner of all headnotes on earth, eagerly printed *United States Code Annotated* (U.S.C.A.). Not only did it print all federal statutes (same title numbers, same section numbers). It also then printed, on a section-by-section basis, all headnotes from all cases interpreting all sections of the Code. Thus, the legal researchers of the world could go to U.S.C.A., find the on-point statute, and then find all on-point cases interpreting that statute.

And then came Lawyers Co-op with its *United States Code Service* (U.S.C.S.), providing the same statutes, same title numbers, same section numbers. It also provided headnotes to *some*, but not all, cases. But then it one-upped the West Company and provided cross-references to law review articles and A.L.R. Annotations. Thus, the legal researchers of the world would now have to buy and use *two* versions of the code: U.S.C.A. as a case finder and U.S.C.S. as a law review article and A.L.R. finder.

Our world of legislation was complete.

Ready to learn how to use this stuff in the real world? Turn the page. You're about to become the law clerk of Judge Clarence Thomas.

CHAPTER 12

LEGISLATIVE RESEARCH: THE THOMAS-HILL CASE

§ 12.1 The Statement of Facts

It is now the summer of 1991. You serve as the law clerk for Judge Clarence Thomas of the United States Court of Appeals for the District of Columbia Circuit. Judge Thomas has recently been appointed by President George Bush to serve on the Supreme Court of the United States. During the first round of hearings before the Senate Judiciary Committee, you provided Judge Thomas with position papers on a variety of constitutional issues. Now the committee has ordered additional hearings on charges made by law professor Anita Hill concerning alleged sexual harassment committed by Judge Thomas when he was the head of the Equal Employment Opportunity Commission. Specifically, Professor Hill alleges that Judge Thomas on several occasions bragged about his sexual prowess and described pornographic movies. Professor Hill does not say that Judge Thomas "propositioned" her in any way or made her participation in these conversations a condition for her continued employment or advancement. She does allege that the conversations made her extremely uncomfortable in her otherwise professional surroundings.

Judge Thomas has called you to his office, has summarized the above allegations, and has asked you to "find out whether this conduct constitutes sexual harassment under the Civil Rights Act of 1964 or any regulations thereunder."[1]

§ 12.2 Finding the Statute

In the real world of the practice of law, your boss—the person responsible for assigning you these seemingly impossible research topics—usually tells you to "hightail it to the library, research the Civil Rights Act, 42 U.S.C. § 2000(e)(2)(a), and find out what constitutes sexual harassment." In other words, in most research

[1]Prospective Justices on the Supreme Court like to use words like "thereunder."

projects, there isn't a "find the statute" phase; you already know the citation to the controlling statute.

But this isn't the real world. This is law school. Or paralegal school. Here, in this strange academic world, you must learn the theoretical—many times to the exclusion of the practical! So, to fit right in with other academic tomes, this work will teach you how to find a statute when all you know is the subject matter or, perhaps, just the statute's name.

Not surprisingly, there are only three things you can do to U.S.C.A. or U.S.C.S. (other than cuss at them): (1) the Index Approach, (2) the Analytical Approach, and (3) the Tabular Approach.

In the following discussion, I will focus on U.S.C.A. (West Company) but point out the features of U.S.C.S. (Lawyers Co-op) that make it an attractive research tool to use in addition to U.S.C.A.

§ 12.2(a) The Index Approach

Like any multivolume lawbook, U.S.C.A. features two indexes: (1) a General Index
{47,48} {47,48}, indexing the entire Code, and (2) Title Indexes, indexing each individual title of the Code (in the volume concluding the title). You will find, I'm afraid, that the U.S.C.A. index is among the worst in all of legal literature, representing classic "over-indexing." Index words that ought to be there, aren't. Index words that ought not to be there, are. Index words that should lead you to the desired statute, don't. The sanity you used to prize, ain't.

But we're stuck with it. When using it, you should keep in mind Good's Rules of Research Nos. 5, 6, and 7. In the highly unlikely event these rules have slipped your mind, here they are again:

GOOD'S RULE OF RESEARCH #5:

When you use an index, always consult the narrowest word first.

GOOD'S RULE OF RESEARCH #6:

When you start an index search at the top of the list, the answer is always found at the bottom. Try to trick it by starting at the bottom? The answer's at the top.

GOOD'S RULE OF RESEARCH #7:

Use a General Index as a "volume finder" and the Volume Index as a "page finder."

Rule Nos. 5 and 7 are especially apt. Choosing the narrowest word first can reduce the amount of time you flail away in the General Index. And using the General Index as a "volume finder," or here a "title finder," can save you scores of stomach ulcers.

When you do find words that cross-reference you to scads of legislative provisions, focus on the recurring numbers, the numbers leaping off the page at you. For example, when you research the Thomas-Hill case, you'll see gobs of references to "§ 2000, etc." in title 42.

That's enough. Don't continue to look for precise references to your exact topic. Bottom line: use the General Index to locate the *likely* title and the *likely* section number. Then shift your looking to the Analytical Approach or the Title Index Approach.

Continuing with the Index Approach, U.S.C.A. provides a separate, more specific index for each title of the Code. You'll find this index in the volume concluding the title (which might stretch over scores of volumes). For some titles, such as the infamous Title 26 (the Internal Revenue Code), the title index sits in a separate pamphlet.

§ 12.2(b) The Tabular Approach

As I mentioned in the previous chapter, many, if not most, federal statutes have a name, usually a given name, found in the enacting clause of the statute, or a "popular name" derived from the sponsors of the statute or other circumstances surrounding its enactment. Often in the real world you'll receive an assignment to research the Civil Rights Act of 1964, the Freedom of Information Act, or the Clean Air Act. No cite is given. Just a name.

In the last volume of the General Index, which is usually the "U to Z" volume, you'll find the "Popular Name Table" {49}. There you can look up the name of your **{49}** statute. Then you'll find the following information: (1) the date of enactment, (2) the *Statutes at Large* citation, (3) the Public Law Number, and (4) *all* locations in the *United States Code* where the statute has been *codified*, that is, reprinted. Item No. 4 will likely cause confusion. Remember that a statute, just like a case, will deal with a variety of subject matters. So a statute, just like a case, must be classified into various subject matter headings. A statute might be carved up and reprinted in several different titles and several different sections for the simple reason that it involves several different subject matters—just like a case, which typically has a variety of headnotes classified to several Main Topics and to several different Key Numbers.

As an aside, although an important aside, this Popular Name Table is the first source we've encountered in this discussion that gives you three pieces of information needed for compiling a legislative history: (1) date of enactment, (2) Public Law Number, and (3) *Statutes at Large* citation. File it away in your brain for future reference that these bits of information are your keys to compiling citations to bills, hearings, committee reports, and floor debate—the legislative history of a federal statute.

§ 12.2(c) The Analytical Approach

Once you've discovered the title containing your statute, it's usually fairly easy to discover the exact sections by using the Analytical Approach. In the front of any volume of U.S.C.A. containing any of the sections of your title, you'll find a complete
{50} analytical breakdown of that title {50}. The title is broken down into chapters, which are divided into subchapters, which are divided into sections. By zeroing in on the names of these chapters, subchapters, and ultimately sections, you can find those sections governing your problem.

§ 12.3 Consulting the Statute

Having used the Index Approach, the Tabular Approach, or the Analytical Approach to locate the Civil Rights Act of 1964, 42 U.S.C. § 2000(e)(2) (1988), the Ace Legal Researcher will then proceed to . . .

HOG THE BOOKS!

By this I mean: the Ace Legal Researcher will use both private codes to consult the federal statute. The Ace Legal Researcher will dash over to U.S.C.A. and to U.S.C.S. and find both volumes containing the same section of the U.S. Code. You might think our Ace Legal Researcher has lost her marbles, but you'd be wrong. Our Ace Legal Researcher is simply recognizing the need for *background legal research* in legislative problems just as she experienced a need for *background legal research* in case law problems. And our Ace Legal Researcher, having already read this sizzling page-turner, knows that U.S.C.S. provides superior cross-references to background materials analyzing the statute and that U.S.C.A. provides superior cross-references to annotations to cases interpreting the statute.

Because you will ultimately use U.S.C.A. for case-finding tasks and for updating tasks, I will focus this section on U.S.C.A. (West Company) but point out the rather attractive features of U.S.C.S. (Lawyers Co-op). I trust that U.S.C.S. book salespeople will not get their noses out of joint and will instead recognize the significant endorsement of U.S.C.S. I make and therefore will choose selected portions of this text (excising all references to U.S.C.A.) for liberal use in their advertising pieces.

Your statute-finding tasks have brought you to the Civil Rights Act of 1964, located at title 42, section 2000(e) et seq. When you seek the correct volume in U.S.C.A., you immediately notice that one single volume of U.S.C.A. (and U.S.C.S.)

contains relatively few sections of the United States Code. The volume (in 1992) containing the Civil Rights Act of 1964, for example, contains sections 2000(e) through 2010, that is, just 11 sections of the Code. Yet the volume contains nearly 1000 pages. Surely the statutory language of a mere 11 sections does not include enough words to fill up an entire volume. Granted, members of the House and Senate can't write, but even they (or their staff members) don't chew up an entire volume for just 11 sections.

Thankfully not. When you visit your first volume of U.S.C.A., you'll find that the vast majority of pages are consumed by references not to the legislation itself but to *headnotes of cases interpreting a particular statute.*

So go ahead and pull the correct volume off the shelf, confident in the knowledge that you won't have to read a 900-page statute. In fact, you'll find that the relevant portions of the Civil Rights Act of 1964 consume no more than a paragraph {51}. It **{51}**
provides:

> It shall be an unlawful employment practice for an employer—
>
> > (a) to fail or refuse to hire or to discharge any individual, or otherwise to discriminate against any individual with respect to his compensation, terms, conditions, or privileges or employment, because of such individual's race, color, religion, sex, or national origin; . . . .[3]

In a word: sex discrimination is against the law. Whether that law outlaws an obscene joke in the workplace is not immediately apparent.

In U.S.C.A., at the end of the statute, you'll find some important information {52}. **{52}**
Immediately following the statute, in parentheses, you'll find the Public Law Number, the date of enactment, and the *Statutes at Large* citation of the original enactment and of any amendments.

Then you'll find a "Historical Note" {52}, showing the significance of amend- **{52}**
ments. Within this "Historical Note" you'll find a bold-faced entry entitled: "Legislative History." This note will then say:

> For legislative history and purpose of [the Act] see [year of the Act] U.S. Code Cong. & Adm. News [page], [page]. For legislative history and purpose of [the Amendment] see [year of the Amendment] U.S. Code Cong. & Adm. News [page], [page].

These are West Company references from one of its books, U.S.C.A., to another of its books, *United States Code Congressional and Administrative News*, known in the trade as USCCAN. USCCAN, you will soon learn, provides an indispensable step in the legislation-updating process. The reference here, after the statute in U.S.C.A., is somewhat misleading, for it seems to say you can use USCCAN to get your hands on legislative history. Well, up to a point, that's true. Beyond that point, it's not true.

USCCAN does let you get your hands on the most important piece of legislative history, the House and Senate Committee Reports. For each significant statute

[3]42 U.S.C. § 2000(e)(2)(a) (1988).

enacted, USCCAN publishes the *full text* of the House and Senate Committee Reports on the bills ultimately enacted. But USCCAN does not enable you to get your hands on other forms of legislative history: bills, committee hearings, and floor debate. It will help you find out where those documents are located *elsewhere* in the law library. But it does not *publish* the text of these legislative history documents. It only publishes the committee reports. We'll return to USCCAN later when I discuss techniques of updating legislative research to the present day and methods of compiling legislative histories.

Following the "Historical Note" you'll find a heading entitled "Library Refer-
{52} ences" {52}. In "older" volumes of U.S.C.A., those, say, before the late 1980s, you won't find much within this heading, just a few lousy cross-references to Key Numbers and to some C.J.S. passages. Big deal.

In more recent volumes, however, you'll find that the West Company has beefed up its Library References feature by providing cross-references to other West treatises
{60} and form books and to "Law Review Commentaries" {60}. Why the change? Because U.S.C.S. started beating the socks off the West Company with its copious notes to A.L.R. Annotations discussing each federal statute and to law review articles discussing each federal statute. Because of these vastly superior research cross-references, you should . . .

HOG THE BOOKS!

Seriously, when you do legislative research, get the U.S.C.S. volume for background research and the U.S.C.A. volume for case law research. Jot down citations to
{53} {54} on-point A.L.R. Annotations {53} and to major law review articles {54}, get that material, read it over, get an overview of the law, and then come back to U.S.C.A. for detailed case law research.

Case law research? Yep. Case law research. Rarely does a federal legislative research problem *end* with the location of a federal statute. Indeed, in the vast majority of situations, the research problem *begins* with the location of the statute. You locate a statute, find out that it outlaws "discrimination . . . on account of . . . sex." Does that include sexual harassment? Does it mean an employer cannot mention a porno movie to an employee? Depending on your political bent, you might want it to or not want it to, but your political bent is irrelevant.

So what does the statute mean? Whatever the federal courts say it means.

Legislative law research, therefore, throws you right back into the thick of case law research. Fortunately for you, you don't have to abandon U.S.C.A. (or U.S.C.S.) to launch your search for case law, for these *legislative* research sources also serve as *case law* research sources. What a deal.

Now comes the fun part. Now comes "piles."

§ 12.3(a) U.S.C.A., A Graphic Depiction

Let's pause to "see" U.S.C.A. and its relationship to legislative law and case law.

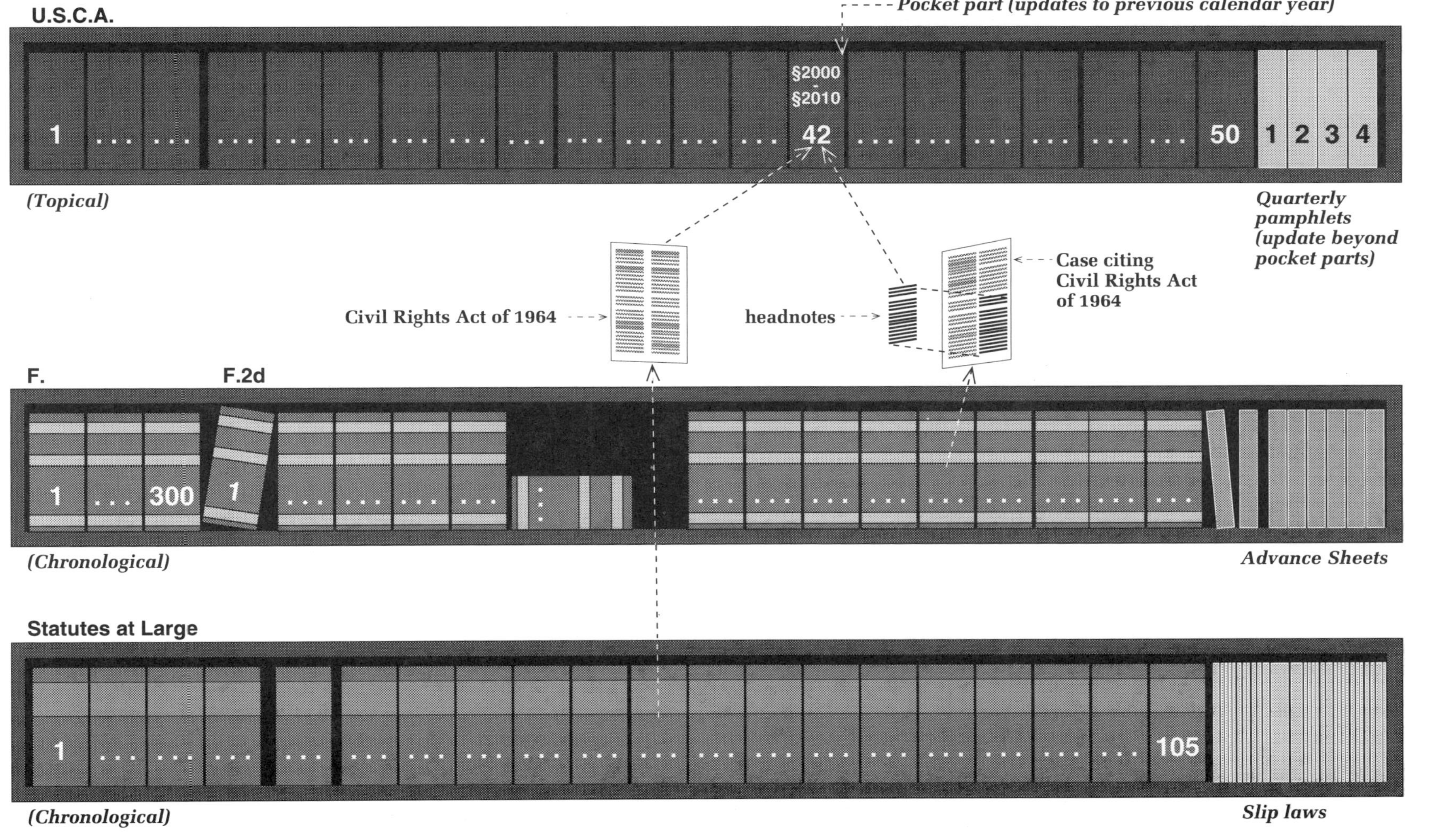

Figure 9

U.S.C.A., A Collector of Statutes and Cases

§ 12.4 Finding Cases Interpreting the Statute

Picture the problem.

Got it? Good.

Now picture the problem faced by the West Company. The West Company decided to publish the entire United States Code. Same titles. Same sections. Word for word. The whole ball of wax. But it realized that attorneys and law students and paralegal students would also want to find cases interpreting every provision of the United States Code. After all, after reading a federal statute, most researchers don't leap out of Archimedes' tub screaming "Eureka! Eureka!" smack dab in the middle of the law library. The words of the statute, after all, don't necessarily *solve* legal problems. Indeed, often they *create* legal problems.

So the problem faced by the West Company was this: how would they publish *both* the individual sections of the U.S. Code and all cases from across the country interpreting each individual section of the Code.

For the West Company, the answer was easy. *Headnotes!* After all, they figured, they already published millions of little paragraphs summarizing each minute point treated in all of American case law. They already published these millions of headnotes in the American Digest System. It would be quite an easy task to order its computer system to spit out just those headnotes coming from cases that interpret sections of the United States Code. Then they could just print the headnotes of the cases interpreting a particular section of the U.S. Code immediately after printing that section of the Code in *United States Code Annotated.*

Piece of cake.

But picture the problem.

Suppose a single section of the Code has been interpreted by 15,000 cases? Great. The computer geeks at the West Company wave their magical computer mouses, or whatever, and . . .

Splat! Here come 15,000 headnotes to the paste-up department for pasting up after pasting up the one-page federal statute. Terrific.

The editors at West (or the paste-up department) faced yet another huge problem of arrangement: how to arrange the zillions of headnotes so that a lonely, befuddled legal researcher could then zero in and find just the right headnotes on any given point of case law surrounding a section of federal legislative law? Not surprisingly, three systems suggested themselves: the Tabular Approach, the Analytical Approach, and the Index Approach.

First, the paste-up department could arrange the headnotes in a tabular way, that is, in a case tabular way, that is, alphabetically by case name.

Not. Not a good way at all, some astute paster-upper pointed out, especially since the researchers wouldn't know the names of the cases they sought.

Second, the paste-up department could arrange the headnotes in an analytical way and provide a subanalysis, much like those in the American Digest System or in the West Company's legal encyclopedia (C.J.S.).

Third, the paste-up department could arrange index words alphabetically and provide cross-references to the headnotes.

They decided on a strange hybrid approach, sort of a cross between an Analytical Approach and an Index Approach. It's a bit difficult to explain, but if you'll play along with me and follow some weird metaphors, you'll understand quite clearly how to use U.S.C.A. to solve the toughest of federal legislative research problems.

§ 12.4(a) *Pile Numbers*

First you must acquaint yourself with . . . *piles*. That's right. *Piles*. And *pile numbers*.

The West Company decided to arrange the headnotes of cases interpreting *each* individual section of the Code into *piles*. And they decided to give each of these piles a *pile number*.

Now you might legitimately ask why I came up with this bizarre term. I respond that I didn't want to use the term *headnote numbers* because you might confuse that term with the term *Key Number*. Because we're definitely not talking about *Key Numbers*, I detected a need to coin a new term. The West Company, by the way, uses *Note Number*, but what could be more boring than *Note Number*? So *piles* and *pile number* it is. Like it or not.

§ 12.4(b) Arranging the Headnotes into Broad Analytical Groupings

Picture if you will the paste-up department at the West Company. There they sit with the fresh typeset of *one* section of the U.S. Code. Now they've added some whistles and bells with the "Historical Note," the "Legislative History," and the "Library References." But now comes the hard part. There they sit, staring at a huge pile of 15,000 headnotes, which they now must arrange in some sort of order so that they can now paste-up and ultimately print these headnotes *and*, most importantly, so that you, the legal researcher, can *find* a given headnote on a given point of law like how many angels can dance on the head of a pin.

The paste-up department, staring at this mass of headnotes, decided to broadly divide them into four or five major groupings, such as "In General," "Private Employer Practices," "Public Employer Practices," and so forth. In your mind, you can imagine dealing the headnotes from one great big pile into four or five smaller, narrower piles.

Great. That's just what the West Company did.

Then the paste-up department decided to take each subdivided category and minutely group the headnotes into . . . into . . . well, into *piles*, that is, into small piles of similar headnotes. One pile might contain the headnotes of cases dealing with dress codes in the workplace or height requirements or weight requirements or marital status of flight attendants or physical tests of firefighters . . . and the list went on and on.

Once the paste-up department had, well, *pileified* the headnotes into these little piles, it then stood back and saw that broad group #1 had, say, 32 piles in it. Group #2 had 73, Group #3 had 231, and so on. Thus, the paste-up department, knowing that case law would grow and that new pile numbers would be needed, divided the 15,000
{55} headnotes this way {55}:

I	Generally	1 - 50
II	Discriminatory Practices—Generally	51 - 150
III	Private Employer Practices	151 - 450
IV	Public Employer Practices	451 - 610
V	Labor Organization Practices	611 - 675

So picture the paste-up department. They had divided the huge pile of 15,000 headnotes onto the tops of five different tables. Then, on each table, they had subdivided the headnotes into little piles called *piles*. They counted the number of piles on each table and then added a bunch of *unused numbers* to accommodate future growth. Then they stuck toothpicks in each pile and made a little paper flag to stick on each toothpick. On each flag, they then wrote down the *name of the pile*, such as "dress codes," "height and weight requirements," "firefighter strength tests," and so on. (One, for example, might be "sexual harassment" or "harassment" or "dirty jokes" or whatever.)

Then the paste-up department wrote numbers next to the names on the flags. These numbers became *pile numbers*! These pile numbers then determined *the order in which each pile would be printed.*

So the paste-up department then arranged the piles of headnotes by pile number and began to paste up the artwork for printing in that pile-number order following the printing of that section of the Code.

Then, to help you, the legal researcher, *find* the right pile number, and hence the right pile, the paste-up department took all the little paper flags, each showing the name of the pile and the corresponding pile number, and alphabetized the list by name of pile.

Then the paste-up department printed that alphabetized list and called it the very
{55} boring "Notes of Decisions" {55}. But when you look at your first federal statute, and read it, and scratch your head and wonder what it means, and begin your first search for cases interpreting that section, you'll know, when you first encounter the "Notes of Decisions," that they are really the alphabetized names of flags on toothpicks sticking in *hundreds* of piles of headnotes, each pile containing the headnotes of cases narrowly defined to just one particular pile.

Then your heart will sink, when you turn the page, and the next page, and the next page, and the next, only to find page after page of alphabetized names of flags on piles.

You know how to search through alphabetical listings of words, through these dreaded legal indexes. That's right: the Nope-Nope-Nope approach. You've got to start at the top of the list and run your *index finger* down the list of names of piles. What fun. This is costing you *how* much in tuition?

§ 12.4(c) A Shortcut: The "Subdivision Index"

As you can see, searching for the right pile number is not a whole lot of fun. Fortunately, there is a shortcut.

When you view the "Notes of Decision" Index, you'll see the broad analytical arrangement at the top, the arrangement of the piles into Roman Numerals. If you can identify one, or perhaps two, of these broad breakdowns as the one (or two) containing your legal issue, then note the pile number beginning that Roman Numeral. Say, for example, that it's 151.

If you'll then skip over the broad "Notes of Decision" Index and go directly to Note 151, you'll find what's called the "Subdivision Index" {56}. This index alphabetically **{56}**
lists *just the names of the piles in your Roman Numeral breakdown*. Necessarily, it's a shorter list, thereby reducing the pain of the Nope-Nope-Nope index search.

§ 12.4(d) Identifying the Right Piles

In your search for cases on point, i.e., for *all* cases interpreting your legislative provision in your factual context, you must exercise great care in your choice of the right pile numbers. Many researchers find one pile number that fits perfectly but neglect to discover other pile numbers equally on point.

The point is this: the paste-up department at the West Company faces the daunting task of dividing 15,000 or so headnotes into six or seven *hundred* subclassifications. Opportunities abound for putting two similar cases in two different piles, thereby tripping up the unsuspecting legal researcher.

Bottom line? When choosing pile numbers, look around, figure that others do exist, ferret them out. Be expansive.

§ 12.4(e) Finding Cases on Point

Finding cases on point, of course, is easy, once you've identified the right pile numbers. Simply consult those pile numbers {57}, read the headnotes of cases **{57}**
classified to those numbers, identify the ones worth reading, jot down their citations, and ultimately retrieve and read those cases.

§ 12.4(f) Finding Secondary Authority on Point

Before running off to read the cases you've found, you should pause and remember the lessons learned in the case law research chapters of this book. As a rule (especially at the beginning of your legal or paralegal career), it's difficult simply to retrieve cases, read cases, and *understand what the heck is going on.* Invariably it makes more sense to find and read some background authority to provide that vital overview of the law so that each individual case fits within the larger context. What you need are A.L.R. Annotations and legal periodical articles.

The *only* place you can find *both* is *United States Code Service* (U.S.C.S.), published by Lawyers Co-op, the competitor to West. U.S.C.S. provides cross-
{53} {54} references to A.L.R. Annotations {53} and legal periodical articles {54} (as well as to a host of "practice aids" of interest to practicing lawyers). Thus, instead of having to make an independent search for on-point A.L.R. Annotations, you can find them right with the statute in U.S.C.S. Also there you'll find references to on-point legal periodical articles.

In U.S.C.S. you'll probably find more than enough legal periodical articles to read, but if you're *thoroughly* researching an issue, you should not rely on the list of legal periodical articles as an *exhaustive list* of articles. The safer approach is to check the *Index to Legal Periodicals,* the *Current Law Index,* or WilsonDisc to make certain you've retrieved *every* on-point article.

If U.S.C.S. is so great, you're undoubtedly saying, then why even use U.S.C.A.? Because U.S.C.S. does not include headnotes to *all* cases interpreting *each* section of the U.S. Code. The case coverage provided by West (because it has already written headnotes for all cases published) far exceeds that provided by U.S.C.S.

Thus, when researching a federal legislative problem, you should use *both* U.S.C.A. *and* U.S.C.S., U.S.C.A. for cases, U.S.C.S. for background authority. In a word: Hog the books!

§ 12.5 Updating the Statute and Cases to the Present Day

It goes without saying (but I'll say it anyway) that when you picked up the volume of U.S.C.A., you undoubtedly followed Good's Rule of Research #11, which admonishes you to check the copyright date of a book *before* using it. Thus, when you use the bound volume of U.S.C.A., your *legislative* research and your *judicial* research is valid as of the year of the copyright date.

That copyright date might be 10 or 20 or even 30 years ago!

"But I thought the U.S. Code was revised every six years?" you moan as you rummage through your old files of applications to Business School.

Well, it is, but simply revising the U.S. Code does not force the West Company to reissue each volume of U.S.C.A. Rather, West keeps each volume of U.S.C.A. up to date via the popular "pocket part" approach to legal supplementation. If a legislative change occurs, that change will be reflected in the Cumulative Annual Pocket Part. And, as new cases are decided interpreting the statutes found within a single volume of U.S.C.A., all West has to do is print the headnotes to those cases each year in the Cumulative Annual Pocket Part.

Each year, of course, that pocket part gets a little bit bigger. But as long as it comfortably fits inside the back cover of the book, West need not reissue the bound volume. In fact, West will only reissue the bound volume when the pocket part gets too big for its britches and won't fit inside the back cover. At that point, the pocket part will become, for several years, a pocket part *pamphlet* sitting on the shelf *next* to the bound volume, which no longer has a pocket part. Then, when that pocket part *pamphlet* becomes the approximate size of a bound volume, the West Company will reissue that bound volume, splitting it into *two* bound volumes by putting some sections in one book and the remaining sections in the other book, each with its own new Cumulative Annual Pocket Part. The pocket part *pamphlet* simply disappears.

Your research, then, is up to date as of the copyright date of the bound volume of U.S.C.A. And that might be 10 years ago. During that time of course, the federal courts of the country have been spewing out cases, many, naturally enough, interpreting *your* federal statute in cases *identical* to your fact situation. In addition, Congress, in its infinite wisdom, might have decided to *amend* your statute or even *repeal* your statute. All you know is what you read in the bound U.S.C.A. And that's old news.

It's time, therefore, to move in the legal research process from the use phase to the updating phase. As you perform these supplementation functions, please note one important fact. You have *two* forms of law that need updating: (1) the statute itself, which might have been amended or repealed, and (2) the cases interpreting that statute. As a general rule, throughout your legal career, you'll find legislative changes *rarely* take place while judicial changes *always* take place. So be prepared *not* to find many legislative changes and *always* to find new, more recent cases interpreting your statute.

Always keep in mind that your research must follow two lines, a legislative line and a judicial line. Fortunately, most of the updating for *both* lines will take place in U.S.C.A. so that looking in one place reveals both legislative law and judicial law. But, as you'll see in the upcoming sections, at some point you and U.S.C.A. must part ways. At that point, the two lines diverge, and you must follow two distinct research trails, one for statutes, the other for cases interpreting that statute.

§ 12.5(a) Checking the Pocket Part or Pocket Part *Pamphlet*

In the back of the bound volume you should find the Cumulative Annual Pocket Part {58}. If one is not there, you should find a "Notice" slipped into the pocket slit, **{58}** pointing out that the pocket part now appears as a pocket part *pamphlet*, in which case you should find it shelved next to the bound volume.

In the pocket part, you simply look up the same legislative section you consulted in the bound volume. Typically you'll find that section number. And typically you'll then see . . .

The Statute That's Not There!

{59} Look very carefully and you'll see the section number {59}. And then, again looking very carefully, you'll see the *statute that's not there*. The *statute that's not there* is the one that isn't printed. See it?

I told you this world of research was weird.

Anyway, in the pocket part, when you find the section number, you typically do not find any statute printed there. The *absence* of a statute printed there, i.e., *the statute that's not there*, means that your statute has *not* been amended or repealed.

Bingo. You've updated the statute.

Now, the cases.

To update the cases, many legal researchers rush off stark raving mad, foaming at the mouth, and head straight for the same pile numbers they identified and used in the bound volume. And they make a drastic mistake by failing to follow:

GOOD'S RULE OF RESEARCH #25

Woe be unto the legal researcher who uses the same pile numbers in a U.S.C.A. pocket part without first checking the list of new pile numbers at the beginning of each pertinent Roman Numeral subdivision.

To understand this vital rule of research, you must orient yourself in time. Your bound volume of U.S.C.A. might have been printed 10 years ago. Since that time, courts have decided a horde of decisions, many dealing with *new* issues. These cases involved subject matter that was nonexistent when the paste-up department at the West Company had to divide all *then-existing* headnotes into piles.

To accommodate these new issues, the paste-up department simply creates new
piles and new pile numbers. It then alphabetizes the names of these new piles and
{61} creates a subdivision index {61}, which it prints after the Roman Numeral grouping
of piles. You should make it a hard and fast rule that you *always* check this subdivision
index *before* dashing off to the pile numbers you used in the bound volume.

After visiting this new index and perhaps picking up one or two new pile
{62} numbers of interest, you turn in the pocket part to the relevant pile numbers {62}. In
the pocket part, you might find the pile number missing, which means that between

the date of the bound volume and the date of the pocket part, no court decided any case on your point of law. If you found sufficient cases in the bound volume, then that's good news. It means you've got fewer cases to read and can spend your time on important things in life. Like taking a nap.

Of course, most of the time you do find the pile numbers, each with additional headnotes of cases on point. Scan the headnotes, jot down the cites to the cases you need to read, cancel your nap, and trot over to the National Reporter System for a real fun afternoon. Or night.

§ 12.5(b) Checking the Quarterly Pamphlets

But wait. Case law research is not over. And neither is legislative law research. When you consult the pocket part, your research is up to date through the autumn of the preceding calendar year. Thus, if you're researching in September, the pocket part brings you up to date as of the *previous* fall.

As a rule, the West Company sends out the pocket parts in March or April of each year. As noted in the previous chapter, the West Company then supplements the pocket part with four (sometimes more) quarterly pamphlets, each updating the *entire* U.S. Code and none cumulating the preceding pamphlet. These quarterly pamphlets appear as red and white paperbacks, numbered, on the spines, 1, 2, 3, and 4. Usually they come out in (1) June, (2) September, (3) November, and (4) January.

You can immediately see that the quarterly pamphlets are not really "quarterly." The first one does not appear until five or six months after the publication of the cumulative annual pocket part. How come? Because Congress rarely passes many laws in the spring of the year (usually fewer than 10). After convening in January, members of Congress have to carefully plan some trips back home to talk with the constituents (fondly referred to as "yahoos" by many inside-the-beltway types!) or perhaps some fact-finding missions to study the foreign aid needs of Tahitians. Whatever the reason, Congress doesn't do much in the spring, so West delays the publication of Quarterly Pamphlet #1.

The steps for using the quarterly pamphlets are identical to those for the pocket part:

1. Find your statutory section number.
2. See the *statute that's not there.*
3. Consult the subdivision index {63}. **{63}**
4. Consult the proper pile numbers {64}. **{64}**
5. Jot down the cites to on-point cases.
6. Cancel your nap.

§ 12.5(c) The Second Most Important Page in All of Legal Research

From February through May or June, your legislative research will consist of two steps: (1) bound volume and (2) pocket part. Then, as the year unfolds, your legislative research will include as many as four additional steps, i.e., consulting each of four
{65,66,67} quarterly pamphlets {65,66,67}.

The point is this, at some point you will run out of U.S.C.A. supplement features. Perhaps the last supplement of U.S.C.A. you can check is the pocket part (February through May or June), or Pamphlet #1 (May or June through July or August), or Pamphlet #2 (July or August through September or October), or Pamphlet #3 (September or October through November or December), or Pamphlet #4 (November or December through January). These dates are not publication dates but rather the dates when the pamphlets actually hit the shelves.

{65} When you do run out of U.S.C.A. supplements {65}, whether it be pocket part or any of the quarterly pamphlets, you must make certain that you follow:

> GOOD'S RULE OF RESEARCH #26
>
> **In the last U.S.C.A. supplement, always check the *second most important page in all of legal research* to ascertain a judicial Stop Cite and a legislative Stop Cite.**

In the front of any U.S.C.A. pocket part and in front of *each* quarterly pamphlet
{68} you'll find the *second most important page in all of legal research* {68}. If you'll recall in Chapter 6, I pointed out how C.J.S. has the table in the front of each pocket part showing the volume and page numbers in *each* court report where Wilbur *stopped* collecting cases. You'll find the same page in all U.S.C.A. supplements.

This page will give you a *judicial* Stop Cite, and, no doubt, you know exactly what to do with the *judicial* Stop Cite (don't worry, we'll review it below). The same page will give you a *legislative* Stop Cite. And you don't know what to do with that.

The point is that you must *separately* update the statute to the present day and the cases to the present day. You've run out of U.S.C.A., which up to this point, has provided a single research tool for both statutes and cases. Thus, you must launch a separate search for cases decided *after* the publication of the U.S.C.A. supplement and for statutes enacted *after* the publication of the U.S.C.A. supplement.

To ascertain where the U.S.C.A. supplement stopped publishing statutes, look at the paragraph at the top of the *second most important page in all of legal research* (at the front of the latest supplement). There you'll find a statement that the supplement
{68} contains new statutes through Public Law Number ____-____ {68}. Such a Stop Cite

might be: Public Law Number 102-255, meaning the 255th public law passed by the 102nd Congress.

Thus, the U.S.C.A. supplement has published statutes for you *through* the Stop Cite. It has not published statutes *beyond* the Stop Cite. But there might indeed *be* a federal statute *beyond* the Stop Cite that either amends your statute or repeals your statute.

Imagine, if you will, citing a federal statute to a federal judge. Further imagine that the statute was recently amended. Further imagine the opponents citing and relying upon the more recent amendment. And then imagine your *failing* to find and cite and rely upon the more recent amendment. Oh, woe is you.

To ascertain where the U.S.C.A. supplement stopped publishing cases, look at
the table in the middle of the *second most important page in all of legal research* {68}. **{68}**
You can pick *any* court report, but for federal research purposes, it's probably a good idea to use one of the federal reports, either the *Federal Reporter* (reporting circuit court cases) or the *Federal Supplement* (reporting district court cases). On the table you'll find the judicial Stop Cites, i.e., the volumes and pages marking the precise moment when Wilbur stopped collecting cases for the U.S.C.A. supplement. As noted above, you can pick any of these Stop Cites, for they all mark the *same moment in time.*

Bottom line? Jot down the judicial Stop Cite (volume number and page number of any given court report) and the legislative Stop Cite (Public Law Number) in your notes. It's now time to update both cases and statute to the present day.

§ 12.5(d) Updating the Cases to the Present Day

Please say you already know how to do this.

Because you do.

In case you've forgotten, however, here it is again.

On the *second most important page in all of legal research* {68} you found your **{68}**
judicial Stop Cite. You simply picked either the *Federal Reporter* or the *Federal Supplement* and jotted down the volume and page number where Wilbur stopped collecting cases. If you choose the *Federal Reporter* and then go to the shelf itself to see how far along the shelf is compared with U.S.C.A. coverage, you're in for a big shock when you discover:

GOOD'S RULE OF RESEARCH #27:

On an average, the *Federal Reporter* has 12 volumes of case law on the shelf *not* yet covered by U.S.C.A.

That's 12 volumes x 1500 pages/volume = 18,000 pages of federal circuit court case law not yet covered by the latest U.S.C.A. supplement. A dangerous NO ZONE indeed.

You can traverse this judicial NO ZONE in two ways. You've already found cases in U.S.C.A. and, presumably, you've at least looked at some of those cases. On their title pages you discovered the Key Numbers that the West Company uses to classify your legal issues. Then, carefully using your new-found skills, you verified your Key Numbers by the Analytical Approach, the Index Approach, and the Peel-the-Label Approach. Finding that your Key Numbers are still valid, you then run the Key Numbers through the NO ZONEs established by the *Federal Reporter* Stop Cite and the *Federal Supplement* Stop Cite. (If you're researching an issue susceptible to Supreme Court review, you'd also have to use a *Supreme Court Reporter* Stop Cite and traverse that respective NO ZONE as well.)

A second approach is also available, an approach that will cut down the size of *all* NO ZONEs. Use any Stop Cite found on the *second most important page in all of legal research* and find out where that Stop Cite is digested in the latest *General Digest.* And how do you find that out? Simple. By using (I hear you all replying in unison):

{69} *The Single Most Important Page in All of Legal Research!* {69}

Remember? At the front of each *General Digest* volume you'll find the table showing where all possible case citations are digested. It's very easy to find out where any Stop Cite is digested. Then you run Key Numbers in those volumes of the *General Digest* digesting cases *beyond* your Stop Cite. (Remember that any Stop Cite is marking the same moment in time.)

Then, after you run Key Numbers in these several *General Digest* volumes, you must find new Stop Cites for each relevant court report and run Key Numbers through *all* of those NO ZONEs.

And please note: *If you fail to run Key Numbers in all relevant NO ZONEs, the day will come (guaranteed) when you miss a case your opponent finds!*

Now let's update the statute beyond the latest U.S.C.A. quarterly pamphlet.

§ 12.5(e) Updating the Statute to the Present Day

Updating a federal statute *beyond* U.S.C.A. coverage requires you to recall another source published by the West Publishing Company: *United States Code Congressional & Administrative News.* Because it's such a mouthful, those in the know have shortened its name to USCCAN. USCCAN is published monthly by West. Each monthly issue appears in a red and white paperback book. At the end of each calendar year, the publishers replace the paperbacks with a series of bound volumes bearing the year as the volume number.

USCCAN publishes a variety of information. Primarily it publishes the *full text* of every public law. In fact, it publishes the public laws and uses the same page numbers that the *Statutes at Large* will use when it finally gets off its derriere and publishes its next bound volume. (Please also note that USCCAN publishes the full text of selected House and Senate Committee Reports.)

In the race to publish federal statutes *chronologically*, the slip laws invariably prevail. Thus, in your law library, you'll find the *latest* federal statutes to be the slip laws, housed in the notebooks, folders, cut-out cardboard boxes, or whatever other high-tech retrieval system the library chooses to use. Then comes USCCAN, publishing the same laws but running a close second to the slip laws. Finally, at some point down the road, the *Statutes at Large* will lumber along in bound-volume form.

The point is that the slip laws and USCCAN are *always* ahead of the latest supplement of U.S.C.A. (or U.S.C.S., for that matter).

You have two choices. Either you can flip through the slip laws, law by law, in search of one amending or repealing your statute, or you can follow:

GOOD'S RULE OF RESEARCH #28:

After the latest U.S.C.A. supplement, use USCCAN Table 3 to update your statute *almost* to the present day.

USCCAN Table 3? Afraid so.

As noted above, USCCAN is published monthly. At the end of each paperback volume (or in a separate paperback volume at the end of the year), you'll find a bunch of tables, including "Table 3." Table 3 provides cross-references from all provisions of the United States Code to the latest chronologically published federal statutes amending, repealing, or otherwise affecting those U.S. Code provisions. The cross-references will be to *Statutes at Large* page number, which, as noted above, is identical to USCCAN page number.

To update your statute, simply locate the latest volume of USCCAN {70} (don't **{70}**
check each one because Table 3 {71} cumulates with each volume). Look up your U.S. **{71}**
Code provision {72}. If it's listed, then it's been affected by an amendment or a repeal. **{72}**
You'll then have to locate the page number listed (in the slip laws or in USCCAN itself) and read the statute to see what changes Congress has made.

Statistically, finding a change in Table 3 will happen to you only a few times in your entire legal career. Quite obviously, Good's Rule of Research #19 comes into play here: check Table 3 and you won't find anything; fail to check it, and a change will be there (waiting for your opponent to find).

Once you've checked Table 3, is your research up to date? Well, unfortunately it's not. You can look on the spine of your USCCAN volume (or sometimes at the top of Table 3) to find out the Public Law Number covered by the USCCAN volume (or the extent of coverage of Table 3). This number will exceed your legislative Stop Cite number. It might exceed it by several hundred Public Law Numbers, or it might exceed it by 20 or 30 or so. But the point is, USCCAN Table 3 gives you a *new* Stop Cite, *which is rarely as up to date as the shelf itself.*

Thus, in the notebook, or folders, or cut-out cardboard boxes, you'll find slip law
{73} Public Law Numbers greater than the Stop Cite provided by USCCAN {73}. This NO ZONE of federal legislative law is traversable only by looking at each individual slip law to determine whether any given slip law amended or repealed any given provision of the U.S. Code. Thus, here you really have to let your "fingers do the walking" and flip through individual slip laws.

Fortunately, researching through the legislative NO ZONE, as a general rule, is only theoretically necessary. As a practical matter, for the vast majority of federal legislative assignments, which typically involve well-known statutes or statutes that your attorneys sleep with every night, the attorney assigning you the research assignment will already know if the statute has been or is about to be amended.

But if you wish to lay claim to the status of Ace Legal Researcher, you must know how to update a federal statute to the *present day.* And now you do.

Actually you don't. If you'll call the Library of Congress, you'll find out that the latest Public Law Number of the latest federal statute enacted is far greater than the latest one on your shelf. But this NO ZONE exists for all forms of law and is not readily researchable except by word of mouth or intensive newspaper reading.

§ 12.6 Federal Legislative Research: A Roadmap for Research

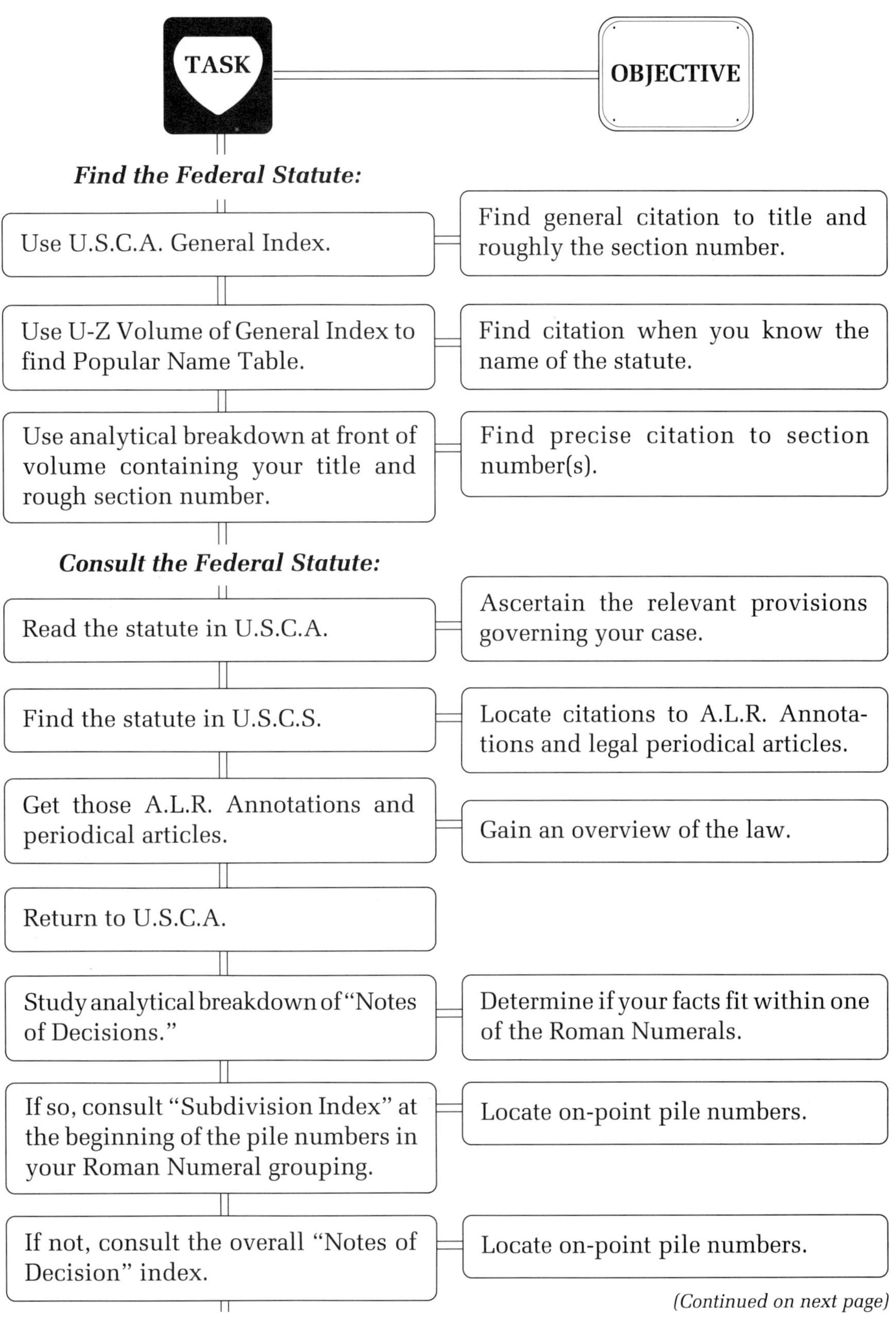

(Continued on next page)

(Continued from previous page)

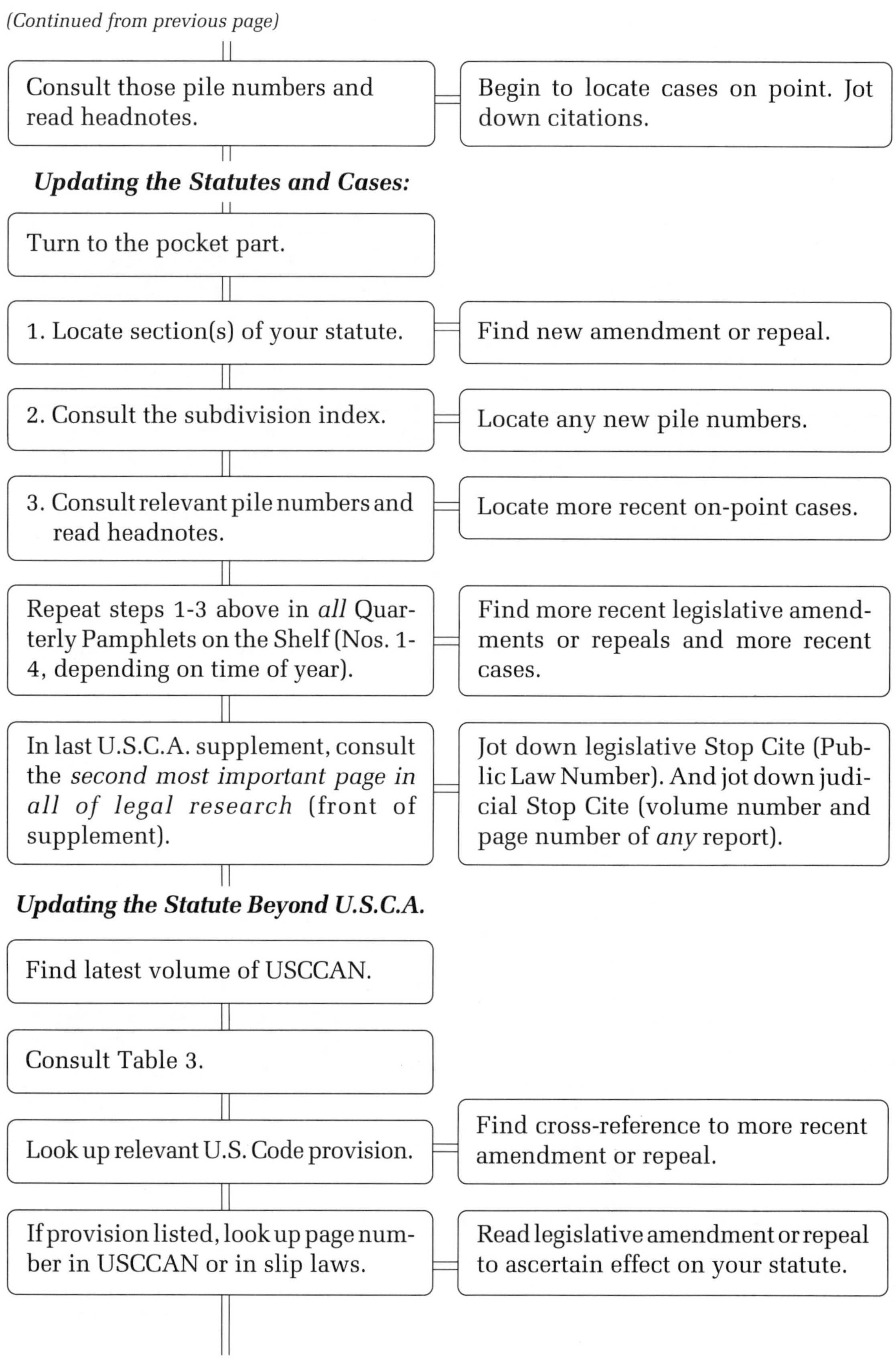

Jot down Stop Cite of latest USCCAN coverage (spine or top of Table 3).

Compare this legislative Stop Cite with slip laws on the shelf.

Peruse those slip laws beyond Stop Cite if necessary, i.e., statute is off-the-wall statute. — Locate more recent amendment or repeal.

Updating the Cases Beyond U.S.C.A.
Find the Correct Key Numbers:

Check title page of case. — Find correct Key Numbers.

Verify Key Numbers:

1. Check Main Topic in latest *Decennial Digest*. — Look for other potential Key Numbers.
2. Check *Descriptive Word Index* in latest *Decennial* or *General Digest*. — Look for other potential Key Numbers.
3. Check spines of latest *General Digest* volumes. — Look for new Main Topics or revised Main Topics.

Run Key Numbers:

1. Check *second most important page in all of legal research* at front of latest U.S.C.A. supplement. — Jot down Stop Cite for any given report (use F.2d as an example).
2. Check *single most important page in all of legal research* at front of latest volume of *General Digest*. — Establish the volume in the *General Digest* where the Stop Cite is digested.

(Continued on next page)

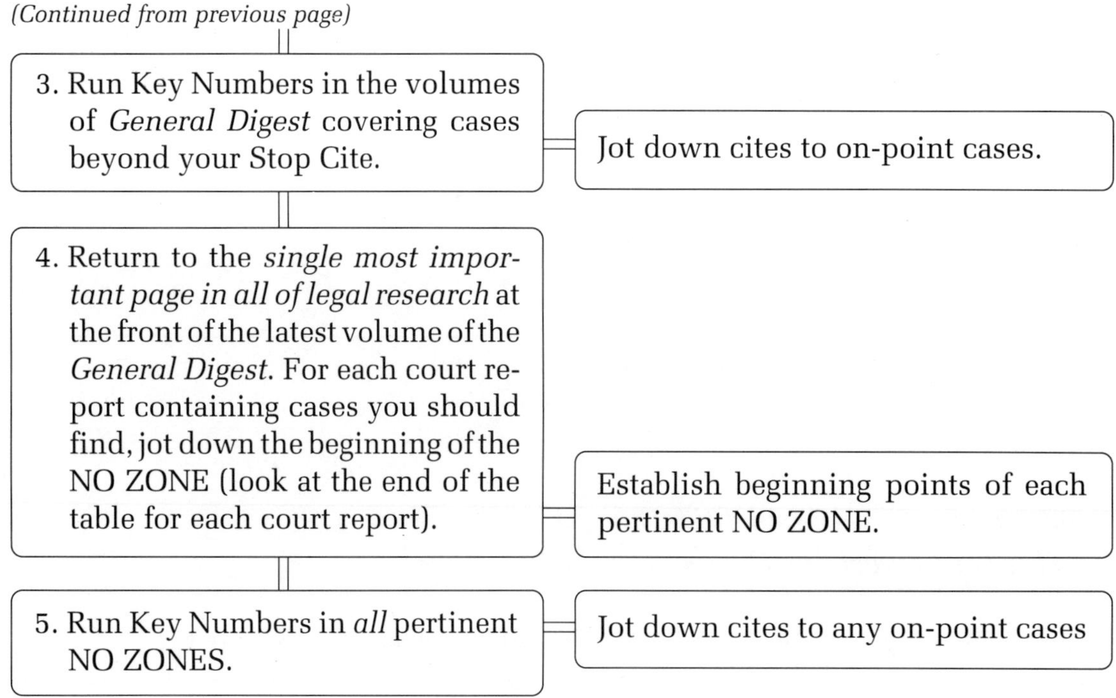

§ 12.7 Legislative Research: Visual Aids {47-73}

In the Visual Aids booklet, I have reproduced selected pages from the variety of sources you would use in researching federal statutes in U.S.C.A. and U.S.C.S. These are pages that you would encounter in researching Judge Thomas and Professor Hill's case. On each page, in the box, you'll find my commentary showing exactly what the researcher is doing to find the federal statute, to consult the federal statute, to find cases interpreting the statute, and to update the statute and the cases to the present day.

Please note that these pages are selective. In the real world of legal research, you would consult many more pages, especially those you'll undoubtedly stumble over in your very first efforts. You will, most likely, go down lots of dead ends, locating irrelevant information, getting frustrated, and, yes, perhaps even *losing your mind.*

But if you'll follow the above instructions, step by step, and study the Visual Aids, page by page, you'll begin to learn how to do legal research *without losing your mind.*

§ 12.8 Legislative History Research

An entire work could be written on the topic of legislative materials, the kind of work that few law students or paralegals would read for the simple reason that they've already got too much to read. When I began this work, I had anticipated omitting any material on legislative histories. I simply did not want the scope of this book to go beyond the ordinary research and writing problems that law students and paralegals face in their courses on Legal Research and Writing. But remembering my own experience in law school, my experience teaching law students at the University of Virginia School of Law, and my experience teaching paralegals at Georgetown University Legal Assistant Program, I know that I should include at least the basics of legislative history research. For I realize that no one can truly claim to be an Ace Legal Researcher without knowing, at a minimum, how to compile a simple legislative history.

§ 12.8(a) A Quick Review

By way of a quick review, please recall the path a bill takes when it winds its way through the legislative process: (1) bill introduced, (2) bill referred to committee, (3) hearing held, (4) committee report written when bill "reported out," (5) bill returned to floor of House or Senate, (6) floor debate held, (7) vote taken, and (8) bill sent to other chamber for similar treatment. As the bill continues along this path, it spins out four basic types of legislative material, broadly referred to as "legislative history":

1. Bills.
2. Hearings.
3. Committee Reports.
4. Floor Debate.

Also recall that much of this information is published separately (bills, hearings, and reports), that much of it appears in the *Congressional Record* (bills, floor debate), and that some is reprinted by other sources (committee reports in USCCAN, as an example). Finally, remember the various numbers used to designate these legislative materials: bill numbers such as H.R. 1304 or S.1243, and committee report numbers such as H.R. Rep. No. 254 or S. Rep. No. 103.

§ 12.8(b) Why Lawyers Want This Stuff

When a case is governed by a federal statute, the court must interpret or "construe" the statute when applying it to a given fact situation. The statute's wording might appear in broad, loosely drafted language that could cover just about anything. The Civil Rights Act of 1964, for example, simply outlaws "sex discrimination" in employment. But what does that mean? Does it include sexual harassment? What does sexual harassment include? Dirty jokes? Who's to know?

So when a federal judge is faced with applying a statute in a given case, that judge wants to interpret that statute in a way that comports with Congress's intent in passing the statute in the first place. And one way that federal courts crawl inside the "minds of the legislators" is by studying the legislative history of the statute.

Before the federal judges can study that material, a lonely legal researcher must first identify the bills that were introduced and that led to the enactment of the statute, the House and Senate committees that held hearings on these bills, the committee reports those committees issued, and the floor debate that took place throughout the legislative process (specifically on the dates when the bill passed the House and the Senate).

Identifying this legislative material is what "compiling a legislative history" is all about.

§ 12.8(b)(i) Why You Want This Stuff

If and when you enter a moot court competition or submit a writing sample for law review tryout or attempt to impress your first boss, you can score some huge points by being able to compile a basic legislative history. That's why.

§ 12.8(c) Two Levels of Research

Legislative history research breaks down into two levels. The first level—the one I can help you with—consists of identifying the legislative documents surrounding any given federal statute. Identifying these documents means (1) discovering the bill numbers of the bills leading to the enactment of the statute, (2) finding out which House and Senate committees held hearings on these bills, (3) identifying the House and Senate committee report numbers of the committee reports issued on the bill or bills, and (4) pinpointing the dates when floor debate likely took place on the floor of the House and the Senate, typically on the dates when the bill passed the House and the Senate.

Once this information is compiled, level two—the one I can't help you with very much—kicks in: getting your hot little hands on this information. Though I can point you in the right direction to retrieve this information, I have been spoiled by the superlative "documents librarians" at the University of Virginia School of Law. On the occasions that I have compiled legislative histories, I simply take the bill numbers and the committee report numbers to the documents librarians, who glance at them briefly, disappear through one door, and—3.2 minutes later—reappear with the documents in hand. How they do it I'll never know. Which is why I can't help you get your hot little hands on the documents themselves: just ask the documents librarians, they're magic!

So follow along and I'll show you how to engage in Level One of legislative history research. Level One, remember, involves identifying the documents themselves. For Level Two (getting your hot little hands on the documents), I'll help the best I can.

§ 12.9 Compiling a Legislative History

Keep in mind what we're doing here. For a given federal statute, we seek to identify and retrieve the bills that led to the statute's enactment, to get our hands on any committee hearings held, to get our hands on the committee reports issued by any House or Senate committee, and to read the floor debate that might have transpired on the floor of the House or Senate (those scintillating speeches televised by C-Span and given by House members or Senators to an empty House or an empty Senate). Keep in mind the "two levels" of research: (1) identifying the documents and (2) retrieving the documents themselves.

§ 12.9(a) An Important Shortcut

Before you ever launch a search for legislative history, you should first find out whether any other poor schmuck has already done the dirty work. On important pieces of legislation, an interest group, a federal agency, or even some wild-eyed academic might have already published a "compiled legislative history." You might find a multivolume book entitled "The Legislative History of the Civil Rights Act of 1964." Now it'd be pretty stupid to spend 30 or 40 hours compiling such a history when it's already been done. Right?

Right. So your first step is to go straight to the Card Catalogue or, you hope, to your Computerized Card Catalogue in search of an already-published legislative history. If you should score, you will have saved untold hours of drudge work. The compiled history will have all the bills, all the hearings, all the committee reports, and all the floor debates—all within one or more volumes. Such a deal.

§ 12.9(b) Another Important Shortcut

If the statute prompting your legislative history research was enacted after 1970, you should consult a source known as the *Congressional Information Service*. This multivolume work provides access to legislative histories on statutes enacted after 1970. Its companion microfilm service provides the actual documents. I will not deal with the ins and outs of using CIS (as it is called) for two simple reasons: (1) it's beyond the scope of this book and (2) I don't know how to use it.

§ 12.10 A Step-by-Step Approach to Identifying the Documents

If either of the above two shortcuts fails to pan out, then you're stuck with doing the work yourself. If you'll follow the steps below, you'll find that compiling a legislative history really isn't all that difficult. Here we go, step by step:

1. Find your statute in U.S.C.A. At the end of the statute, you'll find the following information: date of enactment, public law number, and *Statutes at Large* citation. Jot this information down in your notes.

2. In U.S.C.A., look for the "Legislative History" reference. If one appears, jot down the USCCAN citation. There you'll find the full text of the House and Senate committee reports on the bill or bills leading up to the enactment of your statute. Note that this source provides not only Level One research (identifying the documents) but Level Two research as well (getting your hot little hands on the legislative history material). Note also that the committee report is regarded by most experts as the most important part of the overall legislative history because courts seem to give great deference to the legislative committee considering the bill.

   At this point, you might have the committee reports in your hot little hands. What you lack are the bill numbers, the committee hearings, and the floor debate. To compile this information, you can take either a USCCAN approach or a *Statutes at Large* approach. I'll deal with each in turn.

USCCAN Approach

3. Find the USCCAN volume covering the year when your statute was enacted. Locate the volume containing the various tables. In that volume you'll find Table 4. The table lists the public laws sequentially by public law number. When you find your public law number, you'll then find the following information: (1) the date the statute was approved, (2) the *Statutes at Large* citation, (3) the committee report numbers in the House and Senate, (4) the names of the committees in the House and Senate reporting on the bills, and (5) the *Congressional Record* volume and the dates when the House and Senate considered the bill.

   From this table you can compile references to a statute's legislative history: the committee report numbers, the committees holding hearings (remember, the hearings are separately published), and the dates of consideration (and hence likely floor debate published in the *Congressional Record* on those dates).

   Then take these references to your documents librarians; give them the names of the committees holding hearings; if they're like the ones I know, they'll disappear through one door and emerge immediately with the bills, the committee hearings, and the committee reports. (How they find it, I'll never know.) The floor debate you can find by yourself. Just go to the *Congressional Record* and find the dates when enactment took place in the House and the Senate. Immediately before the vote you'll find a transcription of any floor debate that took place.

Statutes at Large Approach

4. Find the volume containing your statute (remember, you wrote down the *Statutes at Large* citation in your notes when you were consulting your statute in U.S.C.A.). If your volume is 88 or lower, you'll find in the back

of the volume a table entitled "Guide to Legislative History of Bills Enacted into Public Law." This table is virtually identical to the one found in USCCAN. You simply look up your public law number and discover the bills, the committees holding hearings, the committee report numbers, and the dates when the bills were acted upon. Then hop on over to your helpful documents librarians for bills, hearings, and committee reports, and over to the *Congressional Record* for any floor debate.

If your *Statutes at Large* volume is 89 or higher, you'll find that the table at the back of the volume has been discontinued. Instead, you'll find legislative history printed with each statute. So turn to the page number of your *Statutes at Large* citation, find the *last page* of the statute, and there you'll find a reference to "Legislative History," which is the same information contained in the tables in volumes 88 and lower.

§ 12.11 Beyond the Basics

The above discussion focuses only on the basics of legislative history research. In fact it focuses only on the type of legislative history research concerning the identification of documents on actual bills enacted into public law. The vast majority of bills, thank heaven, never make it into law. More than 25,000 can be introduced in any given Congress. Hordes of lobbyists, interest groups, corporations, law firms, foreign governments, and others employ armies of legal researchers to track bills as they wind their way through Congress. Researching the mass of material appearing in the *Congressional Record* and other legislative sources is an art form you might have to master one day. But the skills involved in researching legislative materials on bills that did *not* make it are beyond this book, and, truthfully, beyond this author.

At least I've given you the basics, enough to win Moot Court, make the law review, or impress your boss. The rest is up to you.

§ 12.12 Conclusion

Now you know how to find statutes, consult statutes, find cases interpreting statutes, and update statutes and cases to the present day. You even know a bit about compiling legislative histories on bills that get enacted into public law. Now it's time to turn your attention away from the judicial branch and the legislative branch and toward the executive branch and its unique form of law—Administrative Law.

CHAPTER 13

ADMINISTRATIVE LAW

§ 13.1 Introduction

I've got some good news and some good news. First, the good news: you've already learned the hard parts of legal research—case law and legislative law. The easy part, at least as found in this book, is federal administrative law. Second, the good news: this will be a short chapter.

As you begin to explore the mysteries of administrative law, you will notice many parallels to what you've already learned. Right off the bat, you'll immediately see that administrative law is really a hodgepodge of the kinds of law you've already learned about: you'll find stuff that looks like judicial "cases," and you'll find stuff that looks like legislative "statutes," and you'll find some stuff that seems to be a combination of both, and you'll find some stuff that defies description.

Continuing with these parallels, you'll also learn that one type of administrative law (the one we'll focus on) is published chronologically to satisfy the needs of speed and permanent storage and that this law is then republished in a subject matter arrangement to satisfy the needs of location and ongoing revision.

Finally, by way of introduction, I should point out my intent to deal only with federal administrative regulations in my detailed instruction in the art of finding, using, and updating law. I will mention the other forms of administrative law and point you in the direction of learning how to research such material (primarily through the use of looseleaf services). Such an approach seems justified, especially for the primary audience of this book: the first-time legal researcher. Your legal research topics are not likely to involve highly technical administrative law matters. After all, it's the rare legal research instructor who will assign Food and Drug Law or Mine Safety Law or Tax Law to a first-year law or paralegal student. Your topics, it's safe to conclude, will primarily involve case law and statutory law. If they involve federal statutory law (and many do), it behooves you to learn how to retrieve any federal administrative regulations implementing the provisions (or interpreting the provisions) of your assigned statute.

§ 13.2 The Administrative Process

Although a similar administrative process is at work in the 50 states, I'll focus this discussion on the federal administrative process. Understanding this process requires your familiarity with two American traditions: (1) the constitutional doctrine of separation of powers and (2) the all-American tradition of passing the buck, or put more delicately, the fine art of delegating responsibility and authority.

To prevent dictatorship or royalty in America, the authors of our Constitution separated governmental power among the three branches of government. The Constitution gave to the legislative branch the power to pass laws, to the executive branch the power to enforce and implement laws, and to the judicial branch the power to resolve disputes arising under the laws of the United States. Thus, while Congress can pass a law, it has no power to arrest and prosecute a violator of that law. Although the President can try to influence Congress in its decision to pass certain laws, other than the veto power the President is powerless to control the substance of the laws Congress decides to enact. And although the President has the power to appoint federal judges and Justices of the Supreme Court, and the Senate has the power to confirm those appointments, neither Congress nor the President can control the decisions those judges and Justices render.

Governmental power—the power to make laws, enforce laws, and apply and interpret laws in given disputes—is thus separated among the three branches of government. In the administrative process, however, we see a necessary breakdown of the separation of powers doctrine. Separation of powers had to give way to the American tradition of delegating responsibility and authority.

Take nuclear power as an example. Congress certainly has the power to regulate the design, location, and construction of nuclear power plants. But Congress has neither the time nor the expertise to worry about the scientific "nuts and bolts" of the nuclear industry. Can you imagine your Congress member or Senator in charge of designing safety procedures for storing radioactive fuel? Homer Simpson could do a better job. So Congress creates an administrative agency and delegates to that agency the governmental power to regulate. What kind of governmental power? Perhaps all three types of power—the legislative power to pass laws, the judicial power to adjudicate, and the executive power to enforce. Thus, one administrative agency might have all three types of governmental power. It might have a regulations division responsible for drafting and ultimately promulgating regulations. It might have administrative law judges or certain boards or panels that actually hear cases and resolve disputes. And it might have inspectors all over the country looking for violations of its law so that it can bring enforcement proceedings. The doctrine of separation of powers, thus, has broken down in the administrative process.

Administrative agencies might be one of two basic types: (1) executive branch or (2) independent. Many agencies are part of the executive branch of government, which is divided into 14 departments, the heads of which make up the President's cabinet: Agriculture, Commerce, Defense, Education, Energy, Health & Human Services, Housing & Urban Development, Interior, Justice, Labor, State, Transportation, Treasury, and Veterans Affairs. These departments are broken down into scads of administrative agencies. Take the Department of Transportation, for example. It is divided into the Federal Aviation Administration, the Federal Transit Administration, the National Highway Traffic Safety Administration, the United States Coast Guard (yes, one of the armed services is within the Department of Transportation), and others. As another example, the Department of Treasury is divided into the beloved IRS; the Bureau of Alcohol, Tobacco and Firearms; the Comptroller of the Currency; the United States Secret Service; and others.

Other agencies Congress creates as "independent," intentionally removing them from the executive branch in the hope of lessening abrupt shifts in policy due to presidential politics. Examples include the Securities & Exchange Commission, the Equal Employment Opportunity Commission, the Nuclear Regulatory Commission, and other entities such as the United States Postal Service and the Federal Deposit Insurance Corporation.

Congress creates an administrative agency by passing a statute known as an "organic act," also known as "enabling legislation." This statute paints the broad strokes of legal and illegal conduct and then delegates to the agency the power to implement the provisions of the act by rules and regulations. If Congress does not expressly give legislative power, then the agency may not pass regulations. Congress might also empower the agency to enforce the provisions of the act and to hear and resolve disputes arising under the act. Again, the agency can only wield that type of governmental power expressly given to it by Congress.

Of course, the three types of administrative processes—executive, judicial, and legislative—are producing a substantial amount of law that attorneys must retrieve, read, analyze, and cite in advising clients on matters governed by administrative law or in representing clients appearing before administrative agencies. Although I will provide detailed research instruction only for administrative regulations (legislative information), you should have some idea about executive information and judicial information churning out of the administrative legal process.

§ 13.3 Executive Information

In the federal arena, "executive information" consists of the President's Executive Orders, Presidential Proclamations, and Reorganization Plans. Much of this information is really legislative in nature, but as we'll see in this entire discussion of administrative law, the lines between executive, judicial, and legislative activities tend to blur a great deal.

§ 13.3(a) Executive Orders and Presidential Proclamations

In his Executive Orders or Presidential Proclamations, the President exercises considerable authority, especially when such authority has been specifically delegated by Congress to the President. These Executive Orders and Proclamations are given sequential numbers, which do not begin all over again with the change of a Presidency. The numbering system for Executive Orders began in 1862 and continues to this day. Executive Orders and Presidential Proclamations have no different legal effect, but their publication techniques do vary.

§ 13.3(b) Reorganization Plans

Another type of executive information in the federal sphere is the Reorganization Plan. Acting under authority specifically delegated by Congress, the President has the power to rearrange designated executive agencies below the rank of department. The plan automatically goes into effect unless Congress expressly disapproves of the plan within sixty days.

§ 13.3(c) Publication of Executive Information

Executive Orders, Presidential Proclamations, and Reorganization Plans are published in a variety of places.

Chronologically, all are published in the *Federal Register*, the *Weekly Compilation of Presidential Documents* (since 1965), and *United States Code Congressional and Administrative News* (USCCAN). Proclamations and Reorganization Plans, but not Executive Orders, are also chronologically published in the *Statutes at Large*.

These Presidential documents are then codified as well. Title 3 of the *Code of Federal Regulations* is a codification of Presidential Documents. The Appendix to Title 3 of the *United States Code* and unofficial codes codifies Executive Orders and Proclamations. The Appendix to Title 5 of the United States Code and unofficial codes codifies the Reorganization Plans.

In these codifications in C.F.R., U.S.C., U.S.C.A., and U.S.C.S., section numbers are not used. Consequently, these codifications should be cited by page number.

§ 13.4 Judicial Information

When you think of the judicial process you usually conjure up images of lawyers, a judge, a jury, evidence, rules of procedure, depositions, interrogatories, examination of witnesses, and a whole host of other goings-on. You usually think of a dispute—either a civil case where one party wants the other party's money or a criminal case where a government wants a private party locked up.

In the federal administrative branch of government, many agencies wield judicial power in the classic sense. They resolve civil disputes. They wield this power the same way courts do: they have opposing parties, pleadings, attorneys, hearings, evidence, rules of procedure, depositions, interrogatories, and the same array of activities that take place in state or federal courts.

Indeed, when an administrative agency resolves a dispute, it does the same thing courts do: it writes an "opinion of law." These court opinions, however, in the administrative branch have a variety of different names: rulings, decisions, issuances, opinions, and so on. And, just as court opinions are published chronologically, the opinions of agencies are published by the agency in chronological reports.

An example of a typical judicial proceeding that resolves disputes is a Merit Systems Protection Board case. Congress created the MSPB to hear disputes of federal employees against their employer-agencies. The proceeding, although much less formal than a court case, is very similar to a typical case brought in state or federal court.

Many such disputes *must* be resolved in an administrative proceeding. If Congress creates an administrative remedy, the federal courts will not hear such cases until the aggrieved party has "exhausted administrative remedies." Once the case makes its way through the administrative process, the losing parties might still have an opportunity to bring their case in federal court. The federal courts have the power of "judicial review" over the federal agencies to ensure that the agencies do not exceed the authority given to them by Congress or that their actions do not violate the Constitution.

Many agencies wield other types of judicial power not ordinarily thought of as judicial in nature. A prime example is licensing. Consider the Nuclear Regulatory Commission. If a public utility company wants to build a nuclear power plant, it must apply for a construction permit with the NRC. The NRC has "licensing boards" that undertake judicial proceedings to determine whether the utility has complied with all federal laws in the design of the proposed power plant.

The board conducts a hearing much like a federal court case. The utility's application resembles a "complaint" filed in federal court. There isn't really a "defendant," however. The utility isn't suing the government for its license. Indeed, if the utility meets all requirements, the NRC must issue the license.

To provide an "adversarial" proceeding, however, the NRC has "staff attorneys," who oppose the utility if they think the utility's position is contrary to federal law. To provide additional adversaries, the NRC allows interested parties such as adjoining landowners or special interest groups to "intervene" and oppose the utility in the licensing proceeding.

The "case" proceeds with all forms of discovery, the examination of witnesses, the filing of briefs on points of law, and the ultimate decision of the licensing board. The board writes an opinion, which the NRC calls an "issuance." The opinion is chronologically published in the *Nuclear Regulatory Commission Issuances* (N.R.C.).

The losing party might then appeal to a "licensing appeal board." The board receives appellate briefs, hears oral argument, reaches a decision, and writes an opinion, much like the federal courts of appeal review the decisions of federal trial courts. The losing party then might appeal to the members of the Nuclear Regulatory

Commission itself. The Commission then receives appellate briefs, hears oral argument, reaches a decision, and writes an opinion, much like the Supreme Court of the United States reviews the opinions of the circuits.

§ 13.4(a) Publication of Judicial Information

Federal agencies publish their administrative decisions in chronological reports that resemble official court reports. Some agencies, like the NLRB, publish advance sheets, but the page numbers for the ultimate bound volumes are undetermined.

In the administrative field, there is no overall system of "court reports" publishing *all* decisions of *all* federal agencies. In other words, there is no West System for federal administrative decisions, the reason being that no one would want all administrative opinions. Nuclear energy attorneys want NRC opinions but don't care too much about MSPB decisions.

Following is a list of the most common official administrative publications and their proper abbreviations. You can find a complete list on pages 168-69 of the Harvard *Bluebook.*

Federal Administrative Publications

Agency or Report	Abbreviation
Agriculture	Agric. Dec.
Atomic Energy Commission	A.E.C.
Attorney General Opinions	Op. Att'y Gen.
Civil Aeronautics Board	C.A.B.
Comptroller General	Comp. Gen.
Copyright Decisions	Copy. Dec.
Cumulative Bulletin	C.B.
Customs Bulletin and Decisions	Cust. B. & Dec.
Department of Interior .... Interior	Dec.
Employees' Compensation Appeals Board	Empl. Comp. App. Bd.
Federal Communications Commission	F.C.C., F.C.C.2d
Federal Energy Regulatory Commission	F.E.R.C.
Federal Labor Relations Authority	F.L.R.A.
Federal Maritime Commission	F.M.C.
Federal Mine Safety & Health Review Comm.	F.M.S.H.R.C.
Federal Power Commission	F.P.C.
Federal Reserve	Fed. Res. Bull.
Federal Trade Commission	F.T.C.
Immigration and Naturalization	I. & N. Dec.
Interstate Commerce Commission (valuation)	I.C.C. Valuation Rep.
Interstate Commerce Commission	I.C.C.
Merit Systems Protection Board	M.S.P.B.
Motor Carrier Cases	M.C.C.

National Labor Relations Board .... N.L.R.B.
National Railroad Adjustment Board .... N.R.A.B. (Div.)
National Transportation Safety Board .... N.T.S.B.
Nuclear Regulatory Commission .... N.R.C.
Office of Legal Counsel (Dep't of Justice) .... Op. Off. Legal Counsel
Patents, Commissioner and U.S. Courts .... Dec. Comm'r Pat.
Post Office Solicitor .... Op. Solic. P.O. Dep't
Securities & Exchange Commission .... S.E.C.
Social Security Rulings, Cumulative Edition .... S.S.R. (Cum. Ed. 19__)
Treasury Decisions (customs & other laws) .... Treas. Dec.
Treasury Decisions (Internal Revenue laws) .... Treas. Dec. Int. Rev.
United States Patent Office .... Off. Gaz. Pat. Office

§ 13.4(b) Looseleaf Services: Unique Legal Publications

At this point, you should become acquainted with looseleaf services. We've seen in previous discussions that law is published chronologically to satisfy the need for speed. To satisfy the need for location, law is then republished in subject matter arrangements such as the *United States Code*. In the administrative area, however, law is published by chronology and subject matter simultaneously in looseleaf services.

As mentioned above, nuclear energy attorneys want only the decisions of the NRC, not those of the MSPB. But those same attorneys want not only administrative decisions but court opinions, administrative regulations, state and federal statutes, and even some treatise material. They want all law relating to a given topic. And they want it all in one place.

To satisfy this demand for all law in one place, American publishing companies developed looseleaf services, which publish all legislative, judicial, and administrative law on one particular topic. As their name implies, these services provide binders, which contain separate pages periodically sent to the subscriber. Thus, if a statute is amended, the publisher sends new pages to replace the obsolete pages. The same is true of administrative regulations. As amendments or repeals take place, new pages are sent to replace the outdated ones.

As we saw in the judicial process, in the administrative arena there are more cases coming out than statutes or regulations. And cases don't really "amend" older cases. They may change the doctrine of older cases, but the older cases "stay on the books." So for case law reported by looseleaf services, the publishers do not send new pages to replace older "overruled" or "reversed" cases.

Instead, recent case law is sent to subscribers for them to place in their binders. But as the body of case law grows, the publisher either sends separate hardbound editions of the cases to replace the "loose leafs" in the binders, or it sends "transfer binders" to house the older cases.

Thus, as you can see, often an attorney cites some law to a looseleaf service. That "something" most likely is an administrative decision since the other law published by the looseleaf services—court cases and statutes—is also published in court reports and codes. For this reason, I introduce the looseleaf services here.

The more successful looseleaf service companies are Commerce Clearing House (CCH), Bureau of National Affairs (BNA), Matthew Bender (MB), Callaghan & Co. (Callaghan), Pike & Fischer (P & F), and Prentice Hall (P-H). As a rule, when you learn how to use one CCH looseleaf service, you've pretty much learned how to use all CCH looseleaf services.

These looseleaf services concern highly specialized areas of law, not generally the topics of first-year legal research assignments. Also, to train people in the use of looseleaf services would require detailed instruction on all of the major publishers' services, a task I don't relish tackling. So I won't. I'll simply urge you to review the list of looseleaf services on pages 297-303 of the Harvard *Bluebook* to see the vast array of subject matter covered by these services, all the way from automobile law to the law of human reproduction.

At some point in your legal career, you're going to have to bite the bullet, pick out one of these looseleaf services, and learn how to use it. Not surprisingly, you already know how to use it. You'll find that it consists of three types of finding devices: (1) Analyses (which it might incorrectly call "Indexes"), (2) Indexes, and (3) Tables. You'll find that these looseleaf services contain treatise-like commentary, access to and publication of case law, access to and publication of statutory law, access to and publication of administrative regulations. For the reasons stated above, I will not deal with them in this text.

§ 13.5 Legislative Information

We've already seen that an administrative agency might have executive power and judicial power. The same agency might also have legislative power: the power to pass or "promulgate" regulations. These regulations have the same force or clout as a federal statute; failure to abide by the regulations can result in civil or even criminal liability.

There are two basic types of federal administrative regulations: procedural and substantive. Procedural regulations govern the workings of the agency and, for example, might apply to the internal regulation of employees. Substantive regulations, on the other hand, create legal obligations or legal rights. An IRS regulation, for example, might prescribe the way certain property is to be depreciated for calculating taxes. Depreciate in any other way, and you're in a heap of trouble.

The difference between procedural and substantive regulations has no effect on your legal research technique, for both are published in the same way in the same place. The difference lies in the manner in which the regulation must be promulgated by the agency.

Procedural regulations can be promulgated by the agency with no advance notice to the public. Proposed substantive regulations, however, must first be published in the *Federal Register* so that interested parties may comment on the regulations. The agency must consider comments received, and only then can it promulgate a binding regulation.

§ 13.5(a) Publication of Administrative Regulations

In the 1930s, before federal agencies began to regulate with any intensity, agencies published their regulations on a public notice board. Law firms would send their "runners" around to the agencies to obtain copies of the regulations, which would then be reproduced and circulated in the firm. (Present-day descendants of these same runners are those wild-eyed bicycle guys in Washington who mow down the home folks and small children on their way to the White House tours.) With the onset of New Deal legislation and more intensified regulatory efforts, however, Congress saw the need for systematic publication of all federal regulations. Congress acted and created the Office of the Federal Register.

The Office of the Federal Register faced the same two problems any legal publisher faces when deciding on a method to publish the law: the need for speed and the need for location and revision. Recall that these problems were solved by the *Statutes at Large* (speed) and the *United States Code* (location and revision) for the publication of federal statutes.

The Office of the Federal Register correctly concluded that two publications were needed, a chronological one to satisfy the need for speed and a topical one to satisfy the need for location and revision. It created the *Federal Register* to publish all federal regulations chronologically on a daily basis and the *Code of Federal Regulations* to rearrange these regulations topically and to keep them up to date to reflect amendments and repeals.

§ 13.5(b) *Federal Register*

The *Federal Register* publishes all regulations of all federal agencies on a daily basis. It also publishes proposed regulations, notices of hearings, Presidential information, and other administrative information. Its annual number of pages exceeded 100,000 in the 1970s. Fortunately, the annual number of pages now hovers at a mere 70,000. In the good old days of the late 1960s, the annual number of pages stood resolutely at 15,000.

Each daily issue of the *Federal Register* is published in flimsy paper editions. The pages run sequentially during the calendar year. At the end of the year, bound volumes supersede the paper editions. Each year has a single volume number, but many bound books are needed each year to bind the entire year's output. The page numbers run sequentially throughout the many bound volumes for that year.

§ 13.5(c) *Code of Federal Regulations*

The *Code of Federal Regulations* topically rearranges all federal regulations in the following manner. All federal law is broken down into 50 categories called "titles." These 50 titles are virtually identical to the 50 titles in the U.S. Code. Each title is further broken down into "chapters," each containing the regulations of a given federal agency. Each chapter is further broken down into whole number "parts." Each part contains the regulations governing a particular subject. Each part is then broken down into decimal-numbered "sections," which are the regulations themselves.

Thus, a federal regulation citation might look like this: 29 C.F.R. § 1604.4(a)(i). The "29" means "title 29." The "1604" means "Part 1604." The ".4" means the precise regulation, i.e., the "section," within Part 1604. The "(a)(i)" means that the regulation has been divided into subsections and paragraphs.

The *Code of Federal Regulations* is a much more efficient publication than the *United States Code*. Instead of a total revision every six years, the *Code of Federal Regulations* is revised every year according to the following schedule:

Titles 1-16	as of January 1
Titles 17-27	as of April 1
Titles 28-41	as of July 1
Titles 42-50	as of October 1

Because of this annual revision process, the *Code of Federal Regulations* is published in paperback editions rather than hardbound volumes as used by the *United States Code*. Unfortunately, the Office of the Federal Register has what is called the "Designer Color Committee." This committee meets in strict secrecy and decides on the next color of the covers of the next batch of CFRs. The latest two in a long line of disasters destroying the retinas of legal researchers worldwide can only be described as off shades of vermilion and teal.

§ 13.6 How to Research Federal Regulations

Researching federal regulations is a piece of cake. The process breaks down into the finding phase, the use phase, and the updating phase. We'll take each in turn.

§ 13.6(a) Finding Federal Regulations

§ 13.6(a)(i) The U.S.C.A. or U.S.C.S. Approach

All federal regulations must arise from a federal statute, for no federal agency can promulgate federal regulations without express authority from Congress. In the research process, you will typically search for the federal statute first, then locate cases interpreting that statute, and finally launch a search for any federal regulations implementing or interpreting the provisions of that statute. Fortunately, U.S.C.A. and U.S.C.S. help you in this search.

When you locate a federal statute in U.S.C.A. (or U.S.C.S.), you'll find a cross-reference to "Code of Federal Regulations" {52}. This cross-reference appears imme- {52}
diately after the "Historical Note" and the "Research Cross-References." Hence, in many research projects, you will not have to engage in an independent finding phase of federal regulatory research. Your legislative research reveals the exact citations in C.F.R. you must consult.

I would be shirking my responsibilities as an Ace Legal Research Instructor, however, if I failed to show you how to find federal regulations independently of U.S.C.A. or U.S.C.S.

§ 13.6(a)(ii) The *Finding Aids* Approach

On the C.F.R. shelf you'll find a terrific one-volume book entitled *C.F.R. Index and Finding Aids* {74}. This one volume contains, as you might imagine, (1) an Analysis, {74}
(2) an Index, and (3) various Tables.

The Index Approach is perhaps the most useful and most dominant part of this one-volume book {75}. Its most attractive feature lies in its utter simplicity. It seems {75}
to break all the rules of legal indexing and consequently is a terrific index. It uses ordinary words, not obscure words invented by diabolical legal indexers yucking it up in some dark, dank room and saying, "Boy, they'll never find this reference as long as they live [cackles of weird, insane-like laughter]." As a matter of fact, I have it on good authority that the employment application form for the Index Department at the Office of the Federal Register has the following question on it:

"Have you ever worked as a legal indexer?"

Check the "Yes" box and you're automatically disqualified!

Seriously, you're going to like the Index feature of the *C.F.R. Index and Finding Aids.* Our collective hats are off to one terrific government publication!

The Analytical Approach is somewhat buried in a feature called "List of CFR Titles, Chapters, Subchapters, and Parts" {76}. This feature provides the analytical {76}
breakdown of the entire *Code of Federal Regulations.* By finding the right title, you can then locate the agency's chapter. By looking at the chapter, you can see how it's subdivided into subject areas called "Parts." By looking at the part, you can see how it's subdivided into the individual regulations themselves, which is what you're looking for in the first place.

The Tabular Approach in this one-volume book isn't all that helpful. After all, the "List of Acts Requiring Publication in the Federal Register" isn't exactly the kind of source you make a beeline for first thing Monday morning. If you do, you won't find a line forming. The one table you might use is the "Parallel Table of Authorities and Rules." This table cross-references you from a U.S. Code citation to regulations arising

from that particular provision. But if you already know the legislative provision,
you've already looked up that statute in U.S.C.A. And if you've already looked up the
statute in U.S.C.A., you already have the "Code of Federal Regulations" cross-
{52} reference giving you the C.F.R. citations {52}. Bottom line? You're not likely to use the
Tabular Approach in federal regulatory research.

§ 13.6(b) Consulting the Federal Regulation

When you consult the potentially relevant federal regulations, you'll find the
{77} appropriate designer-color volume in C.F.R. {77}. One volume will contain particular
parts within a particular title, so make certain that you're pulling the right book off the
shelf. When you get the right book, notice that the front cover provides a "Revised as
of" date. Remember that C.F.R. follows a set schedule in revising federal regulations.
Though set out above, it is repeated here for convenience:

Title	Revision date
Titles 1-16	as of January 1
Titles 17-27	as of April 1
Titles 28-41	as of July 1
Titles 42-50	as of October 1

If you have a research problem governed by Title 29, then the book you pulled off the shelf, if it is now September or later, was revised as of the previous July. If it is now July or August, the book you pulled off the shelf was revised as of two Julys ago.

When you consult your federal regulation, read it to determine its potential
{78,79} applicability to your problem {78,79}. Many regulations are horribly written, so your
reading might require a lot of head scratching and brow wrinkling (and nap taking).
Unfortunately, when you consult C.F.R., all you'll find are the regulations. No
annotations to cases are included. Finding cases interpreting or applying the regulations requires an independent step.

§ 13.6(c) Updating the Regulation

Recall in case law research you kept track of time by volume number and page number of any given court report. By having a Stop Cite you could ascertain where Wilbur stopped collecting cases and where you start chronological case research in the West Company's American Digest System.

Recall in legislative law research you kept track of time by Public Law Number. By having a Stop Cite you could ascertain where Wilbur stopped collecting statutes, and you could then pick up in USCCAN with Table 3 and research beyond that Stop Cite. Then by knowing the Stop Cite of USCCAN you could, if necessary, go straight to the slip laws and flip through the Public Law Numbers beyond your Stop Cite.

§ 13.6(c)(i) Stop Cite

Now, in administrative law research, you'll be happy to learn that you'll keep track of time with . . . well, with *time*. On the front cover of the volume of C.F.R. containing your regulation you'll find the "Revised as of" date. This date becomes your "Stop Cite." "Stop *Cite*?" you ask. "A date's not a cite," you astutely point out.

Well, when it comes to the publication of federal regulations, a month-day-year date is a Stop Cite for one simple reason: federal regulations are published *daily*. The *Federal Register* comes out each business day, in daily issues, each bearing a daily date. A month-day-year date, therefore, is, for our purposes, a Stop Cite.

Thus, your initial Stop Cite is the "Revised as of" date on the front cover of your C.F.R. volume. Your updating task is to find out whether your particular C.F.R. provision has been affected in any way from your Stop-Cite day to the *present day*. Doing so is relatively easy.

§ 13.6(c)(ii) The *List of Sections Affected* (LSA)

To update your regulation, you must first find on the C.F.R. shelves some books called
"List of Sections Affected," also referred to as "LSA" {80}. On the front cover of the **{80}**
LSA volume you'll find a breakdown showing, for your title, that LSA covers the period of time from your Stop Cite to . . . a new Stop Cite. You want to select the LSA volume covering the broadest amount of time.

When you find the correct LSA volume, you'll see that LSA is one gigantic cross-
reference table acting just like Table 3 in USCCAN. The LSA table {81} cross- **{81}**
references you from C.F.R. provision to page number in the *Federal Register* where some new regulation has "affected" your regulation. Unlike Table 3 in USCCAN, which does not tell you what the new statute *did* to your statute, the LSA table tells you whether the new regulation amends, revokes, adds to, or otherwise affects your regulation.

Using the LSA tables requires a great deal of care. Depending on the time of year and the size of the time gap you have to bridge between your Stop Cite and the present day, you might have to consult one LSA volume that bridges a one-year time gap and then another LSA table that bridges another three-month time period. Bottom line? Watch out and make certain you consult all pertinent LSA volumes to bridge as much time as you can from your C.F.R. "Revised as of" Stop Cite to the present day.

§ 13.6(c)(iii) The List of Parts Affected (LPA)

At some point, of course, you'll run out of LSA volumes. On the last LSA volume you use, you'll find another "Revised as of" date, which gives you a new Stop Cite. Your updating task now is to bridge the time between that Stop Cite and the present day.

Unfortunately, C.F.R. and its LSA will no longer help you in this updating task. You must, as you have done with all forms of law, go straight to the law itself: here, the *Federal Register.*

Suppose that the latest LSA volume updates your regulation as of the end of June. Suppose that right now is August 7th. Thus, you have to worry that the agency that promulgated your regulation might have amended or repealed or revoked it sometime in July, or during the first seven days of August.

Now, you can sit back and browse through each daily *Federal Register* of July, and seven days in August, *or* you can use LPA.

LPA?

Yes.

{82} In *each* daily issue of the *Federal Register* in July {82}, you'll find a "List of *Parts*
{83} Affected during July" {83}. This list, called the LPA, cross-references you from any
given *part* of C.F.R. to the page number of the *Federal Register* where *any regulation*
{84} *within that part* has been affected in any way by a new regulation {84}. Please note that
your *part* might contain scores of regulations and that you might be interested in only one regulation. It's quite possible that your *part* has been affected by a new regulation when your *regulation,* i.e., *section,* has not been affected.

This LPA list cumulates *each day.* Thus, for any given month, you need only consult the LPA in the *last* (or latest) daily issue of the *Federal Register* for each month between your Stop Cite and the present day. In our hypothetical example, you would consult the LPA in the last daily issue of the *Federal Register* of July, and the latest issue on the shelf in August.

After consulting each of these LPAs, you have updated your regulation to the present day.

§ 13.6(c)(iv) Finding Cases Interpreting the Regulation

It is now possible to Shepardize federal regulations. The Shepard's Company now provides a separate *C.F.R. Shepard's Citator,* which enables you to look up the citation
{85} to your regulation and find cases that have cited your regulation {85}. Because you
already know how to Shepardize, I'll omit any detailed how-to instruction here. If you're hazy, go back to Chapter 9 and follow the steps of Shepardizing. The techniques for Shepardizing cases are easily transferable from one form of law (cases) to another (federal regulations).

§ 13.7 Federal Regulatory Research: A Roadmap for Research

Find the Federal Regulation:

TASK	OBJECTIVE
1. Use U.S.C.A. or U.S.C.S. to locate the applicable federal statute. Consult the cross-reference to "Code of Federal Regulations."	Find on-point regulation.
2. Use *C.F.R. Index and Finding Aids.*	

Analytical Approach:

TASK	OBJECTIVE
Consult "List of Titles, Chapters, Subchapters, etc."	Find on-point regulation.

Index Approach:

TASK	OBJECTIVE
Look up buzz words in the Index.	Find on-point regulation.

Consult the Regulation:

TASK	OBJECTIVE
Find the C.F.R. volume containing your regulations. Note the "Revised as of" date on the front cover. This becomes your C.F.R. Stop Cite.	Read any pertinent regulations.

Find Cases:

TASK	OBJECTIVE
Shepardize the pertinent regulations.	Locate cases interpreting or applying the regulations.

Update the Regulation:

TASK	OBJECTIVE
1. Find C.F.R.'s *List of Sections Affected* (LSA). Pick the one that covers the most time between your C.F.R. Stop Cite and the present day.	

(Continued on next page)

(Continued from previous page)

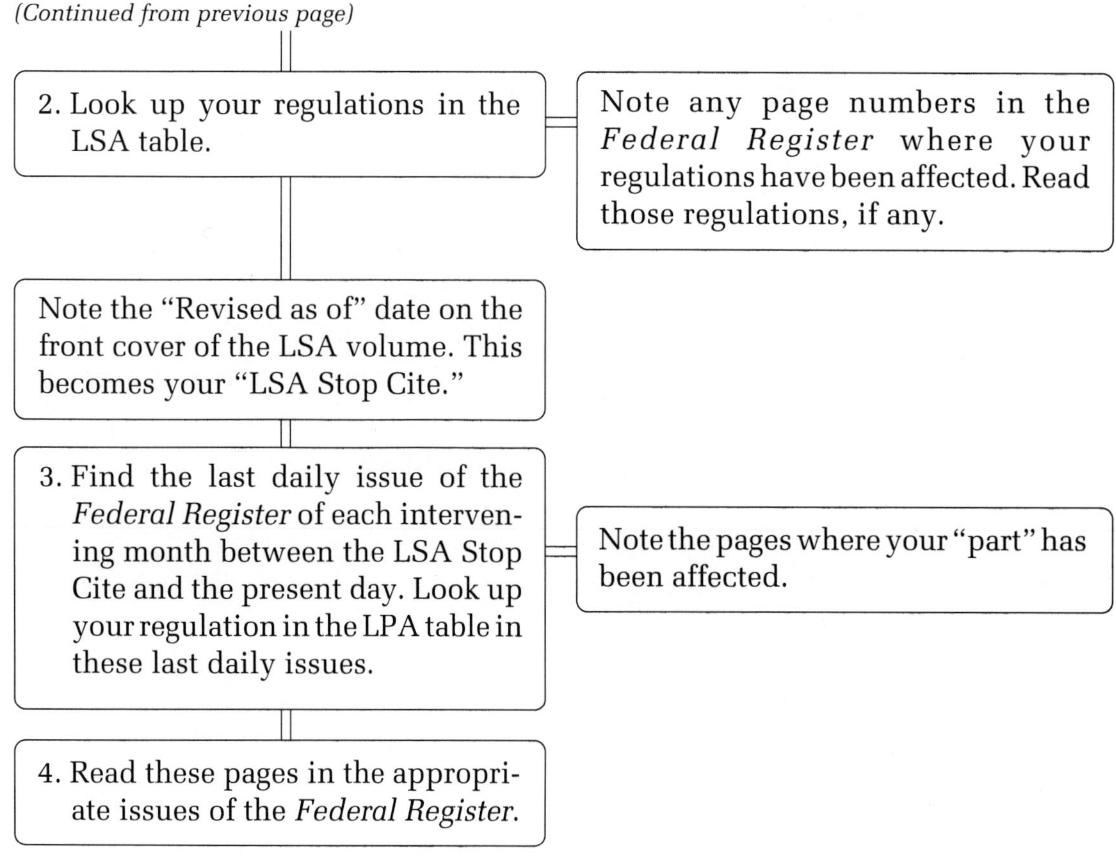

2. Look up your regulations in the LSA table.

Note any page numbers in the *Federal Register* where your regulations have been affected. Read those regulations, if any.

Note the "Revised as of" date on the front cover of the LSA volume. This becomes your "LSA Stop Cite."

3. Find the last daily issue of the *Federal Register* of each intervening month between the LSA Stop Cite and the present day. Look up your regulation in the LPA table in these last daily issues.

Note the pages where your "part" has been affected.

4. Read these pages in the appropriate issues of the *Federal Register.*

§ 13.8 Administrative Law Research: Visual Aids {74-85}

In the Visual Aids booklet, I have reproduced selected pages from the variety of sources and features you would use in researching federal regulations in C.F.R. and the *Federal Register.* These are pages that you would encounter in researching Judge Thomas and Professor Hill's case. On each page, in the box, you'll find my commentary showing exactly what the researcher is doing to find the federal regulation, to consult the regulation, and to update the regulation to the present day.

Please note that these pages are selective. In the real world of legal research, you would consult many more pages, especially those you'll undoubtedly stumble over in your very first efforts. You will, most likely, go down lots of dead ends, locating irrelevant information, getting frustrated, and, yes, perhaps even *losing your mind.*

But if you'll follow the above instructions, step by step, and study the Visual Aids, page by page, you'll begin to learn how to do legal research *without losing your mind.*

§ 13.9 The Final Conclusion

And when you learn all this; when you learn all about case law and its means of retrieval; when you learn all about legislation and its mean of retrieval; when you learn all about administrative law and its means of retrieval; and when you learn how secondary authority comes into play, helps the researcher, and even influences judges and other legal decision makers, you can then, and only then, lay claim to that most coveted of statuses: Ace Legal Researcher.

No longer will you freak out when you see the rows and rows of stacks and the hundreds of thousands of volumes of law. Instead, as you confidently walk into the law library, you can gloat at all those novices as they begin their quests for the same status you've already achieved, that of Ace Legal Researcher.

And when you do, when you begin to help these other fledglings, please don't sell them your used copy of this book. Instead, make them buy their own copy of this runaway bestseller: *Legal Research . . . Without Losing Your Mind.*

Thanks for listening. I hope you learned something.

At least enough to be like Wilbur. Turn the page.

W I L B U R

THE INDEX APPROACH

Note: Entries appearing in italics are publications. Those in initial caps are features within lawbooks or terms coined by *Legal Research . . . Without Losing Your Mind.* Those in initial lower case are words devised by one with zippo experience in legal indexing; they should, therefore, guide you directly to what you seek.